246-8895

1020 Village Drive
Apartment #7
Arkadelphia, AR
71923-2932

246-9607
Jean Thompson

694 Donovan Briley Blvd
North Little Rock, AR
72118

501-753-5783

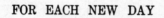

FOR EACH NEW DAY

FOR EACH NEW DAY

SELECTED AND ARRANGED
BY
DELAVAN L. PIERSON

BAKER BOOK HOUSE
Grand Rapids, Michigan

Reprinted 1966 by
Baker Book House Company

PHOTOLITHOPRINTED BY CUSHING - MALLOY, INC.
ANN ARBOR, MICHIGAN, UNITED STATES OF AMERICA
1966

BY WAY OF PREFACE

THE Northfield Conferences have become famous for the rich spiritual privileges which they afford to Christians of every creed for joining in prayer and consultation with men to whom the Holy Spirit has given deep insight into divine truth and marked success in Christian work. These conferences stand for three things—devout and scholarly study of the Word of God, close fellowship with the Son of God, and increased spiritual power for the service of God. It is a matter for regret that all of the most valuable addresses here delivered could not have been gathered yearly in permanent volumes for constant reference; but this has been done only occasionally, and such records as have been prepared are now for the most part out of print. Enough has been printed, however, in newspapers, magazines, and books to form a rich mine, from which we have sought in the present volume to gather *For Each New Day* some of the choicest nuggets of truth for the benefit of those who do not possess the printed reports or who may find them more available in this condensed form.

The power of the addresses has, of course, been greatly increased by the personality of the speak-

ers, even as the attractiveness of Northfield is en-
hanced by the natural beauties of its surroundings.

We send this little book forth in the hope that it
will be the means of disseminating and perpetuat-
ing some of the glorious and heart-searching truths
which have been uttered at Northfield in the years
gone by, and many of which already have been
instrumental in the quickening and strengthening of the spiritual life of Christians at home and
abroad.

DELAVAN L. PIERSON.

PREFATORY NOTE TO SECOND EDITION

A TEXTUAL AND TOPICAL INDEX, prepared at the
suggestion of many friends, has been included in
this edition. It is believed that the book will now
be very helpful, not only as a daily companion, but
also as a collection of choice illustrations for all
branches of Christian work.

Month of January

Therefore being justified by faith, we have peace with God through our Lord Jesus Christ: by whom also we have access by faith into this grace wherein we stand, and rejoice in hope of the glory of God.—Rom. v. 1, 2.

Peace for the past, grace for the present, and glory for the future. Yes, there is glory for the future; nothing before the true believer that isn't glory. I think it would take the wrinkles out of your brow if you would just look into the future instead of into the past.

There are two kinds of people—some that live on the past, and some that live on the future. You never saw a person living upon the past all the time, and always talking about the past, that did not have a good many wrinkles on his brow. Instead of casting all their care on Him that careth for them, they are all the time thinking about their troubles. They go to a meeting, and when it is over they say, "Wasn't it splendid! I enjoyed it so much; I forgot all my cares and all my troubles." They laid their bundle down under the seat, but the moment the benediction was over they picked it up again. Remember that everything before the believer is glory.

D. L. MOODY.

One result of communion with God is to make us tender of all that respects God's honor. Moses forgot himself; he had no room for thought of self; hence God was able to clothe him with a halo of glory. An earthly king likes to clothe his servants in fine robes, and God is pleased when we enable him to bless us.

ANDREW A. BONAR.

As much as lieth in you, live peaceably with all men.—Rom. xii. 18.

A lady who was somewhat quick-tempered, but was very desirous of becoming a Christian, once said to me, "Mr. Peploe, I assure you there is no fault in my case, because I never lose my temper unless I am provoked!" No, and I do not think the devil does! To lose your temper shows that you are out of communion with your blessed Lord. If the peace of Christ ruled in our hearts, we could never again be provoked. Think of that! Moses was so provoked that he spoke unadvisedly, and yet he was the meekest man that ever lived. But Moses had not the risen Christ to dwell in his heart. Be not discouraged or fear lest you may fall to-morrow. You need only live one moment at a time. Can Christ keep you this minute in a good temper? Then he can keep you the next moment, and the next, and so on forever. He can keep you in peace amid the severest trials, even such as he had to bear—in loss of friends, in persecution, in death. H. W. WEBB-PEPLOE.

God's Word teaches us that God does not expect a man to live for one minute as he ought unless the Holy Spirit is in him to enable him to do it. We do not want the Holy Spirit only when we preach, or when we have some special temptation of the devil to meet, or some great burden to bear; we cannot live a right life unless every moment we are guided by the Spirit of God. ANDREW MURRAY.

Much more they which receive the abundance of grace shall reign in life through the one, even Jesus Christ.—Rom. v. 17.

How significant, how exhilarating are these words! Not the life when we have passed the gate of pearl, but the life that is now; not our life when we stand on the brow of the transfiguration mount, but the life at home, or in the daily walks and common places of existence. It is possible that there is a life to be lived in the common round and the daily task, so royal, so radiant, so blessed, that those who live it may be said to REIGN IN LIFE.

Do you reign in life? If not, the reason may be that you do not distinguish between *praying* and *taking*. There is a profound difference between entreating for a thing and appropriating it. You may admit that God's abundant grace is near you through Jesus Christ, and yet you may not quite see the necessity of learning how to take. Some people are always telegraphing to heaven for God to send a cargo of blessing to them; but they are not at the wharf-side to unload the vessel when it comes. How many of God's richest blessings for which you have been praying for years have come right close to you, but you do not know how to lay hold of and use them! Mark, "They which *receive* the abundance of grace shall reign." The emphasis is not on grace, not on abundance, but on *receiving* it; and the whole grace of God may be round your life to-day, but if you have not learned to take it in, it will do you no good.

—F. B. MEYER.

Men sometimes say, "We grant that the arguments in favor of Christianity make its doctrines almost a certitude, but isn't it just barely possible that some other theory is true?" Suppose that it is, what are you going to do about it? A man says to me, "I am going to Europe, and want to know on what vessel I would better go." I say, "Well, there is a vessel down at the wharf which stands A No. 1 at Lloyd's, has a splendid record, safe cargo, fine captain, and picked crew; there is every probability that if you go in that vessel you will have a safe voyage. Here is another vessel, that leaks like a sieve, has a drunken captain and a mutinous crew. I don't think the chances of your making a safe voyage are very bright if you go on that vessel, but of course you can do it if you want to." "Well," he says, "I will think it over." The next day he comes back and says, "Did I understand you that you would make an affidavit that you could prove that this Cunard steamer would go over all right, and that the other vessel was bound for the bottom?" "No," I say; "I didn't say that, but I said there was very great likelihood of it." "Well," he says, "I have been thinking this thing over a good deal, and I have made up my mind that if you could not prove that this vessel is going over safely, and that the other is going to the bottom, I am going to take the leaky vessel." "Oh well," I say, "that is just as you choose. You are taking the risk. If you want to go to sea on a raft or an egg-shell, go; but I have done my duty when I have told you which is the best vessel to go on."

FRANCIS L. PATTON.

We need to apprehend more clearly that for which we have been apprehended. The blind man does not need more light, but more eyes; the deaf man does not need more sound, but more hearing; and the Christian does not need more of the Spirit, but more of the inspiration; that is, the inbreathing of the Spirit. Suppose I go to a man who is sick with the pneumonia, and the nurse says, "Oh, sir, he needs more air." "But the windows are all wide open, my dear woman; he has all the air there is. Do you not see that it is not more air that he wants, but more lungs?" Now the Spirit is *spiritus*, the breath of God, the breath of Jesus Christ; and the church is the lungs of Jesus Christ, if I may say it, and you and I are the cells in those lungs, and if the lungs get closed up, you will have a consumptive church, a feeble church, an asthmatic church, a church that is full of weakness and failure, simply because it does not take in more of the Spirit. It is not that you need more of the Holy Ghost, but the Holy Ghost needs more of you. . . . I believe that the Holy Ghost is in the church in living power. If you will only let him he will do things of which you hardly dream, in the management of the church and the raising of funds, but most especially in the preaching of the gospel. Christ promised that the Spirit was to show us things to come, to bring all things to our remembrance, and to help our infirmities. There is nothing we need that he has not promised to do for us, and it is to me the most real experience.

A. J. GORDON.

13

The Pharisee stood and prayed thus with himself.—Luke
xviii. 11.

This expression is here used to describe this man as
his prayer goes across from himself to himself, sup-
plicated and worshiped and thanked. All that God
gets out of this man is the action of the lips in utter-
ing his name. Self gets the true thanksgiving. He
is bound to say "God," but he thanks and praises
himself. Could not you bite the tongue of somebody
who has been dangerously near that condition in the
house of God? Using holy words, words which in
David's mouth were sobs, or triumphal shouts to God
in heaven, but on your tongue what were they?
Prostituted, debased to this evil use, to inflate your
own conceit.

It is right, my brother, that you should thank God
that you are not like the fellow who reeled past you
last night, the shame of his father's gray hairs and
the heartbreak of his mother. It is right, my sister, that you should thank God that you are not like
the daughters of shame whose presence defiles our
streets. But dost thou thank God? "What hast thou
that thou didst not receive?" "Now, if thou didst
receive it, why dost thou therefore glory as though
thou hadst not received it?" Thank God, and not
yourself.

The Pharisee of Christ's day, as one has said, could
not hold a candle to the Pharisee of to-day. The
New Testament Pharisee said, "I thank God that I
am not as other men are;" but the nineteenth-century
Pharisee knows that that is not orthodox; he plays
the publican, and says, "God, be merciful to me a
sinner," but remains as unhumbled and unhealed as
ever.   JOHN MCNEILL.

Be not drunk with wine, wherein is excess, but be filled with the Spirit.—Eph. v. 18.

Evidently St. Paul had in mind a contrast between the sensual effects of strong drink and that divine intoxication which comes from being filled with the Holy Spirit.

What are the effects of alcoholic inebriation? An expansion of vision, followed by blurring of sight; unnatural exhibitions before the brain; great hilarity, followed by moroseness; on the muscular system, in stimulating to efforts; on the speech, in first loosing the tongue and then muddling language.

How different the effects of the Holy Spirit! The eyes see with truth and power; the mind is aroused to grand efforts of thought, the faculty of speech to most gracious and eloquent utterances; while the whole person is strengthened and the disposition attuned to the Spirit of Christ.

ARTHUR T. PIERSON.

The first thing said of the disciples after Pentecost was that they were "filled with the Holy Ghost." Whenever there was anything important to be done, it says, for example, "Paul, being filled with the Spirit," spake thus; "Peter, being filled with the Spirit," did this. It was characteristic of the apostolic church that they were men full of the Holy Ghost. Is that our privilege? It is not only our privilege; it is our duty. "Be filled with the Spirit" is a command. In Germany a man was once so holy that the neighbors called him the "God-intoxicated man." We want a God-intoxicated church.

A. J. GORDON.

15

The world passeth away, and the lust thereof: but he that doeth the will of God abideth forever.—1 John ii. 17.

There are other thoughts in the Scriptures that catch men up on glorious wings to show them the face of Him whose we are and whom we serve; but there is no thought that more transforms a man's life, more floods over him the transfigured glory of a face touched once on the mountain-top years ago, than the thought that he can tie his life up to the doing of the will of God. Do you seek for an object in life? "I come to do thy will, O God." Do you seek for food? "My meat is to do the will of him that sent me." Do you desire society? "Whosoever shall do his will, the same is my mother, and my sister, and brother." Do you seek for an education? "Teach me to do thy will, O God." Do you wish for pleasure? "I delight to do thy will, O God." Seekest thou for reward? "He that doeth the will of God abideth forever." There will be no change for him. When the wreck of matter comes, and the everlasting heavens are folded up like a garment and laid away for their last sleep, he will still abide. Other things will pass away, but he that is doing the will of God is a part now of a life that shall last forever, of that great, sweeping, flowing life that alone holds this world steady with all that is passing and changing in it. And by and by, when other things shall pass away, his life, instead of grasping in itself the things that are laid aside, will find that it has laid hold of the things that are going to abide forever, the things that alone are worth the seeking, the loving, and the aspiring after.

ROBERT E. SPEER.

Whatsoever is born of God overcometh the world: and this is the victory that overcometh the world, even our faith.—1 John v. 4.

When a battle is fought, we are all anxious to know who the victors are. There is a battle in which we are all interested, and we can prophesy the victory in advance. If we are going to get the victory over the world, we have got to gain it through Christ. I wouldn't think of talking to unconverted men about overcoming the world, for it is utterly impossible for them to do it. A good many Christian people think of the battle as already fought, the victory as already won. They have an idea that all they have to do is to put the oars down in the bottom of the boat, and that the current will carry them into the ocean of God's eternal love; but we have got to go against the current. We have got to learn how to watch and fight, and how to overcome. The battle is not ended; it has only just commenced. The Christian life is a conflict, a warfare against evil, and the quicker we find it out the better. D. L. MOODY.

Who is it obtains the victory over the world? Is it he who is in the midst of favorable circumstances, with nothing to draw him from the right path? No; the victorious man is the man of faith—a faith in God that will overcome difficulties. The more unfavorable our circumstances, the greater our joy and reward if we can stand up for our blessed Master here until the day when we shall hear him say, "Come, ye blessed of my Father, inherit the kingdom prepared for you from the foundation of the world." ANDREW A. BONAR.

The one thing above all else that God desires of men is worship, and yet there are very few in this age who really do worship God. The term is used in our day in a very vague and general and unscriptural way. We speak of the whole service of a Lord's-day morning or evening as "public worship," but there is a great deal in it that is not worship. Reading the Bible and meditating upon it may lead to worship, but, in itself, is not worship. Listening to a sermon is not worship. It is often, I fear, the worship of man; it is not the worship of God. It may lead to worship. Praying is not worship; it may be prefaced or concluded with worship, but prayer is not worship. Singing is not necessarily or generally worship. There are hymns which, if sung intelligently and in the proper spirit, would be worship, but they are comparatively few, especially in the hymnology of the present day, which is more taken up with man's experience and duty than with God and his glory. The worship of God is the soul bowing down before God in absorbed contemplation of himself. Over and over do we read in the Scriptures, "They bowed their heads and worshiped," or "They fell down and worshiped." It has been well said that "in prayer we are occupied with our needs; in thanksgiving we are occupied with our blessings; in worship we are occupied with himself." God would not have us less occupied with our needs or present them less to him; neither would he have us less occupied with our thanksgiving, or return thanks less to him for them; but he would have us, I am sure, more occupied with himself in intelligent worship. R. A. TORREY.

When a man asks me why I believe in miracles, I answer, "Because I have seen them." He asks, "When?" I reply, "Yesterday." "Where?" "In such and such a place I saw a man who had been a drunkard redeemed by the power of an unseen Christ, and saved from sin. That was a miracle." The best argument for Christianity is a Christian. That is a fact which men cannot get over. There are fifty other arguments for miracles, but none so good as that you have seen them. Perhaps you are one yourself. Show a man a miracle with his own eyes, and if he is not too hardened he will believe.

HENRY DRUMMOND.

Sir Isaac Newton had a great intellect, but when he thought it necessary to cut two holes in his barn door—a big hole for the big cat and a little hole for the little cat—then he did not display any great amount of genius. Establish the great miracle, and the lesser miracles will take care of themselves. If the resurrection of Christ took place, then all the other miracles become possible, and the history of the Christian church is exactly what you would expect; if it did not take place, then Christianity, the most stupendous fact in history, stands to-day confessedly upon a falsehood, inexplicable, and with no possibility of a solution. Now whether is easier, to believe that Jesus did not rise from the dead, or to believe, in virtue of the congruous history following the story of his resurrection, and of the specific testimony to the resurrection, and the antecedent presumption in favor of his resurrection, that he did rise from the dead?

FRANCIS L. PATTON.

19

The flesh lusteth against the Spirit, and the Spirit against the flesh; for these are contrary the one to the other; that ye may not do the things that ye [otherwise] would.—Gal. v. 17.

In the best men there is a tendency to do certain things they ought not, but the more they are filled with the Holy Spirit, the more it is true of them that they are kept from doing what otherwise they would.

When I was a boy, I used to go to the Polytechnic in London, where my favorite diversion was a diving-bell, which had seats around the rim, and which at a given time was filled with people and lowered into a tank. We used to go down deeper, deeper into the water, but not a drop ever came into that diving-bell, though it had no bottom and the water was quite within reach, because the bell was so full of air that, though the water lusted against the air, the air lusted against the water, because air was being pumped in all the time from the top, and the water could not do what it otherwise would do. If you are full of the Holy Ghost, the flesh life is underneath you, and though it would surge up, it is kept out.

F. B. MEYER.

We should all condemn sin, as God condemns it, the moment we see it. It is in ourselves, though sometimes it is hid from us. It may be some hidden sin that keeps God from using us more. Let us be honest with God. Let David's prayer be ours: "Search me, O God"—not my neighbors, nor other people, but "Search *me!*"

D. L. MOODY.

If a man therefore purge himself from these, he shall be a vessel unto honor, sanctified, and meet for the master's use, and prepared unto every good work.—2 Tim. ii. 21.

No matter what kind of a vessel a man may be in natural gifts, whether of gold, silver, or merely earthen, if he purge himself he shall be a vessel unto honor.

Sometimes we see a speaker who has brilliant gifts, but who is full of defilement or heresy, and we say, "If that man were only converted, what a power he would be!" Another man, who is a believer, may not glitter with natural endowments; yet, if he will purge himself and become thoroughly sanctified, he may be of far greater service: he may be so used that thousands will bless him. God will use a vessel of wood or earth, if it is made meet for His use, as readily as one of gold or silver. No matter what the vessel is, see that it is clean.   GEORGE C. NEEDHAM.

Christians are apt to fall into two mistakes. One class regard sanctification or consecration entirely with reference to the personal life; they seek simply personal holiness. They are always viewing themselves, and trying to determine whether they have reached perfect sanctification, to the exclusion of thought about service. Others seek consecration only for service, and, in the midst of their arduous and busy work, neglect their personal life. We need both kinds of consecration—purifying and empowering.   GEORGE F. PENTECOST.

21

Whom the Lord loveth he chasteneth, and scourgeth every son whom he receiveth.—Heb. xii. 6.

Suppose that away in South Africa there is a woman whose husband had gone on a long journey into the interior. He is to be away for months, cut off from all postal communications. The wife is very anxious to receive news. In months she has had no letter or tidings from him. One day, as she stands in her door, there comes a great, savage Kafir, carrying his spears and shield, and with a terrible face. The woman is frightened, and she rushes into the house and closes the door. He knocks at the door, and she is in terror. She sends her servant, who comes back and says, "The man says he must see you." She goes all affrighted. He takes out an old newspaper, which he has brought from her husband, and inside the dirty newspaper she finds a letter from her husband telling her of his welfare. How that wife delights in that letter! she forgets the face that has terrified her. Weeks pass away again, and she begins to long for that ugly Kafir messenger. After long waiting he comes again, and this time she rushes out to meet him because he is the messenger from the beloved husband, and she knows that, with all his repelling exterior, he is the bearer of a message of love.

Beloved, have you learned to look at tribulation and vexation and disappointment as the dark, savage-looking messenger, with a spear in his hand, that comes straight from Jesus? Have you learned to say, "There is never a trouble by which my heart is touched, or even pierced, but it comes from Jesus, and brings a message of love"?

ANDREW MURRAY.

There hath no temptation taken you but such as is common to man: but God is faithful, who will not suffer you to be tempted above that ye are able; but will with the temptation also make a way to escape, that ye may be able to bear it.—1 Cor. x. 13.

Solitude has its temptations as well as society. St. Anthony of Egypt, before his conversion, was a gay and fast young man of Alexandria, and when he was converted he found the temptations of the city so intolerable that he fled into the Egyptian desert and became a hermit; but he afterward confessed that the temptations of a cell in the wilderness were worse than those of the city. It would not be safe to exchange our temptations for those of another man; every one has his own.

The attraction of temptation is overcome by a counter-attraction. The love of Christ in the heart destroys the love of sin, and the new song of salvation enables us to despise the siren song of temptation and pass it by. That man alone is really safe who, as he sails the seas of life, carries on board the divine Orpheus, whose heavenly music is daily sounding in his soul.

JAMES STALKER.

The nearer you live in the power of the Holy Ghost, the more keen you are to notice the approach of temptation and the more prepared you are to reckon yourself dead to the world of sin and lust.

F. B. MEYER.

23

Many say, "I heard of this life of rest when I was in bondage to the world, and I came back, made a covenant, and took possession of what I thought was the land of Jerusalem,—the city of peace,—but it has never been a blessing to me. What is wrong in my consecration? I gave myself to God, looked for power; I pleaded for the fullness of the Spirit, asked for a baptism; I thought I had something, but it never came to anything." Brethren, the trouble is this: you have been too much concerned for yourself instead of being concerned with the Lord God Almighty and his work. Remember those striking words, the idea of which occurs so repeatedly in the epistles, "Whether ye eat, or drink, or whatsoever ye do, do all to the glory of God." You ate and drank that you might get strong; you ate and drank that you might get rich and fat in spiritual things; perhaps you took work for the Lord that you might be powerful; you entered upon the position which the Lord accorded to you that you might become great in the eyes of men, and it has been one long failure.

H. W. WEBB-PEPLOE.

Many Christians wonder that they fail; but look at the readiness with which they talk on any subject, and never think that all that may be dissipating the soul's power, and leading them to spend hours not in the immediate presence of God. I fear the great difficulty is that we are not willing to make the needed sacrifice for a life of continual waiting upon God.

ANDREW MURRAY.

The moment that Moses came to years of discretion we read that he "refused to be called the son of Pharaoh's daughter." Take that as the starting-point of the life of service. If your circumstances are making it impossible for you to carry out what would otherwise be the will of God, then drop your circumstances as Moses did; it rests with you to do it. Refuse any longer to be called the son of Pharaoh's daughter. You have been in the courts of men; you may have stood high in the favor of the people of this world, and your heirship may look exceedingly brilliant. You must choose whether you will take the heavenly inheritance or the earthly. There comes a point in every man's history when, if he wishes to be a sanctified vessel, meet for the Master's use, he must decide to drop everything that prevents a holy career and a life of perfect service among the people of the Lord. Would the devil be what he is if he did not gild his bullets, and if he did not find something to boast of to offset the glorious attractions of heaven? Of course Pharaoh's court, with all its grandeur, its learning, its talent, its science, its magnificent prospects and possibilities and power, attracts men, and they are drawn into its snare. Moses, the servant of God, calculated well, and he concluded that it would be better to endure the reproach of Christ than to have all the treasures of Egypt. Put the two side by side, the things of the world in one scale-pan, and the things of God in the other, and see which kicks the beam. Make your calculation, and say deliberately, "I esteem the reproach of Christ greater riches than the treasures of the world."

H. W. WEBB-PEPLOE.

25

Lord, help me.—Matt. xv. 25.

There is a chain of but three links in this prayer of the poor woman of Canaan, but it reaches a long way. Some of the most beautiful prayers ever uttered are very short prayers. This is a very short prayer—any child can say it. There are three links in the chain, mark you. One link is on the throne of God; it is "Lord." The other link is down here; it is "me." And then there is a great link between that and this; it is "help." "Lord, help me." And the greater your need, the more that middle link in the chain will express.   MARCUS RAINSFORD.

Long prayers kill a prayer-meeting. See how short are the prayers recorded in the Bible. "Lord, help me," is one. "Lord, save, or I perish," is another. Why, a man said that if Peter had had as long a preamble as men put into prayers nowadays, he would have been forty feet under water before he would have got as far as the petition for rescue. Prayer is asking God for something, and you can ask it in a few words. If a man will pray fifteen minutes in a prayer-meeting, he will pray all the spirituality out of it. I'd rather have a man pray three times, and only five minutes at a time, than to have him take fifteen minutes all at once.   D. L. MOODY.

If we had prayed more we need not have worked so hard. We have too little praying face to face with God every day. Looking back at the end I suspect there will be great grief for our sins of omission—omission to get from God what we might have got by praying.   ANDREW A. BONAR.

26

Buy the truth, and sell it not.—Prov. xxiii. 23.

The royal diamonds of England cost much, but they are not for sale. The merchantman who found the pearl of great price sold all he had that he might buy it, but it was never on the market again; he would not sell it. So with truth. The Christian, especially the preacher, should be willing to pay any price for it, but it should not be for sale. No inducement should lead him to give up one jot or tittle of truth, moral, religious, or experimental. It often costs no little for a man to be honest and truthful; to contend "for the faith once for all delivered to the saints"; to get the living truth, which he can learn only in the school of trial; but he should be willing to pay the price for it. It is worth all it costs.

A. C. DIXON.

An eagle carrying a serpent in its talons to its nest on the mountain was bitten to the heart, and fell to the ground. Have you ever seen a man or woman in the church fall in the same way? You do not know the secret of the fall, but the omniscient eye of God saw it. That neglect of prayer, that secret dishonesty in business, that stealthy indulgence in the intoxicating cup, that licentiousness and profligacy unseen of men, that secret tampering with unbelief and error, was the serpent at the heart that brought the eagle down.

THEODORE L. CUYLER.

27

They that be wise shall shine as the brightness of the firmament; and they that turn many to righteousness, as the stars for ever and ever.—Dan. xii. 3.

Ecclesiastical orders and titles count for nothing in the kingdom of God. Christ's reward is not to a titled clergy as such, but to "teachers" of the law and the promise. It is not to fruitless preachers, but to "turners of many to righteousness." There is a glory in the kingdom for all, no matter how varied or numerous they are. God's temple rests on many pillars. God's garden has many flowers. God's music has many notes. God's sky has many stars, though differing one from another in glory. A glory belongs to Christ, the central sun, that none of us may claim as our own. Another glory belongs to the church, the moon, that none of us may inherit, a borrowed splendor that covers the whole company of saints. But there is glory that belongs to the individual "glitterers" of the firmament, different in degree; and it is ours so to turn many to righteousness as that neither Alcyone's sheen, nor the stars that burn in Orion's belt, shall surpass our brightness in the resurrection of the just. What a miracle of splendor that will be when sun, moon, and stars all shine in the firmament at the same time! We shall each have our own peculiar glory while yet lost in the "Greater Light" who rules that golden day; for "the righteous shall shine forth as the sun in the kingdom of their Father." The splendor of Christ will augment, not quench, our own. The clear gleam of the saints will be both physical and spiritual— nothing less than the glory of Christ himself. This is the reward which they shall have forever for their brief moment of work and suffering here on earth.

NATHANIEL WEST.

And this is life eternal, that they might know thee the only true God, and Jesus Christ, whom thou hast sent.—John xvii. 3.

Why do not God's people know their God? For this reason. They take anything rather than God, —ministers and preaching and books and prayers and work and effort,—any exertion of human nature instead of waiting until God reveals himself. . . .

Give God his place. Begin in your prayer. The power of prayer depends almost entirely upon my apprehension of who it is with whom I speak. Take time, and get a sight of this great God in his power, in his love, in his nearness, waiting to bless you. Before and above everything, take time ere you pray to value the glory and presence of God. What a wonderful thing our church services and conventions would be if all the worshipers were waiting upon God, determined to let God have his place! I cannot fully give God his place upon the throne, for I cannot realize what that place is; but God will increasingly reveal himself and the place he holds. I know about the sun because I see its light. No philosopher could have told me about the sun if the sun did not shine. No power of meditation and thought can grasp the presence of God. Be quiet and trust and rest, and the everlasting God will shine into your hearts, and will reveal himself.

The abiding presence of God is the heritage of every child of God. The Father never hides his face from his child. Sin hides it, and unbelief hides it; but the Father lets his love shine all the day on the face of his children. The sun is shining day and night. Your sun shall never go down. Come and live in the presence of God.

ANDREW MURRAY.

Go ye into all the world, and preach the gospel to every crea-
ture.—Mark xvi. 15.

Christ never told his disciples to stay at home and
wait for sinners to come to them.

Every Christian of every age and calling is appointed an ambassador for Christ.

The gospel is to be preached to "every creature."
This means personal, hand-to-hand contact with the
unsaved—man to man, and woman to woman. Look
through the Scriptures, and you will be surprised to
see how much springs out of interviews with single
persons. The call is to you personally, and summons
you to personal dealing in the name of Christ with
every creature in the range of your influence. No
matter how low, no matter how foul, a man or woman
may be, no matter how forgotten by the world, your
Master is able to save to the uttermost, and you are
his appointed instrument to proclaim his mercy.
Christ does not say, "Go and address great multitudes;" but he does say, "Go and preach the gospel
to every creature." In looking at some apparently
hopeless case, you may be tempted to think, "Oh,
some creatures are hardly worth saving." But how
do you know that from that very one a rich tribute
of praise may not arise to the Lord Jesus Christ?
In these days Christ may seem to us to be working
in a very strange way, when he is taking up pugilists,
thieves, and illiterate and outcast men, and using
them to bear testimony to the power of his grace.
It is no concern of ours whether the creatures with
whom we deal are prepossessing or not. The command is to "preach the gospel to *every* creature."

JAMES H. BROOKES.

30

Thou wast slain, and hast redeemed us to God by thy blood.—
Rev. v. 9.

We have been redeemed to God. It is a great
thing to be redeemed from sin, from Satan, from this
present evil world, from death; but suppose that redemption stopped there? Suppose that God had said,
"Now you are out of your difficulties; make the best
of it." Suppose that, after taking Israel out of
Egypt, God had left them in the wilderness. No;
he has redeemed us to himself, to sweet and blessed
relations with him; to heaven; to the companionship
of high and holy intelligences; to the nearest place in
his heart; to dominion with him over all the universe.
There is where we lose communion. We realize what
we are redeemed and delivered *from*, but we often do
not apprehend what we are redeemed and delivered
to. If we did, we should not be troubled with that
backward look upon what we are leaving that keeps
us in bondage. We would seek the things that are
above. GEORGE F. PENTECOST.

We are sinful creatures, and our holiest service
can only be accepted through Jesus Christ our Lord.
When we walk in the light, as he is in the light, and
are having unbroken fellowship with God, and God
with us, it is because the blood of Jesus Christ his
Son is cleansing us from all sin. No holy service is
a ground of acceptance with God. Christ alone is
that ground. On the other hand, the fact that our
holiest things need to be accepted through Christ is
no reason why we should neglect to be holy. Though
sinful creatures, we must not be sinning creatures—
a very different thing indeed.
J. HUDSON TAYLOR.

O my Father, if it be possible, let this cup pass from me: nevertheless, not as I will, but as thou wilt.—Matt. xxvi. 39.

Every man who has come to the point where he can swallow a bitter cup because he can feel the breath of Christ on it, and who can say from his heart, "Thy will, not mine, be done," has reached the highest point which he can reach.

The core principle of Christianity is what? Faith? No; more than that, deeper yet than that; the core principle of practical Christianity is obedience— obedience to Jesus Christ. The core principle in the commonwealth is obedience to law; the core principle in every well-regulated family is obedience to parental authority. I am afraid there is not so much of that old filial spirit as there used to be. When a boy has learned the difference between "you may" and "you must," that boy has the first start in genuine manhood. Obedience is the first and the great thing in this school of life in which the Master has placed us. Has not the Master said, "If ye love me, keep my commandments"? The motto for every Christian should be, "Find out what Jesus Christ wants you to do, and then *do* it."

THEODORE L. CUYLER.

To the child of God, yearning for holiness, there is something exceedingly precious and delightful in approaching a command that seems to be naturally impossible; because he realizes that the Lord gave the Word, and that it is for the Lord to make possible of fulfilment in his child that which he commands. Surely we can say with Augustine, "Give what thou commandest, and then command what thou wilt."

H. W. WEBB-PEPLOE.

Freely ye have received, freely give.—Matt. x. 8.

Do not be afraid to call on the Lord's people to give. I know they sometimes complain. "Oh," they say, "it is all the time give, give, give! You are always poking under our noses a collection-box or a hat." Remind them that on the side of the Lord it is always give, give, give to them. It might help parsimonious Christians to look a little over their account with the Lord. It would stand somewhat thus:

Brother John Smith in account with his Master, the Lord of the whole earth.

DR.

To 10 showers of rain on his fields at $25 per shower,	$250.00
2 extra showers at a critical period, $50 each,	100.00
60 days of sunshine at $5,	300.00
	$650.00

CR.

Per contra:	
By given for pastor's salary,	$10.00
Home missions,	.25
Foreign Missions,	.10
	$10.35

Showing a heavy balance against Brother John Smith, and it would be heavy even if he had given ten times as much, for the farm is the Lord's. He prepared its chemical constituents so as to make it a farm at all rather than a patch of desert, and he, too, planted the forest from which John Smith gets the fuel for his fires.   WILLIAM ASHMORE.

Know ye not that ye are the temple of God, and that the Spirit of God dwelleth in you?—1 Cor. iii. 16.

The Jews' temple was an architectural triumph of marvelous beauty and wondrous magnificence. We are likened to it, and told that every believer is a dwelling of the Holy Spirit. What the indwelling power of the Spirit is may be seen in Moses' rod. The rod was a common, insignificant stick,—a bit of acacia,—but when it was linked with the power of God it could do mighty works.

How quickly that power comes! The woman at the well in Samaria went and told of Christ in the power of the Spirit, and immediately there was a great revival. A noted gambler in Chicago was converted. His prayer to God was in gamblers' slang, but God knew what he meant, and received him. The man thought he ought to do something in his Master's service. He told his story; God blessed it; and in the power of the Spirit he has been telling it ever since, with wonderful success. He has won more souls than any man in my church. If the world wants anything, it wants men and women set apart to God, filled with the Spirit, and ready to be used.

E. P. Goodwin.

Are we living habitually in such nearness to the Lord Jesus that the gentlest intimation of his wish comes to us with the force of a command, and with the consciousness that, some way or other, it *is* possible to obey, and that we shall be carried through in any service to which he calls us?

J. Hudson Taylor.

34

He satisfieth the longing soul.—Psalm cvii. 9.

What would satisfy you in regard to religion if you wrote out a catalogue of everything which you felt you could desire, or above all that you can ask or think? Would you not write down at the very beginning, "Peace with God, so that I should not be afraid of him"? You know in your hearts that that is supplied by the sacrifice of Jesus Christ on the cross. You have but to say, "Amen; thank God, it is true. I believe it."

Then would you not write down, "Constant keeping from all evil, and the supply of every need"? The Bible is full of that blessed truth at every point: the keeping Christ, the providing Lord, the comforting Friend, the everlasting Portion of God's people. Whatever you wish, there stands the living God, and says, I AM. God must give; he cannot withhold; he would not be God, any more than a fountain would be a fountain, if he were not perpetually pouring out his fullness upon all the universe.

Suppose that you say, "I want a future that is clear and full of provision for eternity." The Lord is our everlasting Portion; the great God is ever saying, I AM, and what more can men require for the future? The past and the present and the future are all set before us in the living God as being completely and everlastingly supplied. And yet how many souls are satisfied in Christ, how many could say that they have found in him everything that their souls desire? Not many, I fear. Whose fault is it?

H. W. WEBB-PEPLOE.

A good many Christians are kept back from wholly surrendering themselves to God from fear lest he will ask them to do something hard and disagreeable. They think that there will then be no knowing what he may do with them, or what their friends may think of them.

Suppose that a child who had been wayward and wilful were to come and say to a wise and loving parent, "Father, from to-day I will let mother and you choose my life; you shall choose my companions, my amusements, and my books." Would that father say to the mother, "Now, wife, here is a chance to torment our child. What dress does she detest, what companions does she hate, what books does she eschew? Let us select these and pile them into her life." Of course he would not; he would only take from the child the things that were really cursing her, as a cancer might curse a healthy body, and then he would crowd her life with all that would make it one long summer day of bliss. Will Christ, who died for me, do worse?

Friends, you may trust him. He means to do the best for you, and the only thing which can curse and blast your life is to get out of God's hands. When George Stephenson was trying to pass his bill for railways in England, a peer said to him, "Suppose that a cow were to get on the line when one of your newfangled engines was on the road?" "So much the worse for the coo!" said he. If you get into collision with God, it is so much the worse for you. "Woe to the man that striveth with his Maker!" Do not let the devil cheat you out of your inheritance.

F. B. Meyer.

We find no difficulty in distinguishing between the works of God and the works of man. God's works are absolutely perfect; man's are only relatively so. The most perfect needle may be perfect for the work to which it is adapted; but make it a microscopic object, and the smooth hole appears ragged and the needle becomes a honeycombed poker. Take, on the contrary, a hair from the leg of a fly, or the dust from a butterfly's wing. Magnify these, and they are seen to be absolutely perfect.

Now there is no more difficulty in recognizing the Word of God from the word of man than there is in recognizing the work of God from the work of man. You need the minute examination and the anointed eye that can perceive its beauties, which do not lie on the surface. In this way God's Word contains the best evidence of its own inspiration. It could not have been forged or manufactured.

J. HUDSON TAYLOR.

My friends, you needn't borrow any trouble about the old Book; it is going to stand. Some people think it is a "back number"; you and I will become back numbers, but this Book is going to remain. The Word of God is just lighting up the nations of the earth. Some one asked a young convert how he could believe that the Bible was inspired. He said, "Because it inspires me." That is a short cut to inspiration. I would doubt my existence as quickly as I would doubt the truth of that Book.

D. L. MOODY.

But if the Spirit of him that raised up Jesus from the dead dwell in you, he that raised up Christ from the dead shall also quicken your mortal bodies by his Spirit that dwelleth in you.— Rom. viii. 11.

Everywhere the Holy Spirit stands related to Jesus Christ. How was Jesus begotten? The angel Gabriel said to Mary, "The Holy Ghost shall come upon thee, and the power of the Highest shall overshadow thee: therefore also that holy thing which shall be born of thee shall be called the Son of God." How did Jesus receive the enduement of power? "Jesus also having been baptized, and praying, the heaven was opened, and the Holy Ghost descended . . . as a dove upon him." Ask how he wrought miracles, and I answer in his own words: "I by the Spirit of God cast out devils." How did he complete the work of atonement? "Who through the eternal Spirit offered himself without spot to God." How did he give the great commission? I reply in the language of the Acts: "After that he through the Holy Ghost had given commandments unto the apostles." How was he raised from the dead? He was "declared to be the Son of God with power, according to the Spirit of holiness, by the resurrection from the dead."

A. J. Gordon.

The answer of God to the heartfelt, sincere surrender of the whole being to the possession of Jesus Christ is the filling of the whole man, spirit, soul, and body, with the Holy Spirit. How insignificant in comparison the human side, and yet how unspeakably important, since the fullness of the Spirit's presence depends upon it! C. I. Scofield.

My soul, wait thou only upon God; for my expectation is from him.—Psalm lxii. 5.

There is no joy like the joy of communion. Living apart from God is misery. Look at Gethsemane; see the Saviour's face; how sad with sorrow because of the Father's wrath! But on the Mount of Transfiguration, when the Father said, "This is my well-beloved Son," the person of Christ glistened with glory.

Communion with God has the effect of making us joyous. The Lord does not like to see any of his disciples looking sad. . . . When men seek to entice you to forego communion with God and to follow the world with them, let your face shine with the brightness that comes from your communion with the Master, and they will cease to trouble you. Christians can sometimes do more by shining for God than by speaking for him. ANDREW A. BONAR.

What folly it is to imagine that I cannot expect God to be with me every moment! Look at the sunshine! Have you ever said, "Oh, how can I keep that sunlight, and be sure that I shall have it to use while working?" Is not God, who made the sun to shine, also willing and able to let his light and his presence so shine through me that I can walk all the day with God nearer to me than anything in nature? Praise God, he can do it.

Why then does he do it so seldom, and in such feeble measure? There is but one answer: you do not permit it. You are so occupied and filled with other things—religious things perhaps—that you do not give God time to make himself known, and to enter and take possession. ANDREW MURRAY.

O Church of Christ, behold at last
    The promised sign appear, —
The gospel preached in all the world;
    And lo! the King draws near.

He shall reign from sea to sea;
    When he girds on his conquering sword,
All the ends of the earth shall see
    The salvation of our God.

With girded loins, make haste! make haste!
    Thy witness to complete,
That Christ may take his throne and bring
    All nations to his feet.

And thou, O Israel, long in dust,
    Arise, and come away!
See how the Sun of Righteousness
    Sheds forth the beams of day.

Thy scattered sons are gath'ring home,
    The fig-tree buds again;
A little while and David's Son
    On David's throne shall reign.

Then sing aloud, O Pilgrim Church,
    Brief conflict yet remains,
And then Immanuel descends
    To bind thy foe in chains.

A. J. GORDON.

Month of February

Howbeit when he, the Spirit of truth, is come, he will guide you into all truth.—John xvi. 13.

A man once asked me, "Is not conscience a safer guide than the Holy Spirit?" I just took out my watch and said, "Is not my watch better than the sun?" Suppose that I said to you, "I will tell you the hour by my watch, and you must always take the time from me." That is conscience. It is the sun that is to rule the time. Conscience is fallen and corrupt. If we had an unfallen conscience, like holy Adam, it would be as if my watch were always to agree with the sun. But now it is a most unsafe guide. Sometimes we hear men say, "I don't see any harm in this practice; my conscience doesn't condemn it." It is not your conscience or your consciousness that is the rule of right and wrong; the law is the standard. By the law is the knowledge of sin. Sin is the transgression of the law, not of conscience.

ANDREW A. BONAR.

It is a great sin that multitudes of Christian believers are going to human sources for the things which the Spirit has promised to give to them at first-hand.   H. M. PARSONS.

When people say, "I want more of the Holy Ghost," I answer, "The Holy Ghost wants more of you." The question is not, how much you can take in of the Spirit, but how much the Spirit can take possession of you. If you will yield yourself to the living God with the conviction that he is all that every man can want, not one good thing shall fail, any more than it has failed in the past, of all that the Lord our God has promised to give us.

H. W. WEBB-PEPLOE.

41

Tarry ye in the city of Jerusalem, until ye be endued with power from on high.—Luke xxiv. 49.

The apostles had taken a four years' course in the best theological seminary that ever existed, in which the Lord Jesus Christ himself was the chief and sole instructor; they had been eye-witnesses of our Saviour's miracles, his death, and his resurrection, and were in a few moments to witness his ascension. Yet Jesus said that they were not ready to work. The world was dying; the apostles were the only ones who knew the saving truth; but they were not to stir a step until they had received something further—the baptism with the Holy Spirit. Now if those men, with such an exceptional training, were not allowed to enter upon their work until they had received the baptism with the Holy Spirit, should we dare to undertake that service until we have been so baptized?

In Acts we read, "God anointed Jesus of Nazareth with the Holy Ghost and with power: who went about doing good, and healing all that were oppressed of the devil; for God was with him." That refers to the time when, as Jesus stood at the Jordan, the heavens were opened and the Holy Spirit descended upon him in the form of a dove. Now if Jesus Christ, "the only-begotten Son of God," did not enter upon his public ministry until he was baptized with the Holy Ghost and power, it seems to me very closely akin to blasphemy for a man to undertake Christian service until he has received this baptism.   R. A. TORREY.

Ye are dead, and your life is hid with Christ in God. . . . Mortify therefore your members which are upon the earth.—Col. iii. 3, 5.

An awful responsibility lies with us of making dead practically by the Holy Ghost what Christ made dead judicially. You are ashamed to tell of the jealousy, the lust, or the covetousness which is dragging you down. Brethren, give it to the grave. Does not Jesus say that you would better pluck out your eye or cut off your right hand rather than that your whole body should be cast into hell? Put your passions to death. They will rise up if they can; they have terrible taproots, and you will never pull them all up; but your determination must be to destroy them. You may have to do it openly. I have known men who have had to lose all their character to win their souls. It is a solemn process. There are downright damnable things in most men who call themselves Christians, and they are cherishing them. Bring them out and put them to death.

H. W. Webb-Peploe.

There is no way of being delivered from this life of self but one: we must follow Christ, set our heart upon him, listen to his teachings, give ourselves up every day that Christ may be all to us, and by the power of Christ the denial of self will be a blessed, unceasing reality. Never for one hour do I expect the Christian to reach a stage at which he can say, "I have no self to deny." His fellowship with the cross of Christ will be an unceasing denial of self every hour and every moment.

Andrew Murray.

Religion is communion between man and God—the finite "I" and the infinite "I AM." Christianity is religion plus the incarnation. . . . If you eliminate the supernatural from Christianity, you will at once get a new religion, a new Christianity, that has no reference to the next life, no salvation; simply a moral philosophy, a theory of life, and the present life at that; a Christianity that is simply a philanthropy; and the immortality of the individual having been given up, the next thing will be to give attention to the immortality of the organism. Hence it is that some men at the present time are saying very little about the salvation of the soul, but a great deal about the salvation of the life and the regeneration of society. Hence it is that a great deal of practical Christian endeavor, that used to be addressed to the question of making men sorry for sin and leading them to seek pardon from God, is expending itself in providing soup-kitchens and more comfortable environment for the poor.

Now, when we are told, as we have been, that the church does not understand Christianity, that the Young Men's Christian Association does not understand Christianity, that Christianity does not understand Christianity, the meaning is that those who make this allegation have a fundamentally false view as to the philosophy of life, as to the place that Christianity is designed to serve in our world's history. We must understand the underlying philosophy of these men if we would appreciate their anti-evangelical attitude.

FRANCIS L. PATTON.

44

As in the case of the temple of Israel, so with the believer, the temple of the Holy Spirit, our whole natures should be consecrated to God. "Present your bodies—the court—a living sacrifice;" "Let the peace of God rule in your hearts"—the holy place; "Casting down imaginations, and every high thing that exalteth itself against the knowledge of God, and bringing into captivity every thought to the obedience of Christ"—the mind, the holy of holies.

Perhaps our conception of consecration has been poor and inadequate. We have been thinking of service simply, and that in connection with the body; we have said, "Take my hands; take my lips; take my feet," and so on in a kind of sentimental, anatomical way. We have not thought of being God-filled, God-possessed, quite apart from considerations of service. I grow weary of the perpetual spurring on of God's people to service,—as if any father ever cared so much to have·his children toiling for him as loving and trusting him,—and the more so as the God-possessed Christian invariably does serve. There is a higher thought: the enthronement of Jesus as Lord of all, and once for all; there should be no call for reconsecration in the Christian's experience.

C. I. SCOFIELD.

In full consecration to God it is a joy to recognize all our members, all our faculties—every fiber of our body and faculty of mind and appetite and propensity—all as his, for his service and glory; and as his children to do all to the glory of God.

J. HUDSON TAYLOR.

45

Christ was once offered to bear the sins of many.—Heb. ix. 28.

There is this mistaken view of the atonement: that God would not forgive his creatures but for a vicarious atonement; that for this sin-offering he took Christ, his Son, and that his pain and intense suffering brought the pardon.

That is not it. There was sin in the world. Death was the penalty. Who would pay the wages of sin? Christ was the volunteer. He trod the wine-press alone because there was none holy enough to stand with him. God is not hampered by his own attributes. Justice never forgives; it exacts punishment. The defaulter cannot wipe out his crime by the multiplication table. If there is a world where five times five make fifty, then there may be a world where the wages of sin is life. If a friend gives a defaulter fifty thousand dollars, he may pay the money back and gain forgiveness. Christ paid the debt contracted in the currency of earth in the higher currency of heaven.

A Russian officer could not make his accounts come right; there was a heavy balance against him. In the rigid despotism of the empire he feared the consequences and the severe penalty if he could not make it good. Poring over the figures at his table one day, in his worry and despair he began scribbling. He wrote on the paper before him, " Who will make up this deficit?" He fell asleep. The czar passed; he saw the officer, and, curious, read the scrap of writing; he seized the pen and wrote underneath, "I, even I, Alexander."

Who can pay the deficit of human sin? "I, even I," said Christ on the cross.   A. J. GORDON.

Whatsoever a man soweth, that shall he also reap.—Gal. vi. 7.

In the natural world a man expects to reap if he sows; he expects to reap the same kind of seed; he expects to reap more than he sows; and ignorance of the kind of seed sown makes no difference in the reaping. The man who sows his "wild oats" will find that the same is true in his experience.

D. L. MOODY.

Never trifle with one sin. It is like a little cloud which, as a poet has said, may hold a hurricane in its grasp. The next sin you commit may have a mighty effect in the blighting of your life. You do not know the streams that may flow from that fountain; for sin is a fountain—not a mere act, but a fountain of evil. ANDREW A. BONAR.

Have you ever thought of the power of sin to perpetuate and multiply itself? In Genesis thistles are mentioned as a part of the earth's curse. One seed is the first crop, twenty-four hundred the second, five hundred and seventy-six million the third. So it is with sin: "By one man's disobedience many were made sinners." This stands as a law of nature, natural and spiritual—"yielding fruit after his kind." Man was created holy; had he remained so there would have been "fruit after his kind." But he sinned, and Adam begat a son in his own likeness—not in God's likeness. Then see the power of sin in producing defiance of God. Cain is an example; he is the first-fruit of the flesh—the first child born into the world. It is not necessary to go through five hundred and seventy-six million thistle-seeds in their growth and development to know their nature; they are all alike.

D. W. WHITTLE.

Look at God. Who is God? He is the great Being for whom alone the universe exists, in whom alone it can have happiness. It came from him; it can find no rest or joy outside of him. Oh, if only Christians understood and believed that God is nothing but a fountain of happiness and perfect, everlasting blessedness, the result would be that every Christian would say, "The more I can have of God, his will and his love and his fellowship, the happier." If they believed that with their whole heart, how they would with the utmost ease give up everything that might separate them from God! . . .

Look at man's nature. For what was man created? Simply to live in the likeness of God, and as his image. Now, if we have been created in the image and likeness of God, we can find our happiness in nothing but in what God finds his happiness. The more like to him we are, the happier we shall be. In what does God find his happiness? In two things: everlasting righteousness and everlasting beneficence. "God is light, and in him is no darkness at all." The kingdom, the rule of God, will bring us nothing but righteousness. Seek the kingdom of God and his righteousness. If men but knew what sin is, and if they really longed to be free from everything like sin, what a grand message this would be! Jesus comes to lead men to God and his righteousness. We were created to be like God, in his perfect righteousness and holiness and love.

ANDREW MURRAY.

It is far less important to die the martyr's death than to live the martyr's life.   R. E. SPEER.

When man ends then God begins. When all the
world had become guilty before God; when Hebrew
righteousness had utterly failed to fear God and keep
his commandments; when the Greek by his wisdom
knew not God; when the Roman had stupefied his conscience and liked not to retain God in his knowledge,
even though there was still taught by Hebrew and
by pagan creed, by seer and sibyl, the coming of a
day of wrath and the impending judgment of Gehenna;
then God, in his love, wisdom, and power, made himself manifest, a just God and a Saviour.

W. J. ERDMAN

Christ came into this world not simply as a moral
reformer, or as a moral philosopher, though he was
both, but as a Saviour. Christianity is salvation, and
the Bible gives us the plan of salvation. There is
either no peril at all, in which case we do not need
any religion, and need not trouble ourselves; or there
may be peril, and no salvation at all, in which case
we may trouble ourselves, but it will do us no good;
or else " there is none other name under heaven given
among men, whereby we must be saved;" and " other
foundation can no man lay than that is laid, which
is Jesus Christ."

FRANCIS L. PATTON.

If we are going to get salvation, we have got to
get it upon God's terms and not upon our own; and
that is why I fear that a good many people will not
get it—simply because they can't have their own
way about it.   D. L. MOODY.

49

How shall we, that are dead to sin, live any longer therein?—
Rom. vi. 2.

We have been redeemed, like the people of Israel,
from bondage, and then have been led through the
Red Sea of Christ's blood, and should know that our
enemies are practically drowned there. Every man
who desires to have contact with the flesh is putting
his arm across the Red Sea, and is shaking hands
with the survivors of the Egyptians, which are the
flesh, across the grave of Christ. Did you ever think
that when you made a concession to the flesh you
had to reach over the buried Son of God to get back
to your old lusts and appetites? No wonder that
Satan's hand is stronger than yours, and that he
pulls you over. Were you redeemed to go on living
in the wilderness forty years, supplied, like beggars,
every day with bread and water? God never lets his
children starve to death; he manages to give them
bread and water; but, after all, that is a tasteless
supply to most Christians. I hear Christians say,
"I suppose we must go through a howling wilderness
all the days of our life." It is a pilgrimage, my
brother. There is something far better than the old
bondage of Egypt, or than merely lingering on in a
howling wilderness, supplied with bread and water.

H. W. WEBB-PEPLOE.

He who begins by halving his heart between God
and mammon will end by being whole-hearted for the
world and faint-hearted for Christ. We are so constituted that it is impossible for us to exercise a
divided allegiance; we must be out-and-out for God,
or we shall be in-and-in for the world and all its interests.

A. J. GORDON.

And we are his witnesses of these things; and so is also the Holy Ghost, whom God hath given to them that obey him.—Acts v. 32.

Obedience means surrender, absolute surrender. I come to God and say essentially, "Heavenly Father, thou hast bought me with a price; I acknowledge thine absolute ownership. Take me, send me where thou wilt, use me as thou wilt." Here we touch the hindrance in many lives. Many desire the baptism with the Holy Spirit who are not conscious of any definite sin, but there is not total surrender. One minister wishes the baptism that he, in the power of the Holy Spirit, may preach in Boston; another that he may preach in New York; another in Chicago. Ah, God may want you in Africa or in India or in the islands of the sea; and before you can have the Holy Spirit's power anywhere you must be willing to go anywhere.

R. A. TORREY.

Obedience means marching right on whether we feel like it or not.   D. L. MOODY.

We hear much these days about God's sovereignty and man's free agency. Christ said to the woman of Canaan, "Be it unto thee even as thou wilt." Here is something that looks like human sovereignty and divine agency. Free to do what we please because we please to do God's will. Such is the free agency of faith that takes hold of the arm that moves the world. Such free agency Moses had when the Red Sea was no obstacle in the way of his progress. The walls of Jericho fell before this free agency of faith. By means of it any little David is more than a match for the strongest Goliath. Armed with it, Gideon and his three hundred were invincible.

A. C. DIXON.

Have you a capacity for the law? Christ himself is an Advocate. Come, practise in the supreme court; expound the law of God. He will open your eyes and show you wondrous things out of his law. Go forth and teach men to obey this law.

If you are fond of working among conveyances and title-deeds, go and help multitudes of people to get, or to clear up, their title-deeds to mansions in the skies. You will not get your fees in this world, but you will in the next.

Have you a talent for medical work? Christ was the great Physician. Come, heal the wounds that sin has made; open blind eyes; unstop deaf ears; make the lame to leap; raise the dead. God himself will furnish you the medicines: the balm of Gilead, the Water of Life, the anointing salve for the eyes, the leaves of the Tree of Life, which are for the healing of the nations. You will receive your fees for pouring in oil and wine, and for bringing to the great inn above many a poor sinner who has fallen among thieves as he wandered away from Jerusalem to Jericho.

Have you been thinking of a business life? Here is a "merchandise better than the merchandise of silver, and the gain thereof than fine gold." Men go far from home to Brazil or South Africa, and toil in the mud and mire of the mines to dig up diamond stones, which they sell to kings and princes for merely an earthly reward. Would you not, then, go far away and assist to gather these gems which, when washed in the blood of Christ and cut and polished by the Holy Spirit, shall adorn the crown of him who is King of kings, and flash back the glory of the living God? WILLIAM ASHMORE.

Elijah said to Elisha, "Is there anything you want? Don't be afraid to ask. You seem to be very timid." Elisha replied, "Yes, there is something I want." "Well, don't be afraid to ask; you shall have whatever you want." A blank check! How did he fill it out? Did he ask for as much of the Spirit as Elijah had? That would have been a great thing. Talk about kings! Elijah had power over kings. Kings are in the habit of ordering their subjects around. Here was a subject who was in the habit of ordering kings around. Talk about the power of Cæsar, Napoleon, Alexander, the great generals and warriors of this earth! Why, it is nothing to the power of the man who is in communion with God. Elisha was not going to ask for a small thing. He says, "I want a double portion of thy spirit." I can see Elijah turn round to him in surprise and say, "You have asked me a hard thing." But he says, "If you see me when I am taken from you, you shall have it." "Then," says Elisha, "you'll not get away without my seeing you." He wanted a double portion of Elijah's spirit, and he was determined to get it. So he took good care to see him in the chariot, and he did see him. Elisha performed twice the number of miracles that Elijah did.

Jesus Christ has come down from heaven since then, and is it so wonderful to ask for the power of the Spirit? We ought to have a hundred times more power than Elijah and Elisha had.

D. L. MOODY.

When God takes possession of a slow tongue, he can make it fast if he wants to, but you will get none of the credit.　　　　　　H. W. WEBB-PEPLOE.

You will never possess any more of Christ than
you claim as your own. You do not gain God's blessing by storing away books full of notes; you must
take God's truth into your very soul and feast upon
it. What good will abundance of food or water or
money do you if it is unclaimed and unused? The
money that a man takes from the bank is his enjoy-
able possession, that which he has in the bank is only
his lawful possession. You cannot pass through the
riches of God except by the study of this blessed
Book and by constantly dealing with God in prayer.

H. W. WEBB-PEPLOE.

The difference between Christians is not so much
a difference of endowment as it is a difference of
apprehension and appropriation. A man once owned
a small farm. He did his best to till it and rear a
family, but after working hard all his life he died a
poor man. The farm was inherited by his eldest son.
The son discovered a gold-mine and became immensely rich. The property he had was the same
that his father had; but the father didn't know what
was in the land, while the son found it out.

That is the difference between Christians. Through
the atonement of Jesus Christ God hath made us heirs
to all things, but only the Holy Ghost reveals our
riches. A. J. GORDON.

"Let us come boldly to the throne of grace, that
we may obtain mercy and find grace to help in time
of need." How many of God's people who have the
bank of heaven to draw on, and could come boldly to
the throne of grace and get help in time of need,
have thus far been living on a few crumbs.

D. L. MOODY.

I distinguish very clearly between a *doctrine* as essential to salvation, and the *belief* of that doctrine as essential to salvation. If Christianity is worth anything at all, there could have been no hope for you and me except upon the ground of the doctrine of the incarnation of our Lord Jesus Christ; for it is the fact of the incarnation, together with what is involved in it, that makes salvation possible. But it is one thing to say that salvation is conditioned upon a doctrine, and another thing to say that my salvation is conditioned upon my belief in that doctrine. I do not raise an inquiry here as to the minimum of belief, though I hold some belief to be necessary; but the question is, whether there is anything of a dogmatic nature, in the content of the Christian religion, which is obligatory upon all who profess and call themselves Christian.

FRANCIS L. PATTON.

A great many men are waiting for feeling; but feeling never saves, and the most unsatisfactory Christians are those who are governed altogether by their sentiments. D. L. MOODY.

There are three things: feeling, faith, and fact. You may have put them in this order: feeling, fact, faith; or fact, feeling, faith. You must change, and put them thus: fact, faith—and feeling a hundred years after, if you like. You have been trying to feel God's fact, but you must take God's fact on faith—the great fact that Christ has come through the grave into a new world. Upon your apprehension by faith of that fact as revealed in the Bible the whole structure of your deliverance depends.

F. B. MEYER.

55

And I, if I be lifted up, . . . will draw all men unto me.—
John xii. 32.

If you put yourself before the cross, you may hold
up the cross and yet obscure it. But the man that
will get behind the cross,—who is willing to get behind Christ and the Bible, so that men will not see
him, but only the exalted Word,—that is the man
whom the Holy Ghost is likely to endue with great
power. Like the Statue of Liberty in New York
harbor, we are to be light-holders; and if we stand
on a high pedestal it is that we may hold the light a
little higher. May God truly endue us with power
by his Spirit and for his service!

ARTHUR T. PIERSON.

One day a friend of mine, in passing down a Glasgow street, saw a crowd at a shop door, and had the
curiosity to look in. There he saw an auctioneer
holding up a grand picture so that all could see it.
When he got it in position, he remained behind it and
said to the crowd, "Now look at this part of the
picture, . . . and now at this other part," and so on,
describing each detail of it. "Now," said my friend,
"the whole time I was there I never saw the speaker,
but only the picture he was showing." That is the
way to work for Christ. He must increase, but we
must be out of sight. ANDREW A. BONAR.

Christ spake his parables *unto* the people. To
speak *unto* people is a thing that some commentators
and preachers never by any means try. They speak
over or under them, or past them, or all round about
them, but *unto* them they never tried yet.

JOHN MCNEILL.

And I, brethren, could not speak unto you as unto spiritual, but as unto carnal, even as unto babes in Christ.—1 Cor. iii. 1.

The apostle here speaks of two stages of the Christian life, two types of Christians: the spiritual and the carnal. Those to whom he wrote were all Christians,—in Christ,—but, instead of being spiritual Christians, they were carnal.

In the wisdom which the Holy Ghost gives him St. Paul feels, "I cannot write to these Corinthian Christians unless I know their state, and unless I tell them of it. If I give spiritual food to carnal Christians I am doing them more harm than good, for they are not fit to take it in. I cannot feed them with meat; I must feed them with milk."

In the church of Christ you will find two classes of Christians. Some have lived many years as believers, and yet always remain babes; others are spiritual men, because they have given themselves up to the power, the leading, and to the entire rule of the Holy Ghost.

If we are to receive a blessing, the first thing needed is for each one to know on which side of the line he stands.   ANDREW MURRAY.

"Every one that useth milk is unskilful in the word of righteousness: for he is a babe." It is to be feared that many Christians are content with the forgiveness of sins, and do not care to take another step. "I write unto you, little children," says John, "because your sins are forgiven you." Are we going to be content to remain little children, without going on to do the young men's battle with the wicked one? "I write unto you, young men, because ye have overcome the wicked one."   ANDREW A. BONAR.

The trouble with us is, our proud hearts refuse to accept the position in which God's Word places us. It charges us with sin and corruption, and we would like to excuse ourselves and harp a little upon the dignity of human nature. God tells us that without him we can do nothing. We are apt to think that by our reasoning powers and high culture we can ourselves do wonders. Not until we accept the position of sinfulness and weakness are we prepared to receive his blessing. A. C. DIXON.

Some Christians make a great deal of themselves and little of Christ, while others make a little of themselves and a great deal of Christ. When a person considers that he is growing little in the sight of the Lord, in reality he is finding the true grace and goodness of the God of mankind. D. L. MOODY.

Allow God to take his place in your heart and life. Luther often said to people, when they came to him about difficulties, "Do let God be God." Let God be all in all, every day in your life, from morning to evening. No more say, "I and God;" let it be "God and I." God first, and I second; God to lead, and I to follow; God to work all in me, and I to work out only what God works; God to rule, and I to obey. Even in that order there is a danger, for the flesh is so subtle, and one might begin to think, "It is God and I. Oh, what a privilege that I have such a partner!" There might be secret self-exaltation in associating God with myself. There is a more precious word still—"God and not I; not God first, and I second; God is all, and I am nothing." Paul said, "I labored more abundantly than they all, though I be nothing." ANDREW MURRAY.

There is no truly Christian man who keeps an unconverted pocket-book. God's universal law of unselfish service is as supreme in the domain of material possessions—in the realm of that wealth which extends a man's power "to bring things to pass"—as it is in any other department of man's possible efforts. The unvarying law of God, which attaches an obligation to every opportunity and places a duty over against every right, makes no exception of wealth with its vast powers of service. God has so ordered the social life of our race that no man can make the most of his powers of mind and heart and will until he employs those powers in the service of his fellow-men. This is an accepted law in the realm of mind and spirit. It is no less binding upon the power which material wealth places at a man's disposal. No man has the slightest right to say of his wealth, "It is mine; I may use it selfishly if I will." No man has arrived at a true conception of the responsibility that attaches to the possession of property, until his relations through it to his fellow-men fill a larger place in his views of life than does his ability by his wealth to serve his own selfish ends. No man is free to make an option as to whether he or his property shall come under God's law of service. He and his property are of necessity under that law, as he is of necessity a member of society and of the state, without his leave having been asked. In the use of his property, as of all his other powers, he owes steady allegiance to that law of service; and though in managing his property he may disregard this obligation, he can never escape it.

MERRILL E. GATES.

That Christ may dwell in your hearts by faith.—Eph. iii. 17.

One of our poets, speaking of our birth, beautifully says, "Every soul leaves port under sealed orders. We cannot know whither we are going or what we are to do till the time comes for breaking the seal." But I can tell you something more beautiful than this. Every regenerated soul sets out on its voyage with an invisible Captain on board, who knows the nature of our sealed orders from the outset, and who will shape our entire voyage accordingly if we will only let him.　　　　　　　　　　A. J. GORDON.

If your heart is empty, if you have only sent the devil out by a pledge or a resolution, he will surely come back and say, "Is there any one inside?" If there is silence he will smash open the door through all your good resolutions, and he will bring seven other devils along with him, and will fill your heart with riot and sin. But if, when he comes back, Christ says, "I am here," that is enough. Do you mean to tell me that Christ can keep that sun full of light, and cannot keep your heart full of light? I believe, if Christ wished it, that he could make Niagara leap back, and I believe that he can come into your life and can take your passion and stay it. Do not be afraid; Christ can keep. Put him in possession, and he will keep his own.　　F. B. MEYER.

Take the position of power and privilege which God offers to you; no longer dare to vilify Christ in the eyes of the world by saying "I cannot." No one ever said that you could. Say once for all, "I cannot, but Christ can."　　　　　H. W. WEBB-PEPLOE.

God be merciful to me a sinner.—Luke xviii. 13.

Sometimes in the darkness a man's foot kicks against the ladder that slopes through the darkness up to God. He takes the first round of it. It is not the top of the ladder—justification; but it is a big jump upward from where he has been lying in the dirt at the bottom of the pit of iniquity. He is clean out, altogether out, and up one rung on the ladder, and will take the rest. For whom He calls, them He also justifies; that is the first round, and the publican took it in that prayer. And whom He justifies, them He also sanctifies; that is a rising up the ladder. And whom He sanctifies, them He also glorifies.

The publican is in heaven. May we meet him there, through the rich grace of Him who, a few months afterward, died on the cross that the publican's prayer might be heard and answered exceedingly abundantly above all that he could ask or think.

JOHN MCNEILL.

A soldier once said that, according to his idea, repentance was, "Halt! About face! Forward! March!" Repentance is not lopping off particular sins. If I have a vessel full of holes, and stop only part of them, the vessel will sink just as surely as if I did not stop any. We must break off from all sin and turn unto God.

D. L. MOODY.

To repent means to change your mind about sin, and especially about Christ. Peter says, "Repent;" change from the Christ-rejecting to the Christ-accepting attitude of mind; accept Christ as Saviour and as Lord.

R. A. TORREY.

I would rather aim at perfection and fall short of it than aim at imperfection and fully attain it.

A. J. GORDON.

"Daniel purposed in his *heart*." That's the trouble with a great many people; they purpose to do right, but they only purpose in their heads, and that doesn't amount to much. If you are going to be Christians, you must purpose to serve God away down in your hearts. "With the *heart* man believeth unto righteousness."

D. L. MOODY.

The purpose of our life should be twofold: first, to understand what is our position in Christ, and then by faith and by the power of the Holy Ghost to be lifted to that level.

F. B. MEYER.

Many men have high aspirations, but not the right motive. A man desires the baptism with the Holy Spirit simply that he may be a greater preacher or a greater personal worker, or that he may become renowned as a Christian. One of the subtlest errors that Satan leads us into is that where we are longing and crying for this most solemn of all gifts that we may be greater preachers or that our church may be built up. The desire must not be for any glory that comes to me or my church, but because God and Christ are being dishonored by my life and lack of power, and by the sin of the people around me, and because he will be honored if I am baptized with the Spirit.

R. A. TORREY.

Philosophical doubt, although it has done harm, has also done good; good results have come with the spirit of investigation that has been developed. It was no great credit to Thomas that he did not believe the resurrection of Christ as the others did, and yet what a wonderful chapter in the evidences of Christianity was opened by his skepticism! It was no great credit to men that they called in question the authenticity of the four gospels, but how their skepticism has stimulated scholarly inquiry and strengthened the defenses of the gospel narratives!

When the elevated railroad was first started in New York the people were a little timid about riding on it; so the proprietors of the road took great pleasure in apprising the public of the fact that this road had been subjected to a most abnormal and enormous tonnage, and that consequently people of ordinary weight might deem themselves quite safe in traveling over that road. I feel the same way about the four gospels—that I can take my way to heaven above the din and dust of daily life because this elevated road has had all Germany upon it, and that as yet it has given no sign of instability.

FRANCIS L. PATTON.

If you stand on the mountain of faith and look down, things will seem easy to you; but if you are in the valley of doubt they will look like giants. What the church wants and what it is looking for are men and women of faith.

D. L. MOODY.

63

There are men who tell us that a revelation from God is impossible. I simply ask them, How do you know? Because if God exists it is not impossible; all things are possible with him.

Others say that a revelation is not needed. If I should ask a dozen men for the time of day, and each watch should mark a different time, it would be difficult to tell which one was right; they might be all wrong, but it would be clear that only one of them could by any possibility be right. A man might claim the gift of infallibility for his own watch, which would not be modest; or we might say, "There is no telling what o'clock it is," which would be uncomfortable; or we might say, "It would be convenient if there were a big town clock by which we could all regulate our watches." What we want in this universal conflict about moral questions is a town clock to tell us the time of day.

Others say that there is so much in the Bible that could not have come from God; that this or that, for instance, is not God's style. I don't know just what God's style is, but it seems to me that what is fair for one is fair for the other; and when I ask that my verifying faculty be allowed the privilege of eliminating from the Bible what I do not like, I am fair enough to say that my next-door neighbor may have the same privilege. It may turn out that his eclecticism has not hit upon the same thing to take out or keep in as mine has. Now when we have all taken out what we do not think could have come from God, I should like to know how much of the Bible would be left except that for which the bookbinder is responsible.

FRANCIS L. PATTON.

An hour alone with God isn't lost time.
D. L. Moody.

Persevering prayerfulness—day by day wrestling
and pleading—is harder for the flesh than preaching.
Andrew A. Bonar.

Real prayer is need packed till it takes fire.
A. C. Dixon.

"Thy will be done" is the key-note to which every
prayer must be tuned.
A. J. Gordon.

"Praying in the Holy Ghost" (Jude 20). Not
simply the Holy Ghost praying in you. You are im-
mersed in the Holy Ghost. The atmosphere you
breathe is what you give out. It is wrong to imagine
that prayer is only speaking to God. Often the most
precious part of it is God speaking to us. On Jacob's
ladder angels descended as well as ascended. The
closet is the place of revelation.
Arthur T. Pierson.

Prayer is the most necessary and wonderful thing
in the spiritual life; yet we know neither how to pray
nor for what to pray as we ought, so the Spirit prays
for us with groanings unutterable. We often do not
know what the Spirit is doing within us; but God,
who searches the hearts, finds out, and answers the
prayer of the Spirit because it is according to his will.
What a solemn, blessed, comforting thought!
Andrew Murray.

65

Receive with meekness the engrafted Word, which is able to save your souls.—James i. 21.

God has given only two perfect things to this lost world: one of them is the incarnate Word, which is the Lord Jesus Christ; the other is the written Word, which is the Holy Scripture. There is a divine element and a human element in both.

JAMES H. BROOKES.

Believe God's Word as it stands; you need not interpret God's words until you have altogether changed their meaning, as some expositors do.

H. W. WEBB-PEPLOE.

The best way to be equipped for the work is to be deeply taught in the Word. If we want the work "well in hand," we must have the Word "well in hand." But it is one thing to have the Bible in the hand, and quite another thing to know how to handle it. The Word of God is called by Paul "the sword of the Spirit." Any one can hold a sword, but only an expert can use it skilfully. . . .

A man might come from hell, his eyes bursting with terror, his flesh scorched with the fires of perdition, fly through your congregation as you preach, and cry, "Flee from the wrath which is to come." He might be followed by another, clad in white, from the heavenly city to tell of the joys about God's throne. And if the Spirit of God is not there it will pass without effect from your people.

W. W. CLARK.

God is a Spirit: and they that worship him must worship him in spirit and in truth.—John iv. 24.

The only living that is acceptable to God is living in the Spirit. The only walk that is acceptable to God is walking in the Spirit. The only service that is acceptable to God is serving in the Spirit. The only praying that is acceptable to God is praying in the Spirit. The only worship that is acceptable to God is worshiping in the Spirit. Would we worship aright, our hearts must look up and cry, "Teach me, Holy Spirit, to worship," and he will do it.

R. A. TORREY.

The service of the Israelites was very similar to that of surrounding nations; but whereas the latter kindled the fires upon their altars, God distinguished his service by sending down fire from heaven. That is the difference between true religion and its counterfeit. Natural religion depends on the energy of the flesh. Supernatural religion depends on the energy of the Spirit of God, which comes down from above. It is quite possible to be perfectly right in the forms of our service, and yet destitute of divine power. GEORGE F. PENTECOST.

It is a blessed privilege to fall before our Saviour and worship, though all his dealings with us are as dark as night. A. C. DIXON.

Those who are in communion with God live, those who are not are dead. HENRY DRUMMOND.

67

Go ye into all the world, and preach the gospel to every creature.—Mark xvi. 15.

There is the great commission, "Go ye." Where men are ordered to enroll themselves as soldiers, it is their business to do so thereupon. If they are exempt, the onus probandi as to exemption rests upon them and not upon the executive. It is for us to do; as when Deborah and Barak called for troops, "the people willingly offered themselves. Let us recognize our obligation and offer ourselves.

WILLIAM ASHMORE.

There is no question that if we had a human imperial authority we could go around the globe in a year, and promulgate this gospel decree all through the world. And yet we stand still when the King of kings is saying to us, "Go ye into all the world, and preach the gospel to every creature."

ARTHUR T. PIERSON.

If we could only put ourselves into harmony with God, how easily the great work of carrying the gospel into all the world would be fulfilled, and the time brought near when our Redeemer shall come as a King to reign and to judge the poor with equity! There is something wrong when one man can sit in a palace while another is perishing with hunger at his door.   W. E. BLACKSTONE.

Work enough at home? There will be more work at home if we don't take hold of missions more in earnest. . . . Christianity is nothing if it is not missionary. *Your* Christianity is nothing if it is not missionary.   JOHN A. BROADUS.

Month of March

The sins of teachers are the teachers of sins. Beware of the bad things of good men.

ANDREW A. BONAR.

No amount of praying or psalm-singing will cover up a sin. A lady once said to me, "I am more irritable than I was five years ago. Can you help me?" I answered, "The next time you are angry with a person, go and confess it, and ask forgiveness." "Oh," she said, "I shouldn't like to do that." Of course not. I shouldn't like to take cod-liver oil, but I should do it to save my life. When people do with their souls as they would with their bodies, there will be something accomplished.

D. L. MOODY.

Many of us would love to have sin taken away. Who loves to have a hasty temper? Who loves to have a proud disposition? Who loves to have a worldly heart? No one. You ask Christ to take it away, and he doesn't do it. Why does he not do it? It is because you wanted him to take away the ugly fruits while the poisonous root remained in you. You did not ask him that the flesh should be nailed to his cross, and that you should henceforth give up self entirely to the power of his spirit.

Do you suppose that a painter would want to work out a beautiful picture on a canvas which did not belong to him? No. Yet people want Jesus Christ to bestow his trouble upon them in taking away this temper or that other sin while as yet they have not yielded themselves utterly to his command and his keeping.

ANDREW MURRAY.

69

Love not the world, neither the things that are in the world.
—1 John ii. 15.

We are living under a materializing influence that
is disastrous to a more serious and devotional view
of life. In the minds of a great many good people
the ideal of human existence is a great deal of material comfort and a large surplus of pleasure that
can be purchased in the form of desirable surroundings. These ideals rise in the scale of magnitude and
grandeur every year, and men say, "When I can
realize this ideal of earthly paradise, I am going to
devote a great deal of time to devotional preparation
for the next world." The trouble is that they no
sooner get their house on the sea-shore than they
want a house in the mountains, and when they have
that they want a house somewhere else. They say,
"Wait till my cat-boat grows into a sloop, and my
sloop into a schooner, and my schooner into a steam-
yacht; then I devise liberal things." But the "then"
never comes. Meanwhile they have become so im-
mersed in this world, and so filled with the spirit of
this world, and so absorbed in the pursuit of this
world's pleasure and comfort, that they have no time
to read this Bible as they ought to read it.

FRANCIS L. PATTON.

Love not this world, because if you love it you
cannot love Him. Love not this world, because if
you love it you love something that by and by will
be ashes, and, while you thought you were grasping
the honors of the world that now is and is to come,
you will find you have grasped only the hot, dusty
ashes of the world that is to come.

ROBERT E. SPEER.

Daniel purposed in his heart that he would not defile himself with the portion of the king's meat, nor with the wine which he drank.—Dan. i. 8.

Modern travelers commonly do not get half-way to Babylon before they conclude that it is more prudent to follow the example of the multitude, on the drinking question, than to stand out by themselves, as did Daniel, Shadrach, Meshach, and Abednego; so they drink the wines of the European tables, as "everybody else does." When they have come to that conclusion they are in a good state to consider further whether it is wise to be cast into a den of lions or a fiery furnace of invidious comment rather than conform to the universal custom of the country they are in, as to times and modes of worship, as to local amusements, and as to a courteous recognition of the images which King Fashion has set up to be admired and extolled.

HENRY CLAY TRUMBULL.

Will the Christian find that he gets peace and joy so long as he tries to satisfy his soul by saying that his worldly taste is "only a little one"? I do not say that it is wrong to smoke or for a Christian to go to the theater. *That* is for each one to settle with his God. But when Christians draw quibbling distinctions between great and small sins, between one theater and another, one dance and another, it is clear that the conscience is not at rest, and there can be no rest till God's voice is fully and heartily obeyed.

H. W. WEBB-PEPLOE.

Let the wicked forsake his way, and the unrighteous man his thoughts, and let him return unto the Lord.—Isa. li. 7.

If you ever expect to enter the kingdom of God, you must give up your thoughts and accept God's thoughts, give up your ways and accept God's ways; for his thoughts and ways are as high above ours as is the heaven above the earth.

D. L. MOODY.

Get the love of Jesus into your heart, and the lust for woman and man, the lust for gold, and the lust for drink will be crowded out. Money! It was for money that Zaccheus was damning his soul; but Jesus so took possession of his heart that he virtually said, "Lord, as to money, I will fling it away by the shovelful, now that I know thee; I will restore fourfold." You say that you are converted. Show me your hands; show me your purse. Do not pretend that you know Jesus if you have a purse as tight as a miser's fist. You say that you are converted. Are you delivered from that which before was dragging you down to the pit? Folks go about scorning conversion. Nobody in Jericho scorned and scoffed at the conversion of Zaccheus. It had all the signs of a genuine turning of the man inside out and outside in. He was radically changed, and it was the love of Christ that did it. Zaccheus came out of curiosity to see this man Jesus. He saw him, and he got such a close look at him that his heart rose up and said, "This is the Lord." That was faith, saving faith. It works by love and purifies the heart and overcomes the world.

JOHN McNEILL.

The law was given by Moses, but grace and truth came by Jesus Christ.—John i. 17.

The law slays the sinner, grace slays the sin.

ADA R. HABERSHON.

Our first union was with the law; and the law said, "Thou shalt love the Lord thy God with all thy heart, and with all thy soul, and with all thy strength, and with all thy mind. Thou shalt love thy neighbor as thyself." We never brought forth one single particle of fruit to God during such connection. Knowing that "cursed is every one that continueth not in all things that are written in the book of the law to do them," we have never continued for one mortal hour in all things or in any of the things written in the book of the law to do them. We could bring forth no fruit to God in our connection with the law. That is why he sent the law—that we might learn this truth. Some people think they can be justified by the law that condemns them to eternal torment. It is impossible; we must look for justification to some one who was able to satisfy the demands of the law and of justice.

MARCUS RAINSFORD.

The law produces legal conviction and leads to despair; the gospel produces evangelical conviction and leads to hope.

A. J. GORDON.

If we confess our sins, he is faithful and just to forgive us our sins, and to cleanse us from all unrighteousness.—1 John i. 9.

Some one has said, "Unconfessed sin in the soul is like a bullet in the body." If you haven't power, it may be there is some sin that needs to be confessed, something in your life that needs to be straightened out. No amount of psalm-singing, no amount of attending religious gatherings, no amount of praying, no amount of reading your Bible, is going to cover up anything of that kind. If I have too much pride to confess my sins, I needn't expect mercy from God or answers to my prayers.

"He that covereth his sins shall not prosper." He may be a man in the pulpit, a priest behind the altar, or a king on the throne—I don't care who he is; he will fail. Man has been trying it for six thousand years. Adam tried it and failed; Moses tried it when he buried the Egyptian, but he failed; David tried it; priests and kings and princes and the best men that ever trod the earth have tried it, but all have failed. "Be sure your sin will find you out." You cannot bury your sins so deep that there will not be a resurrection by and by, if they have not been blotted out by the Son of God. What man has failed to do for six thousand years you and I would best give up trying to do.

The reason that some people's prayers go no higher than their head is because they have some unconfessed sin in their lives. You may pray and weep and pray and weep, but it will do no good. First confess to the one you have wronged, then go to God and see how quickly he will hear you.

D. L. MOODY.

All Scripture is given by inspiration of God, and is profitable
for doctrine, for reproof, for correction, for instruction in
righteousness: that the man of God may be perfect, thoroughly
furnished unto all good works.—2 Tim. iii. 16.

The Bible contains a complete rule for the whole
life of man. It tells a man how he should conduct
himself with reference to God, to the Lord Jesus, to
the Holy Spirit, to the Word which God has given,
and to the church which he has established. It
directs him how he should treat his wife and care
for his children; how much he should pay his hired
man, and when he should pay him. It teaches the
hired man how he should conduct himself with reference to his employer. It tells men how to loan
money and how to collect debts as well as how to
worship. It teaches a man what kind of a citizen
he should be, how he ought to vote if he is in a self-
governing country. If he is a magistrate it directs
him how he ought to exercise authority, and says
that God will call him to account for the manner in
which he executes his office.

We are apt to narrow down the teachings of the
Bible and the business of the church, and to suppose
that they have to do chiefly with the work of the
Sabbath, and that they have little or nothing to do
with our pleasures, our business, or our political and
our industrial relations; but the testimony of the
Word of God is that this Book is given by inspiration
of God, and that it is "profitable for doctrine, for
reproof, for correction, for instruction in right doing:
that the man of God may be perfect, thoroughly furnished unto every good work," not simply to some
good works.

CHARLES A. BLANCHARD.

There are graces within our reach that we will never seek until we are hard pressed by temptation in the opposite direction. It is a profound mistake merely to resist the tempter; a better policy is to turn from the temptation to acquire the opposite grace. If you are tempted to impurity, claim purity; if you are tempted to impatience, claim patience; if tempted to weakness, claim strength.

We must watch not only our weak points, but our strong points, for many of the great Bible heroes failed on their strong points; Moses in his meekness and Job in his patience. There is nothing in which men are naturally strong that can stand against the power of our great adversary. Yielding is the result of long previous decline; the sin which breaks out in the manifestation has far-reaching roots, and to be confessed properly one needs to go back from the act to the intention, and from the intention to the purpose, through the weeks or months of previous life, until one gets at last to the beginning of the sin; then confess it in order that it may be expiated before God.

There is this blessed thought—that there is reciprocity between Christ and ourselves; and in this the tempted man finds succor, first, that he is in Christ, and, second, that Christ is in him. If you are in Christ you are in the one under whose feet the devil is. Abide there and you too are above the devil, and therefore—now mark—the whole energy of the devil is directed to solicit, to seduce men out of Christ.　　　　　　　　F. B. MEYER.

Some people ask how a man is to know that he is saved. How do you know anything? Suppose that I am dealing with an inquirer who has accepted Christ, but has not the assurance which a believer should have. Do I ask him to kneel down and pray and pray until some happy feeling comes into his heart? If I do, I do not know how to lead a soul to Christ. No; I take God's Word and put it into his hand, and say, " My friend, will you read the thirty-sixth verse of the third chapter of John: 'He that believeth on the Son of God hath everlasting life.'" I say to him, " Who has everlasting life?" " He that believes on the Son of God." " Do you believe on the Son of God?" " I do." " Have you everlasting life?" " No; I do not *feel* it!" " Will you please read that again?" And he reads, " He that believeth on the Son of God hath everlasting life." I say, " Who has everlasting life?" He looks at the Book and says, " He that believeth on the Son." I say, " Do you believe on the Son?" " I do." " What have you?" " Why, I do not know that I have anything." " What does that verse say that the one that believes on the Son of God hath? How many of those who believe on the Son have everlasting life?" " All of them." " How do you know it?" " It says so." " Do you believe on the Son?" " I do." " What have you?" " *Everlasting life!*" " How do you know it?" " Because God says so." It is only after he rests on what God says in his Word that he has the testimony of the Holy Ghost. Faith in the Word of God comes first.   R. A. TORREY.

77

With what weapons do the missionaries propose to do this mighty work of conquering the heathen world for Christ? With nothing but "a little book." That is like Moses going down with a sheep-crook to conquer Pharaoh and all his host. Any weapon is enough if the Lord is only behind it. The little Book is enough if the Lord only helps you to use it. A Christian warrior should always carry his fighting Testament in his pistol pocket. If you cannot carry around with you a double-barreled Testament, always carry a single-barreled one.

WILLIAM ASHMORE.

When a man is giving a lecture with a map or illustrations, he often uses a long pointer to indicate the places or illustrations. Does the audience look at that pointer? No. It might be of fine gold, but the pointer cannot satisfy them. They want to see what the pointer points at. The Bible is nothing but a pointer pointing to God; and Jesus Christ came to point us, to show us the way, to bring us to God.

I fear that there are many people who love Christ and trust in him, but who fail to see the one great object of his work; they have never understood the Scripture, "He died that he might bring us to God." There is a difference between the way I am going and the end I have in view. I might be traveling amid beautiful scenery, in delightful company, but if I have a home which I long to reach all the scenery and company around me cannot satisfy me. God is meant to be the home of our souls.

ANDREW MURRAY.

Men tell us sometimes there is no such thing as an atheist. There must be. There are some men to whom it is true that there is no God. They cannot see God because they have no eye. They have only an abortive organ, atrophied by neglect.

HENRY DRUMMOND.

A good many people live on negations. They are always telling what they don't believe. I want a man to tell me what he does believe, not what he does not believe.

D. L. MOODY.

Young gentlemen, believe your beliefs and doubt your doubts; do not make the mistake of doubting your beliefs and believing your doubts.

CHARLES F. DEEMS.

Nothing cuts out the roots of the Christian life so much as unbelief.

ANDREW MURRAY.

Hinder not the will of God by a spirit of unbelief, by limiting the Holy One of Israel, because you thereby reject his holy counsel and purpose for you. Train your souls in a spirit of receptivity and by the exercise of faith to take all that God himself can give. Be determined that "your whole spirit, soul, and body"—whatever department of your being you can deal with—shall be placed submissively at the disposal of God, to know, to receive, and to enjoy everything that God can possibly give you.

H. W. WEBB-PEPLOE.

Christianity stands out as a kind of "spiritual highland" and headland for the human race, a system which, the more it is studied and experienced, is the more highly prized; its path is always the path of peace, knowledge, elevation, emancipation, salvation; a system various in manner, flexible in its circumstantials, while most inflexible in its essence; full of strength for the weak, of consolation for the sorrowful, of hope for the discouraged, of stimulus for the sluggish, of defense for the defenseless, of authority for the many, of terror for the evil, of reward for the good, of pardon for the penitent; a system which can satisfy all the desires that human want awakens, which can enter all dark places and leave them full of light by conquering despair and instituting its wonderful miracles of renovation; a system which can convert dens of thieves into bethels of the Holy Ghost, and which can cast out its legion of devils, and say to wretches whose brains have been in a perpetual "craze" and whose hearts have been filled with all sorts of villainies, "Peace, be still;" a system which can stand by the bedside of the dying, quell every misgiving, wipe away the death-sweat, and leave the brow calm and serene as heaven; a system which can perfect the individual, bless the family, correct and purify society, and civilize the world; which can, in fine, do everything it promises to do, and promises to do everything essential to human happiness here and hereafter— such a system has the unencumbered guaranty of all times.

L. T. TOWNSEND.

God has given us two sets of scales in our mental and moral constitution. One of these scales is intended to weigh evidence and subject it to rational proofs; the other is to weigh right and wrong and to ascertain the difference between morality and immorality. Reason's office is to weigh evidence; conscience's office is to weigh right and wrong.

ARTHUR T. PIERSON.

If a man is morally color-blind he is likely to be wrong—conscientiously. That faculty or element in our nature which we call "conscience" is set within us as a *monitor*, not as a *teacher*, in the school of morals. Conscience tells us that we *ought to* do right, but conscience does not tell us *what* right is. The compass is safe to steer by as long as its needle points where it ought to point; but the compass-needle may be forcibly deflected from the pole, or it may be drawn aside by the influences of its surroundings, and then, of course, it is untrustworthy.

It would be well if all of us understood just how far from the true meridian *our* moral compass-needles were deflected by the attractions of gold or pleasure or appetite or ambition or love or hatred or by the social atmosphere of our immediate neighborhood.

HENRY CLAY TRUMBULL.

Conscience is not a safe guide, because very often conscience won't tell you you have done wrong until after you have done it, but the Bible will tell you what is wrong before you have done it.

D. L. MOODY.

Faith is totally distinct from trust. By faith we claim; by trust we prove that we have taken, and that the gifts of God have become to us what God in his omnipotence intended them to be.

Faith takes into our soul what God in his mercy reveals, and believes God against all comers. Trust hands over to God what God has given us, and says, "Keep, Lord, and use, for I cannot." Then comes a holy confidence and assurance which prevents us from being disturbed under any circumstances whatever, and out of which comes a boldness which enables us to act for the glory of God. Faith when it has conceived brings forth trust, and trust when it is finished brings forth confidence and boldness.

Alexander the Great had a physician who was his bosom friend. One day there came an anonymous letter on a waxed tablet to the king. "O king, there is treachery in thy home. Thy physician purposes to kill thee by the draft which he gives thee to-morrow under the plea of healing thee." The king put that waxed tablet into his breast, and the next day, when the physician came to give him the draft, he put out his left hand and took the cup, and with his right hand handed the tablet to the physician and said, "Friend, I trust thee," and drank the potion without stopping a moment to see the effect upon the physician. It is not enough to believe that Christ is the great Physician; you must trust him. We trust the cook every day. What fools we are that we cannot trust God!

H. W. WEBB-PEPLOE.

My little boy, since taken to heaven, once asked me, "Papa, how is it that one person, Christ, could atone for the sin of millions of men?" We were in a garden at the time. I replied, "Suppose that there was on the ground there a handful of worms; don't you think that you would be more valuable than those worms?" "Yes," he said. "Suppose that that wheelbarrow was full of worms; would you not be more valuable than all of them?" "Yes." "Suppose all the millions of worms in the earth were gathered together; would you not still be more valuable than they, no matter how many?" "Yes; I am sure I would." "Then is there not a far greater difference in the scale of being between Christ and man than between man and the worm? We are creatures; God is the Creator. Had many other worlds sinned as well as ours, the blood of Christ would be more than sufficient to atone for them all."

R. C. MORGAN.

Let us consider for a moment our standing with Christ. Again we must distinguish. The death of Christ has two aspects: one toward the guilt of sin, the other toward the power of sin. The aspect toward the guilt of sin is that by his one oblation and sacrifice he has put the guilt away forever, and the thunder-clouds that lower over his cross spend themselves on Calvary, and his cross is a lightning-conductor to draw away what men might fear. But Christ not only died *for* sin, but he died *unto* sin.

F. B. MEYER.

It has taxed many minds to explain what Jesus could have meant when on the cross he cried, "My God, my God, why hast thou forsaken me?"

It seems to me that we may see its meaning more clearly in the light of an incident which happened in the eastern part of Massachusetts some years ago. A judge was obliged to try his own son, who had been charged with some crime. There was great anxiety to know how that judge would conduct the case. To the astonishment of everybody, the judge was just as impartial and unmoved as if the young man had had no relation to him. When he had heard the evidence he charged the jury with just the same exactness and carefulness as if he had not known the accused. People were astonished. They said he had no heart. But when the jury uttered the words "Not guilty" the judge jumped up, reached out his hands, and cried, "Come up here, my boy." He took his son right into his seat on the bench.

Notice that in Gethsemane Jesus says, "*Father*, if it be possible, let this cup pass from me." He also prayed, "Father, forgive them." But when he reached the culmination of his agony, when he stood before the judge bearing the sins of the world on his shoulders,—a great culprit,—he could say "Father" no more. For once it was, "My God, my God!" But when it was all over and he rose from the grave, once more he is filled with the full radiance of the Father's love, and the Father places him at his own right hand.

A. J. GORDON.

If the amount of energy lost in trying to grow
were spent in fulfilling rather the conditions of
growth, we should have many more cubits to show
for our stature. . . .

The stature of the Lord Jesus was not itself
reached by work, and he who thinks to approach its
mystical height by anxious effort is really receding
from it. . . .

If God is adding to our spiritual stature, unfold-
ing the new nature within us, it is a mistake to keep
twitching at the petals with our coarse fingers. We
must seek to let the Creative Hand alone. "It is
God which giveth the increase." . . .

The life must develop out according to its type,
and, being a germ of the Christ-life, it must unfold
into the image of Christ.

HENRY DRUMMOND.

It is one thing to be innocent; it is another thing
to be virtuous. It is one thing to be like Adam,
created after the image of God in perfect purity and
simplicity; it is another thing to be like the perfected
Christ, who was tried and tempted in all points like
as we are, yet without sin. Remember that, while
the blood of Jesus Christ cleanses us from all sin,
conformity to the image of Christ wrought in us by
the Holy Spirit means that we, being changed from
glory to glory, may become like the Son of God, and
at last be actually one with him, seeing him as he is,
and being exact facsimiles of his perfect image.

H. W. WEBB-PEPLOE.

All things are possible to him that believeth.—Mark ix. 23.

Faith is simply claiming from God what God bestows, and thankfully accepting the benefits thereof.

H. W. WEBB-PEPLOE.

Don't let experience judge your faith; let your faith judge your experience.

MARCUS RAINSFORD.

Always put your "if" in the right place.   In the case of the man who wanted Christ to cast the dumb spirit out of his son, the father said, "If thou canst do anything;" but the Lord answered him, "If thou canst believe."   Christ straightened out the "if" and put it in the right place.

D. L. MOODY.

The ten spies differed from Caleb and Joshua in their report of the land of Canaan.   There are three words here beginning with G—the word "God," the word "giant," and the word "grasshopper."   Now, note, these spies made a great mistake as to the position of these three words; they compared themselves with the people of the land and said, "And in their sight we were as grasshoppers."   If they had compared the people of the land with God, they would have come back, as Caleb and Joshua did, who said in effect, "We have compared the giants with God, and the giants are as grasshoppers."

F. B. MEYER.

No man can serve two masters: for either he will hate the one, and love the other; or else he will hold to the one, and despise the other. Ye cannot serve God and mammon.—Matt. vi. 24.

We become inevitably and insensibly assimilated to that which most completely absorbs our time and attention. One cannot be constantly mixed in secular society without not only losing something of his interest in the divine society of God and angels, where he belongs by his new birth, but also becoming himself secularized. "Our citizenship is in heaven," says the Scripture. It is a sublime conception that even while here in the flesh we hold residence among seraphs and saints of the New Jerusalem. It is for us, therefore, scrupulously to keep to our heavenly fellowship, to pay taxes where we live, and to refuse to be assessed by any rival system to Christ's true church—simply because a divided loyalty is impossible. . . .

A man cannot be two without ceasing to be one; a Christian cannot subdivide himself among many interests without subtracting himself from some one interest. . . .

The true disciple is bound to adopt the double motto, "I believe and I belong."

A. J. GORDON.

When a man lives up to what he preaches, then his testimony has weight.

D. L. MOODY.

Whom the Lord loveth he chasteneth, and scourgeth every son whom he receiveth.—Heb. xii. 6.

It sometimes seems hard to find out any reason for God's dealings with his children. We may not be able to find out why we are afflicted, and may think that perhaps it is because of some undiscovered sin; but I do not think that God often deals with us in that way. He generally likes to let his people know their faults when he chastises them. You remember how when Absalom could not get Joab to come and talk with him, he burned up his corn-fields and then Joab came. Now the Lord often sends sore afflictions upon his children in order that they may come and talk with him more. You remember that Christ took away Lazarus in order that the sisters might send for Him, and that the people through all ages might get a wondrous discovery of Him as the resurrection and the life. And you remember, too, how John the Baptist was taken away from his disciples in order that they might rather go to Christ.

ANDREW A. BONAR.

When the devil tries our faith it is that he may crush it or diminish it; but when God tries our faith it is to establish and increase it.

MARCUS RAINSFORD.

The man who has fallen most and wandered most and caused God most trouble is the man who may get some good out of his sins by learning to deal with other men as God has dealt with him, and to teach them the infinite love and mercy of God.

F. B. MEYER.

Thou openest thine hand, and satisfiest the desire of every living thing.—Ps. cxlv. 16.

Look away from self to God. The God who took Israel through the Red Sea was the God who took them through Jordan into Canaan. The God who converted you is the God who is able to give you every day this blessed life. God does not disinherit any of his children. What he gives is for every one. God is waiting to bestow it.

ANDREW MURRAY.

There is no favoritism with God; just as the spring flowers, the sunshine, and the pure air are for all, as free to the beggar as to the sovereign, so God's abundant grace is for every man and woman, and there is nothing that any one has ever had which you may not have if you will. The same stream is passing your door, though you may not utilize the power to drive your water-wheel; the same electricity is in the air, though you have not learned to make it flash your messages or do the work of your home. The same grace that made a Luther, a Knox, a Latimer, a Frances Ridley Havergal, or a Spurgeon is for you to-day, and if you are living a low-down life, beaten and thwarted and dashed down and constantly compelled to admit shortcomings and failure, understand it is not because there is any favoritism on God's part; because all the Holy Ghost's power, and everything which is stored in Jesus Christ, is waiting to make you a saint and to lift you to the level which you pine for in your best moments. It makes a great difference when a man understands this.

F. B. MEYER.

The spiritual man having passed from death unto life, the natural man must next proceed to pass from life unto death. Having opened the new set of correspondences, he must deliberately close up the old. Regeneration, in short, must be accompanied by degeneration.

HENRY DRUMMOND.

Christ had no sinful self, but he had a self, and that self he actually gave up unto death. In Gethsemane he said, "Father, not my will." That unsinning self he gave up unto death that he might rise out of the grave from God, raised up and glorified. Do you expect to go to heaven any other way than Christ went? Beware! Remember that Christ descended into death and the grave, and it is in the death of self, following Jesus to the uttermost, that the deliverance and the life will come.

ANDREW MURRAY.

Dead with Christ, and buried with him in baptism! Our baptism is the burial service of the old man. Then what business have we ever unearthing a stinking corpse? H. W. WEBB-PEPLOE.

There is a law of dynamics to the effect that for every action there is an equal and opposite reaction. There is a law in Christianity that the ascent is equivalent to the descent; that the lower we get the higher we rise; that the deeper we drink in the cup of our Saviour's death the deeper we shall drink in the cup of his resurrection and ascension to glory.

F. B. MEYER.

The waters of God's blessings flow downward, and he who would drink them must stoop.

Our faith can never afford to approach God in robes of royalty. Sackcloth and ashes are always its proper clothing. Faith can never grow too strong to pray, "God be merciful to me a sinner." We are all Pharisees by nature, publicans only by grace, and let us shun as we would a viper all claim to sinless perfection. Paul never reached it, or if he did he was far from being conscious of his high attainment. When a comparatively young Christian he wrote, "I am the least of the apostles." After he had grown in grace a few years he could say, "I am less than the least of all saints." When he had grown old in God's service he could subscribe himself the "chief of sinners." A certain Methodist bishop, in charging a class of licentiates, said, "Aim at perfection, but I charge you, in God's name, never to profess it." The place for true faith is on its knees before a holy God, weeping tears of penitence for its sins and rejoicing only in his righteousness.

A. C. DIXON.

When a man's face really shines like Moses' he wists it not.   F. B. MEYER.

It is not the sight of our sinful heart that humbles us; it is a sight of Jesus Christ. I am undone because mine eyes have seen the King.

ANDREW A. BONAR.

The wind bloweth where it listeth, and thou hearest the sound thereof, but canst not tell whence it cometh, and whither it goeth: so is every one that is born of the Spirit.—John iii. 8.

We know that the wind listeth to blow where there is a vacuum. If you find a tremendous rush of wind, you know that somewhere there is an empty space. I am perfectly sure about this fact: if we could expel all pride, vanity, self-righteousness, self-seeking, desire for applause, honor, and promotion,—if by some divine power we should be utterly emptied of all that,—the Spirit would come as a rushing, mighty wind to fill us.　　　　　　A. J. GORDON.

We must distinguish what the Bible clearly separates: the difference between having the Spirit as an indwelling presence, and the baptism with the Spirit as a working power. I care not how full of imperfections your life may be, just as surely as you are a child of God the Spirit of God dwells in you. But it is one thing to have the Spirit of God *dwelling* in you, and quite another thing to have the Spirit of God *filling* you. There is a great difference between having a tenant in the house and having a tenant take possession of the house. Now, while we do not need, if we are saved, to pray that the Spirit may dwell in us, we do need to pray that he may dwell in us more fully.　　　　　　R. A. TORREY.

Just as little as you should be drunk with wine, just so little should you live without being filled with the Spirit.　　　　　　ANDREW MURRAY.

Neither pray I for these alone, but for them also which shall
believe on me through their word; that they all may be one; as
thou, Father, art in me, and I in thee, that they also may be one
in us: that the world may believe that thou hast sent me.—
John xvii. 20, 21.

Now, if the Lord Jesus Christ has had his prayer
answered,—I suppose no one will doubt it,—and all
who believe upon him are, according to the Lord's
word and his Father's word, in union with him, then
see the consequences that follow. I never—I *never*
can be alone. I have joys. I never can have them
all to myself. He rejoices with me. I have sorrows.
I cannot monopolize them. Jesus knows them—
sympathizes with me in them. I have temptations;
he is touched with the feeling of them, for he was
in all points tempted like as I am, yet without sin,
that I might have a merciful high priest, and might
go to him with confidence and present my petition
to him. In this life I can be in no position of lone-
liness. Where I am he is with me. Lying down on
my bed, he is beside me. Rising in the morning, he
is with me. Walking through the weary paths of
life, he is with me—cannot be separated from me.
Otherwise this union is not true. As nothing that
concerns me can concern me alone, even so nothing
that concerns Jesus concerns him alone. He is interested in all that concerns me, and I am interested
in all that concerns him, or there is no real union.

MARCUS RAINSFORD.

Every Christian should be *like* Christ, should live
with Christ, and find the fountains of his being *in*
Christ. Through such lives Christ can speedily win
the world to himself.   R. E. SPEER.

Love is a wonderful thing. When a man tries to love he has no real love, but the more opposition true love meets the more it triumphs, for the more it can manifest itself the more it rejoices. Beware, above everything, of being unloving. If there is one thing that grieves God and hinders the Spirit (the fruit of the Spirit is love) it is the want of lovingness. Love is rest, and rest is love, and where there is no love the rest must be disturbed. The joy of the Holy Ghost is the joy of always loving, of losing my own life in love to others.

ANDREW MURRAY.

There is a day coming in which God will bring to light every little hidden service of his children, and will let assembled worlds see the delight he has had in that which has met no eye, but which has gladdened the heart of our Father in heaven. For he is a Father indeed, and it is delightful to realize that all that fatherhood ever has been or has produced, all that motherhood has ever brought to our notice, all, indeed, that is noble and pure and tender and true, is but an outcome of the great, loving heart of our heavenly Father. There is more light in the glorious sun than in any of the thousands of reflections in the little dewdrops. So there is more love and complacency and gratification in his children in the heart of our heavenly Father than all the gratification that earthly parents and earthly friends have ever felt in the objects of their affection.

J. HUDSON TAYLOR.

Paul says that we are to be sound in faith, in patience, and in love. If a man is unsound in his faith the clergy take the ecclesiastical sword and cut him off at once. But he may be ever so unsound in charity, in patience, and nothing is said about that. We must be sound in faith, in love, and in patience if we are to be true to God.

D. L. MOODY.

How many there are to-day pretending to be loving both God and the world, men and women trying to touch the things that they should hate, and yet pretending to be living in the closest friendship of Jesus Christ! It is easy to put on the garments, but it is easier to see through the thin, mocking gauze of them the true impossibility of such living. Just so truly as God and the world are at war, so the moment our lives are laid down in uncompromising obedience to him they are laid down in utter and uncompromising contrariety with the things he has told us we are not to love. We must choose between the evil love of the world and the overflowing love of God.

ROBERT E. SPEER.

Contemplate the love of Christ, and you will love. Stand before that mirror, reflect Christ's character, and you will be changed into the same image from tenderness to tenderness. There is no other way. You cannot love to order. You can only look at the lovely object, and fall in love with it and grow into likeness to it.

HENRY DRUMMOND.

95

As long as we dare to think that secular life must be a separate existence from the spiritual, that earthly engagements cannot be fulfilled in uninterrupted communion with God, just so long are we living outside the purposes of God, contradicting the majesty of our true nature, and denying the efficacy of the gospel of the Lord Jesus. There may be a manifold manifestation of the great purposes of life, but throughout all these manifestations there ought to run one great unity of principle, one purpose, one idea, and, unless that unity of life pervades every operation in which we engage, it is no wonder that we lack communion with God the Father, and with his Son, Jesus Christ, that religion is divorced from business, and that what men call the privileges of the gospel are in their minds disassociated with the duties and the demands of daily existence.

H. W. WEBB-PEPLOE.

The first and chief need of Christian life is fellowship with God. The divine life within us comes from God and is entirely dependent upon him. As I need every moment afresh the air to breathe, as the sun every moment sends down its light afresh, so it is only in the direct living communication with God that my soul can be strong. The manna of one day was corrupt when the next day came. I must every day have fresh grace from heaven, and I obtain it only in direct waiting upon God himself. Begin each day by tarrying before God and letting him touch you. Take time to meet God.

ANDREW MURRAY.

It would be well if the Christians of to-day would learn a lesson in prompt obedience from the servants of Ahasuerus in publishing the king's decree concerning the Jews in Persia. This was one of the greatest empires of antiquity, reaching from the borders of the Mediterranean Sea to the Indus, and from the Caspian Sea to the Persian Gulf. It was fifteen hundred miles east and west, and a thousand miles north and south—as large as the Congo basin is to-day. The messengers of Ahasuerus had to reach all the provinces with the utmost haste. They had no postal facilities, no telegraphs or telephones, no steam-vessels or steam-cars; nothing but dromedaries, camels, and horses to depend upon. They had to translate this decree into all the various languages in all the one hundred and twenty-seven provinces—not only translating it, but transcribing it by hand, for they had no printing-presses. The messengers had to publish the decree to every individual in all the provinces. How long did it take to accomplish this work? Upon the thirteenth day of the twelfth month the commandment had been published to all the people, and the Jews were ready on that day to fight for their lives. In other words, it took ten days less than nine months to do it. And we have taken nineteen hundred years nearly to carry the gospel to one quarter of the human race, when we have the command of the King of kings to do the King's business in haste. Now that is a burning shame to Christendom, and we shall not honor the Lord if we do not get stirred up on this subject to do our duty in the evangelization of the world.   ARTHUR T. PIERSON.

Word and work—the two W's. You will soon get spiritually gorged if it is all Word and no work, and you will soon be without power if it is all work and no Word. If you want to be healthy Christians there must be both Word and work.

D. L. MOODY.

It is by steadfast drilling into the bed-rock of the Word that we are able to bring up the drafts which we can pass to others.

A. F. SCHAUFFLER.

If we are going to have the true secret of Christian leadership we must study that leader of Christian leaders, Jesus Christ. There we find the secret that he came not to be ministered unto; he went about as one that served; he taught that he who would be greatest must be the servant of all: that is the secret of enduring leadership in things spiritual.

JOHN R. MOTT.

A telegraph-wire must be completely insulated before it can convey the electric communication. So we must be separated from the world before God's message to sinners can have free course through us. When Saladin looked at the sword of Richard Cœur de Lion, he wondered that a blade so ordinary should have wrought such mighty deeds. The English king bared his arm and said, "It was not the sword that did these things; it was the arm of Richard." We should be instruments that the Lord can use, and when he has used us the glory should all be his.

GEORGE F. PENTECOST.

We are the members of the "body of Christ"; he
is the head.   Be careful, then, for the head suffers
with the body.   J. WILBUR CHAPMAN.

Nothing is more dishonoring to Jesus Christ than
a church that is apostate and worldly and unconse-
crated.   A man died some years ago, a very eminent
literary man, who had a magnificent head, lofty
browed and intellectual; but by a sad misfortune he
had that head upon a crippled body. He was a dwarf,
a hunchback, and you could not look upon him without pity.   "What a splendid head," you would say,
"but alas, that it rests upon such an unsightly
form!"   Shall Jesus Christ be so dishonored that
he shall have a body unsanctified and misshapen,
concerning which the angels might exclaim, "Alas!
what a noble head, but what an ignoble body!"
                        A. J. GORDON.

The church is compared to the body of which
Jesus Christ is the head; therefore, endeavor to
keep the unity of the Spirit in the bond of peace.
Men make a great mistake in trying by their evangelical alliances and their compacts to make a unity;
it would be a great deal better if they would do
their best to keep the unity that the Spirit of God
has made.   We are members of one another because
we are members of the same head.
The hand may say the foot is not in the body, but
it cannot help its being in the body, and after I have
got to heaven my High-church friend will see that
I have been in the body all the time, and he will be
sorry he didn't recognize me before.
                        F. B. MEYER.

My Jesus, I love thee; I know thou art mine;
For thee all the follies of sin I resign;
My gracious Redeemer, my Saviour art thou;
If ever I loved thee, my Jesus, 'tis now.

I love thee because thou hast first lovèd me,
And purchased my pardon on Calvary's tree;
I love thee for wearing the thorns on thy brow;
If ever I loved thee, my Jesus, 'tis now.

I will love thee in life, I will love thee in death,
And praise thee as long as thou lendest me breath;
And say when the death-dew lies cold on my brow,
If ever I loved thee, my Jesus, 'tis now.

In mansions of glory and endless delight,
I'll ever adore thee in heaven so bright;
I'll sing with the glittering crown on my brow,
If ever I loved thee, my Jesus, 'tis now.

A. J. GORDON.

Month of April

A stanza from an old hymn says that Jesus Christ "burst the bars" of the grave and "tore its bands away." If a man bursts the bars of State's prison all the police force of the commonwealth is after him to bring him back. If, on the contrary, he has served out his full time, all the power in the State cannot retain him a single hour longer. Jesus Christ must remain in the grave three days "according to Scripture," but after the three days had expired there was not power enough in heaven or in hell to retain him another moment.

Bunyan writes graphically about "the terrible Captain Sepulcher and his standard-bearer, Corruption." I think I hear those two talking over the situation on the night that Jesus Christ was buried. Corruption says to Sepulcher: "Hold fast to that man in Joseph's tomb yonder! There is a rumor that he proposes to break forth from the grave. Do not let him go till I can fasten upon him." But Corruption fails to touch him, because it had been written, "Thou wilt not suffer thy Holy One to see corruption." Then hell from beneath cries out, "Hold fast to this man! If he comes out he will make a breach in the walls of death through which all the prisoners of Hades will escape." And "he that hath the power of death, even the devil," exclaims in fright, "If thou let this man go, thou art not Satan's friend!" But vain the seal, and vain the watch, and vain the grip of death, and vain the doors of the tomb. As it began to dawn the first day of the week there began to be a mighty stir in the sepulcher; terrible Captain Sepulcher tightens his grip, but in vain. "It was not possible that he should be holden of death."   A. J. GORDON.

101

If Christ be not raised, your faith is vain; ye are yet in your sins.—1 Cor. xv. 17.

The belief in the incarnation stands or falls with the doctrine of the resurrection of Jesus Christ. You may just as well shut up the Bible, recall the missionaries, pull down the churches, and let us eat, drink, and be merry, for to-morrow we die and don't know what is coming next, if it be not true that Jesus Christ rose from the dead.

If a man should tell me now that a man who had been buried two days ago had been seen to-day I should not believe it. On an ordinary question I will believe the testimony of men; but if I should be told that an ordinary man who had been in his grave two days had come out, I should say the presumption against it was enormous. But Jesus Christ was not an ordinary man. We take the specific evidence after the resurrection of Christ as an argument for that resurrection; but the Old Testament also creates a presumption in behalf of the resurrection of Jesus Christ in advance. The ordinary man dying and going into his grave, it is presumable that he will not rise from the dead. Jesus Christ stands so manifestly at the climax of Jewish history, and is so organically related to it, that when he came into the world he came as an *exceptional* man, and when he died there was an antecedent presumption of his resurrection as was the case with no other man. So that you can say, as it is said in the Acts, "It was not possible that he should be holden of death."

FRANCIS L. PATTON.

I beseech thee for my son Onesimus, whom I have begotten in my bonds. . . . If he hath wronged thee, or oweth thee aught, put that on mine account.—Phil. 10, 18.

We may draw most helpful lessons from the study of Paul's letter to Philemon, as illustrating in the characters of Philemon and Onesimus and Paul, master, slave, and friend, the relation of the sinner to God and Christ.

The sinner is the property of God. He has fled from God, and is now under the curse of alienation and separation. Not only so, but he has wronged God, and has robbed him besides. The law of God provides no right of asylum for the sinner. He is the absolute property of God—both a bond-slave and a criminal. This ownership is not made void by the sinner's flight. He may break the relationship he sustains to God, but he cannot break the obligation. There is but one thing conceded to him; that is the right of appeal. He may run to Christ, who is the partner of God, and through his intercession seek mercy. Jesus receives him. He comforts him. Not only so, but he manumits him by adoption—begets him in bonds as his own son. And then he sends him back to the Father to be received as himself, and he says, "If he hath wronged thee, or oweth thee aught, put that on my account;" and with his own signature, written in blood, he says, "I will repay." The reception of the sinner is exceedingly abundant—more than he can ask or think.

ARTHUR T. PIERSON.

For if the blood of bulls and of goats, and the ashes of a heifer sprinkling the unclean, sanctifieth to the purifying of the flesh; how much more shall the blood of Christ, who through the eternal Spirit offered himself without spot to God, purge your conscience from dead works to serve the living God?—Heb. ix. 13, 14.

That is the great central thought of the atonement: the sacrifice of Christ's own blood, not the blood of bulls and goats, shall "purge your conscience from dead works to serve the living God."

JOHN A. BROADUS.

There are two things which we must uphold and hold fast—the sacrifice of Christ upon the cross, and the priesthood of Christ in heaven.

ANDREW A. BONAR.

The great strength in us and the great stumbling-block by which the devil himself will be overthrown is the blood. By the blood of the Lamb we are saved, we are strengthened; by the blood of the Lamb we are misunderstood, we are scoffed at.

JOHN MCNEILL.

The last that the world ever saw of Christ, he was hanging on the cross. The last business of his life was the saving of a poor penitent thief. That was a part of his triumph; that was one of the glories attending his death. No doubt Satan said to himself, "I will have the soul of that thief pretty soon down here in the caverns of the lost." But Christ snapped the fetters of this soul and set him at liberty. Satan lost his prey. "The Lion of the tribe of Judah" conquered the lion of hell.

D. L. MOODY.

I am the vine, ye are the branches.—John xv. 5.

We know how close is the union between the vine and its branches. The same life that nourishes the root nourishes the most distant spray on the most distant point of the most distant branch. When our dear Lord was here he was the vine—he bore all the fruit himself. But now that he is transplanted into heaven and on the throne, he bears all his fruit in his branches. But all the life in all the leaves and all the blossoms and all the fruit borne here comes down from him as the root. It is the natural order reversed. How shall I call it? The root above, and the branches below. That is what we ought to be—branches in Jesus, growing out of his fullness, spreading his name and his fragrance over this whole world. Till we are in Christ we cannot serve Christ. Vital Christianity in the doctrine is union with the Son of God. Till we have union with him we have no power. Corrupt trees cannot bring forth good fruit, and we are corrupt to the core. Christianity in the practical is just the manifestation of union with the Son of God in our walk and conduct in the church and in the world.

MARCUS RAINSFORD.

Adam had rest and fellowship with God, but Adam fell because he was not so perfectly linked to God as to prevent the possibility of Satan injuring him. But we are so linked unto God in Christ Jesus that it will be impossible for us to fall from that position.

H. W. WEBB-PEPLOE.

There was a famous sculptor in Paris, who executed a great work which stands to-day in the Galerie des Beaux Arts. He was a great genius, and this was his last work; but, like many a great genius, he was very poor and lived in a small garret. This garret was his workshop, his studio, and his bedroom. He had this statue almost finished in clay when, one night, a frost suddenly fell over Paris. The sculptor lay on his bed, with the statue before him in the center of the fireless room. As the chill air came down upon him he saw that if the cold got more intense the water in the interstices of the clay would freeze. So the old man arose and heaped the bedclothes reverently upon the statue. In the morning, when his friends came in, they found the old sculptor dead; but the image was saved!

Preserve at any cost the image into which you are being changed by the unseen Sculptor, who is every moment that you are in his presence working at that holy task. The Spirit of God is busy now re-creating men, within these commonplace lives of ours, in the image of God.   HENRY DRUMMOND.

Christ said, "Peter, deny yourself." Instead of doing that Peter denied his Lord. Just think of it! It was a choice between that ugly, cursed self and that beautiful, blessed Son of God; and Peter chose self. No wonder that he wept bitter tears.

Christians, look at your own lives in the light of the words of Jesus. Is there self-will, self-pleasing? Remember this: every time you please yourself you deny Jesus. It is one of the two. I must please him and deny self, or please myself and deny him.

ANDREW MURRAY.

In many a man's life in that harbor out of which he sails his little boat two vessels arise. One vessel has the sound of laughter, rich and full, upon it; the sound of music and dancing upon it; gaudy colors float from its mastheads: it is the ship of the "World and its Lusts." Another ship lies in the offing, a good, stanch boat, free from things that are for the pleasures of the flesh, but filled with a royal crew, captained by One who never failed to lead his vessel safely through to the desired haven. Upon one of those two boats you and I must embark. Most of us have already put off our little boats on the sea with the Brittany fisherman's prayer, "Keep me, O God; the sea is so large, and my boat is so small." But perhaps some are still halting between the choice of the world and the good will of our God. The two boats put out to sea; the sky is blue, the Father's face is sweet and tender, and the sea is sweet and peaceful; and the two vessels sail quickly over the waters. By and by the wind comes, and that rocky cape which every vessel must round before she reaches her haven looms up in the gathering darkness. There, while the clouds surge heavy overhead, and the night-birds sweep, and the waters pitch and toss tempestuously beneath, the "World and its Lusts" has passed away, but the good ship of the "Will of God" rides on. The storms go down and the clear sun shines out lovingly after the rain, and by and by the light breaks upon the hills of the better country, and the "Good Will of God" casts anchor in the haven of my Father's land at the very threshold of my Father's house.

ROBERT E. SPEER.

Upon the coast of France, the sailors say, there is a buried city; and on quiet nights, as they are rocked upon the deep, they think that they can hear the tones of the buried bells coming up from the steeples far down in the ocean depths with muffled sound. So in the hearts of men of the world who have lived lives of self-indulgence and evil there are muffled tones from the depths of their nature, ringing in the steeples of conscience, that tell them to choose what is right and to shun what is wrong.

Conscience is not simply the knowledge of right and wrong; it is the judgment-seat of God in miniature. Every Christian carries the judgment-seat inside of him, and day after day he stands before it; and the Son of man, to whom all judgment is committed, sits upon the throne of this inner court, and not only tells us that this or the other is right or wrong, but he goes further and he pronounces sentence with a kiss of infinite delight or with a look of infinite sorrow. He says to each of us, "Come, thou blessed soul, loved of my Father and me; come into the joy that I have prepared for you;" or, "Depart into the darkness of unfellowship and broken communion, O thou who hast disobeyed the dictates of the inner voice!" We cannot doubt that there is a judgment to come when we carry a judgment in miniature within us.   F. B. MEYER.

The more you know of God's Word, the more you can know God's Word; and the more you are living by God's Word the better you can understand God's Word. But if you keep it at arm's-length, and dally with it, and play around it, then years may pass without your having progressed one whit.
                    JOHN A. BROADUS.

There is, I grant, a place for the reason in considering this question about the information given to us about salvation; there is also a place for the church as the great agency in transmitting this information; but the greatest place, the most conspicuous place, the supreme place, belongs to the Bible, and it will not do to say that the reason, the church, and the Bible are coördinate, because they do not stand in any such relation to one another. It is very absurd to put the reason and the church in such relation to the Bible as to imply that either could be a substitute for the Bible.

Suppose that a man gets a telegram to-day from his friend in China, sad or happy as the case may be, and he says, "I don't need any message. I have my own reason, and I can excogitate out of my own consciousness all that I need know of my friend in China." "Oh no," you reply; "your reason is the condition of your being able to read this message, but it is no substitute for the information, and will not give you the information which the message contains." But he replies, "I don't need any message; I have an unbroken continuity of telegraph-wire from here to the antipodes." "No," you reply; "the telegraph-boy is useful and the telegraph-wire is an important thing as making the connection between you and the message, but what you needed was the *message.*"

Your reason is the condition of your being able to read the message which your heavenly Father has sent you; and the church has performed a most important function in transmitting the message; and the Bible, my friends, is the message.

FRANCIS L. PATTON.

Look at that man, Paul. Men called him a madman.
I wish we had a lot of that kind of madness now.
Some one has said, "If he was mad, he had a good
keeper on the way, and a fine asylum at the end of
the route." He could afford to be mad; he was a
man that turned the world upside down—it was
wrong side up before. There was a man who consecrated his life to God. He had one motto: "This
one thing I do." He hadn't forty aims; if he had,
you would never have heard of him. He threw his
whole life into one channel. "This one thing I do,
forgetting those things which are behind, and reaching forth unto those things which are before, I press
toward the mark for the prize of the high calling of
God in Christ Jesus."

The world looked down upon him, but the world
wasn't worthy of him. He is well known in heaven.
If you had asked the rich men in Corinth what kind
of a man Paul was, they would have said, "Huh! he
is a fanatic—gone clean mad. He's honest enough,
but he is a madman." He has been gone eighteen
hundred years, and now his epistles are going to the
very corners of the earth. Let us get right on
Paul's platform, and have one aim: "One thing I
do." Let the kingdom be first in everything, and
everything else will be added. We needn't be
bothering our heads and troubling our minds about
what our future is going to be. If we are wholly
given up to God, he will lead us. Paul never marked
out the path he was going to tread. Hold your reins
loosely, and God will guide you.

D. L. Moody.

The light of Christ strikes down on our hearts
and lives, and, as in Switzerland the sun at dawn
only strikes the loftiest mountains and leaves the
valleys as yet unreached, so, when Christ first begins
to deal with a soul, he does not show the soul the
whole of its depravity, but he deals with one or two
or three outstanding sins. Directly the soul sees
that, it says, "I will give that up to God," and it
shoots up on to another level, and for some happy
weeks or months lives upon a higher level of Christian enjoyment than ever before. Then there comes
another moment. It may be a month or a year
after, and the great light of God's revelation within
reveals something else which has never been noticed
or suspected, which the soul has done comparatively
innocently; but instantly that sin stands out before
God as the one thing to be dealt with. The soul
shudders for a moment and then says, "I treat that
as I treated the former one; I yield it," and it shoots
right up again and goes on to a higher level than
ever. The process is repeated upon that higher
platform. So life is one great stairway upon our
dead selves as stepping-stones to higher things.
My growth is simply because God Almighty is constantly revealing things deeper and deeper. As a
line is made up of a number of dots, so Christian
life is made up of a number of surrenders to God,
but you do not think them to be surrenders because
your heart is so taken up with what he is giving
that you drop the thing that holds you to take the
better thing he gives. God wants to deal with you
as his child.

                                    F. B. MEYER.

Take heed therefore, that the light which is in thee be not darkness.—Luke xi. 35.

Beware of moral color-blindness! A man's thinking that he sees the truth aright does not shield him from the consequences of his error. Conscientious wrong-doing is never safe doing. In moral color-blindness there is moral peril, and you may be morally color-blind without knowing it. The Mosaic law declared, "If any one sin, . . . though he knew it not, yet is he guilty, and shall bear his iniquity." The lips of the loving Jesus said also of the sinning servant, "He that knew not, and did commit things worthy of stripes, shall be beaten," although with fewer stripes than the conscious transgressor.

If a color-blind engineer mistakes a red signal for a white one at an open drawbridge, the resulting calamity is as terrible to himself and the train-load of passengers as if he had deliberately defied a token of danger which he read correctly.

One's danger of misreading the signals along his personal life-course is no less in the moral world than in the physical. Man's conscience, like a ship's compass, should be corrected according to a divine standard. It must be set right by comparison with the true standard of the Sun of Righteousness, rated frequently by the Bible record, and guarded watchfully, lest by careless usage its accuracy be lost and the soul in mid-ocean be without a guide. Unless you know how much your conscience chronometer slows or quickens in the various latitudes where you sail, you will never be able to learn your bearings accurately or to lay your course correctly.

HENRY CLAY TRUMBULL.

Come out from among them, and be ye separate, saith the Lord.—2 Cor. vi. 17.

That command means not only *come* out, but it means also *stay* out. Some come out and then go back. Some come out and straddle the line. Christ draws sharp lines. "He that is not with me is against me." Some church-members have their roots on one side of the church wall and their boughs all hang over and drop the fruit on the world's side. It is not only a question of where your roots are, but where the boughs hang and the apples fall. We want more in these days of clear, distinct, emphatic, Christly religion, so that we do not need to look into the church-roll to find out whether a man is a Christian or not. THEODORE L. CUYLER.

Probably the most of the difficulties of trying to live the Christian life arise from attempting to half live it. HENRY DRUMMOND.

We can and do make it hard for Christ to confess us. For as the devil of old came into the presence of God accusing Job, so now the devil in a sense enters the courts of heaven accusing us before the Father. Here is some poor trembling, faltering sinner who walks unworthy of the vocation whereunto he is called. The devil comes before God, and says, "Ah, yes; that is one of yours, who promised to serve you and be faithful, and yet see how he is living." Christ's reply is, "Well, he has confessed me before men, and I promised to confess him before my Father. Yes; he is one of mine, and I am hoping that this and that will remove every trace of evil." It is a hard thing for Christ to confess us in the face of our many inconsistencies, but he is faithful to his promise. A. J. GORDON.

113

Suppose that you see a mother with a beautiful little babe, six months old, rosy and chubby. It cannot speak, it cannot walk; but we are not troubled about that, for it is natural. Suppose, however, that a year later you find the child not grown at all, and three years later still the same; you would at once say, "There must be some terrible disease;" that baby, that at six months old was a joy to every one, has become to the mother and to all her friends a source of anxiety and of sorrow. It was quite right, at six months old, that it should eat nothing but milk; but years have passed by, and it remains in the same weakly state.

Now this is just the condition of many believers. They are converted, they know what it is to have assurance and faith; they believe in pardon for sin, they begin to work for God, and yet, somehow, there is very little growth in spirituality, in the real heavenly life. You come into contact with them, and you feel at once there is something wanting; there is none of the beauty of holiness or of the power of God's Spirit in them. Is it not sad to see a believer who has been converted five, ten, twenty years, and who has yet no growth and no strength and no joy of holiness!   ANDREW MURRAY.

There are a great many church-members who are just hobbling about on crutches. They can just make out that they are saved, and imagine that is all that constitutes a Christian in this nineteenth century. As far as helping others is concerned, that never enters their heads. They think if they can get along themselves they are doing amazingly well. They have no idea what the Holy Ghost wants to do through them.   D. L. MOODY.

As long as the soldier slinks outside the battle he carries a whole skin; but let him plunge in and follow the captain, and he will soon have the bullets flying about him. Some of you have had a good time because there was no use in the devil wasting powder and shot upon you; you haven't been doing him any harm; but directly you begin to wake up and set to work for God, the devil will set a thousand evils to worrying you, or he may come himself to see to you. F. B. Meyer.

If Satan was dangerous when Paul wrote his epistles, how much more dangerous must he be now, for he has so much more experience!
Andrew A. Bonar.

"*Stand fast therefore in all the armor of God.*" We are in the heavenlies to fight the devil and all the principalities and powers who are trying to draw us out from our fortress where God has placed us. There can be no peace between us and the devil; we must fight him to the very end, because he is always assailing our souls and trying to draw us out of our high place in Christ Jesus. From the pit of darkness to the throne of God Christ Jesus raises us, and, putting us above all principalities and powers, says, "Having done all, stand." But mind that you take the *whole* armor of God; don't omit one piece. The devil is crafty; let him see one spot without its covering, and he will hurl a fiery dart that will make you groan with pain, and would wound you unto death, perhaps, were it not for the oil and wine which the good Samaritan deigns to pour in. H. W. Webb-Peploe.

The pleasure of sin may seem very great to you when you are young, but what will be the end?

H. W. WEBB-PEPLOE.

The biggest lie ever uttered in hell is that the devil is an easy master and God a hard one. I would like to drive that lie back into perdition; and I testify now that my God is not a hard master and the devil an easy one. I take up that old Book, and read, "The way of the transgressor is hard;" and looking around me, I see that it *is* hard. Go down to yon prison, and ask the prisoner if it is not hard. Go with me to the gambler, the drunkard, the forger, who has lost everything, and ask if the way of the transgressor is not hard. D. L. MOODY.

When a man begins to argue with his conscience, he is sure to be in the wrong. Are you trying to justify yourself in an act? You may be sure that that act, in your deepest consciousness, is not what it should be. May I go deeper down? Is it not a fact that with some of us there are sins which we permit, but which we condemn? We excuse ourselves by saying that they are hereditary, and that we cannot help them. We say, "We have a strong nature; we are swept by the winds of passion; some men were born good, but we were born with a crook in us." These excuses will not be accepted by God; his grace is sufficient; Christ can take a Simon and make a Peter of him. F. B. MEYER.

There are many sins which must either be dealt with suddenly or not at all.

HENRY DRUMMOND.

There is an awful responsibility in the gospel.
It damns a man if he will not accept it. God
makes provision for a free pardon, but what if you
decline to take it? Here it is; God holds it out to
you—take it; if you do not there are awful consequences, and the fault is yours, not God's. If you
turn your back on God you set your face toward the
devil. If the gospel needed to be preached to Cornelius, then a man's own righteousness will not save
him; Cornelius must close with God's bargain; he
must take God's gift; that was all he had to do, and
all was right. H. W. WEBB-PEPLOE.

A sinner, telling of his conversion, may at one
time say, "If it had not been for that sermon, I
would have been a sinner still." Another time, "If
it had not been for that person." Another time,
"If I had not turned." But when he looks solemnly
into the whole case, he says, "Unless He who is
exalted a Prince and a Saviour had called me, and
the Holy Spirit had brought home the Word, I
should have been a lost sinner still." Let us cease
giving credit to ourselves and depending on ourselves. ANDREW A. BONAR.

No man can believe on Jesus without repentance
toward God; but mark this: you never find repentance *toward Jesus* spoken of in the Bible. Faith in
Jesus Christ produces repentance toward God; for
we do not know God till we come to Jesus.
MARCUS RAINSFORD.

117

Blessed is he whose transgression is forgiven, whose sin is covered.—Ps. xxxii. 1.

There are two ways of covering sin, man's way and God's way. *You* cover your sins and they will have a resurrection sometime; let *God* cover them, and neither devil nor man can find them. There are four expressions in the Bible with regard to where God puts sins. He puts them "behind his back." If God has forgiven me, who shall bring a charge against me? "He has blotted them out as a thick cloud." You see a cloud to-night, and to-morrow there isn't a cloud to be seen. "He casts them into the depths of the sea." Some one has said, "Thank God that it is a sea and not a river; a river might dry up, but the sea cannot." The greatest blessing that ever comes to me this side of heaven is when God forgives me. Have you been forgiven? The fourth expression is that he removes them "as far as the east is from the west." Do you know how far that is? Perhaps some good mathematician will figure that up. "If we confess our sins, he is faithful and just to forgive us our sins, and to cleanse us from all unrighteousness." Then make sure that you are forgiven. D. L. MOODY.

If God had waited until we repented and asked his pardon for our sins before he gave his Son and brought to bear upon us all his loving-kindness to bring us to repentance, we should have spent eternity in hell. If you know that you hold any ill will toward any one, and you wish God to work a mighty work in your soul, get down and ask God to cast the bitterness out of your heart.

R. A. TORREY.

118

God resisteth the proud, and giveth grace to the humble.—
1 Pet. v. 5.

It is pride—unwillingness to admit that there is
any fundamental lack in our experience—that keeps
many back from spiritual blessing. Many preachers
of the gospel fail of the Holy Spirit's power simply
because they are unwilling to come right out and
humbly and frankly confess that there is such a
thing as the baptism with the Holy Ghost, which
they have never received, and that they have been
preaching all these years without that power which
Jesus commanded his disciples to wait for before
they stirred a step.   R. A. TORREY.

Pride changed an archangel in heaven into a devil
in hell, and pride was the cause of all the wretchedness of man. Pride is the root of every sin; we
need to see that above everything we must be saved
from pride and self-will. It is good to be saved
from lying and stealing and murder and every other
evil; but a man needs, above all, to be saved from
the root of all sin.   ANDREW MURRAY.

There is a false humility, which is marked by two
signs: first, a reluctance to enter upon the work of
God, on the ground of incapacity. The true soldier
of Christ says, "These are not my words or my
works; I am doing my Master's work, and using my
Master's weapons in my Master's service." False
humility is detected, secondly, by self-consciousness.
If you *think* you are humble, you never *are*.
                                    ARTHUR T. PIERSON.

119

Let us lay aside every weight, and the sin which doth so easily beset us, and let us run with patience the race that is set before us.—Heb. xii. 1.

Of course sins are weights, but all weights are not sins. A sin necessarily impairs or destroys all communion with God and all spiritual life, but a weight is something which is not necessarily a sin, but which is a hindrance. The author of this epistle says, "Seeing the race which is set before us, let us not only lay aside the sin which makes all holy running impossible, but let us lay aside every weight which prevents all rapid racing."

ARTHUR T. PIERSON.

God is willing to do for any man or woman all that he ever did for any one. If there is not a mighty work of God in us, it is our own fault. Find out what these hindrances are, and put them away.

R. A. TORREY.

Sometimes professing Christians are beset by special hindrances to their usefulness—tendencies of speech or action that mar the beauty of holiness most sadly. What are you going to do with the evil habit, or the half-dozen, which are hindering you? Fight them one by one; that is one way. What did you do last winter when the panes of the window were covered with frost, and you could not see out of them? Did you scratch them off with a knife? That would take too long. Heat up the room and the frost goes off the pane. Warm up the soul with the love of Christ and the bad habits will run off. That is what Chalmers calls the "expulsive power of a new affection." Bring Jesus Christ into the soul and you will overcome the evil habits.

THEODORE L. CUYLER.

God is love; and he that dwelleth in love dwelleth in God, and God in him.—1 John iv. 16.

The landscape is very much affected by the glass through which you regard it. If that glass is yellow, everything looks yellow. If it is blue, everything looks blue. If it is somber, everything looks somber. Now, the man who is living a life of love looks out upon his life through the love of God, and the love of God has such a mysterious property in it that it takes away from terrible things their terror, from dreadful things their dread, and from the malignity of man his spite; and the soul looks with a calm serenity upon all the circumstances of life, and finds itself hushed and calm.

F. B. MEYER.

You are not very holy if you are not very kind.
ANDREW BONAR.

Christ's love to God and his love to man were not two great passions, but one. He loved man because he saw God in him. This must ever be the pulse of a powerful philanthropy—to see God in man. In the humblest—aye, in the most sinful human being —we see one whom God loves, whom the Saviour died for, and who may be an heir of the glory of Christ. JAMES STALKER.

Love stops not to think how much must be given and what may be kept; it gives all. What is your most precious possession? Money? Will you give it up to him? Your voice? Give it up to him. You must strip yourself, and God must have all.

H. W. WEBB-PEPLOE.

121

Thou, O Lord, art a shield for me; my glory, and the lifter up of mine head.—Ps. iii. 3.

God is whatever you need him to be. There is an old tradition among the Jews that the manna tasted like whatever you were hungry for every morning. If you woke up, for example, hungry for Egyptian cucumbers and leeks, and did not murmur after them, but thankfully took your manna, the manna tasted like them. And God, he is our life; he is all our strength and stay, and is whatever we need him to be. Do you want a friend? God is a friend. Do you want a guide? God is a guide. Do you want somebody to be, as it were, your leader in battle? The Lord is a man of war. Do you want somebody to be your advocate, to stand in the high court and plead your cause? We have an Advocate. Our God adapts himself exactly to the very shape and body and color of our wants.

JOHN McNEILL.

What God the Father was to his Son, Jesus Christ is prepared to be to every one of us. In reading the gospel, if you will substitute the thought of Christ's relationship to yourself every time Jesus speaks of the Father's attitude to him, you will find that the gospel will have a new emphasis and meaning.

F. B. MEYER.

God wants all his sons and daughters to be very happy, but he wants them to be happy in a way that will help and not hinder them.

D. L. MOODY.

I can do all things [I am all-prevailing] in him that strength-eneth me.—Phil. iv. 13.

A great Methodist preacher in Manchester once entered his pulpit, gave out this text, and began solemnly reading in measured tones: "'I can do all things'—Paul," he said, "you are a liar. 'I can do all things'—Paul, thou art a terrible liar. Oh, I beg your pardon, Paul; I see it now—'through Christ which strengtheneth me.' That is quite another thing. Paul, you are quite right—'I *can* do all things through Christ which strengtheneth me.'" This is a secret worth learning, even though a man has to be shut up in a prison with a galling chain on his wrist in order to learn it. H. W. WEBB-PEPLOE.

Ah, if we but knew the power that worketh in us and the power that worketh for us, there would be less talking and more working, and things that seem to be, from the point of unbelief and panic-stricken-ness, almost too big to attempt, would be seen to be natural and obvious. JOHN MCNEILL.

There is a good deal of difference between social power, political power, and a kind of religious power. Strength is one thing, and power is another. The giant of Gath had strength, but David had power. It would be a good idea when a man or woman wants to join the church to ask him if he wants to be a member with or without power. If he says, "Without power," it would be well to say, "We have plenty of that kind of church-members. What we want is a few with power." D. L. MOODY.

We have a supernatural work to do, and we must have supernatural power with which to do it.
A. J. GORDON.

123

Every man who desires the pearl of great price must sacrifice his all to buy it. It is not enough to see the beauty and the glory and almost to taste the joy of this wonderful life; you must become the possessor of it. The man had found and seen, desired and rejoiced, in the pearl of great price, but he did not have it until he gave up everything and bought it.

Ah, friends, there is a great deal which must be given up: the world, its pleasure, its favor, its good opinion. The world rejected Jesus and cast him out, and you must take up the position of your Lord, to whom you belong, and follow with the rejected Christ. You have to give up all that is good in yourself, even your past religious life and experience and successes, and to be humbled in the dust of death. The blessed Spirit cannot teach us more effectually only because the wisdom of man prevents the light of God from shining in.

Some Christians may be holding fast some doubtful thing, not willing to surrender and leave behind the whole of the wilderness life and lust.

You cannot live every day in perfect fellowship with God without giving up time to it. Hours and days and weeks and months and years are gladly given up by men and women to perfect themselves in some profession or accomplishment. Do you expect that religion is so cheap that without giving time you can find close fellowship with God? You cannot. But, my brothers and sisters, this pearl is worth everything. If you find that there is a struggle within the heart, never mind. By God's grace, if you will lie at his feet, you may depend upon it deliverance will come.   ANDREW MURRAY.

In these days the work of rescuing the individual sinner is very popular, but it is not so popular to point out and put down the evil that destroys him, because there are material interests involved. Men are trying to save a few wrecks here and there, while thousands go down and the wreckers keep plying their trade. It is better to hang or reform the wreckers than to save one wreck.

CHARLES A. BLANCHARD.

Possibly the most eloquent passage that Dr. Guthrie ever uttered was one in which he said little. He was pleading for a ragged school, and a large congregation of conservative people were opposing him. One man said, "I am utterly opposed to this plan. You intend to go down among those people who are the very offscouring of the earth, dirty, filthy, intemperate, and vicious, expecting to make decent folks of them. I for one do not care to spend my money in trying to accomplish what is impossible. The very rags on which your feet step as you go along the street are better than they." Dr. Guthrie, filled with indignation, took a piece of white paper and waved it before them. "My friends, what is this paper made of? Is it not made of those very rags that you trample under your feet?"

A. J. GORDON.

Never despair of any man. Seek him out to save him, even though he be as the vilest reptile. Go and die for him if necessary.

H. W. WEBB-PEPLOE.

125

When you are discouraged, when you see how much worldliness there is in the church, defections in doctrine and defections in the members, when you see how little impression has been made on this world by nineteen centuries of Christian history, do you not think that it is an encouragement and a help for the child of God to feel that he has a conception of God's work, in which he is simply working for God along the lines that God projected? He has to do what God gives him to do, and leave the result to God. He does not estimate his success by figures, but he says, "I am commanded by my Lord to go into all the world and preach the gospel to every creature; I go as I am bidden, and leave the strategy to my Lord himself. What he means, he knows, but what he commands, I do."

ARTHUR T. PIERSON.

O church of the living God, awake!—arise from your lethargy, and spring forward to the conflict. Give your choicest sons, your loveliest daughters, to this war of Immanuel. Consecrate to him your silver and your gold. Fill up the mission treasuries to overflowing. Let a shout go forth that shall leap over seas and continents, and reach the ears of your waiting hosts in those distant lands. And what shall that shout be? Shall we catch the cry, "March onward! Seize every point of vantage. Call upon the enemy to surrender. Reinforcements five thousand strong are on the way; supplies in abundance are coming. March on, and conquer the land for Christ "? This is the shout that we long to hear, but it has not come. Shall it be long delayed?

JACOB CHAMBERLAIN.

There was a defect in the faith of many who came
to Christ to be healed. But it was not the strength
of their faith Christ looked to, but the reality of it.
They got the cure though the hand that touched
him trembled.　　　　　ANDREW A. BONAR.

Our faith needs strengthening, and it would be
an unkindness for God to give us great answers
to wavering faith. If we have not faith enough to
remove a mountain, we may climb it step by step,
and, when we reach its summit, our spiritual muscles will be greatly strengthened, and from the
height thus gained we may breathe a purer atmosphere and get a broader view.　　　A. C. DIXON.

I heard of a woman in Scotland who was intro-
duced to a minister by another minister as a woman
of great faith. She instantly rebuked him by saying, "No; I am a woman of little faith with a great
God." She had the right idea. If I have even a
little faith I have the power of the Almighty behind
me.　　　　　　　　　　　D. L. MOODY.

The faith that rests in Jesus is the faith that
trusts itself to him with all it has. In our homes,
in our business, in society, everywhere, let Christ be
the one object of our trust. If you want power in
your house, in your Bible class, in your social circle
and your nation, or in the church of Christ, then
come into contact with Jesus in this rest of faith
that accepts his life fully, that trusts him fully for
yourself, and you will be able by faith to influence
your family, by faith to overcome the world, by
faith to bless others, by faith to live a life to the
glory of God.　　　　　　ANDREW MURRAY.

If we really believe that God loved us with his whole heart, what a help it would be to us in our daily lives! We would then feel that we could go at any moment into the presence of a loving Father, who cared as much for us as if he had nothing else to care for. A child may come into the presence of its earthly father, except when the parent is occupied. Our heavenly Father is never so occupied. At all times he will bestow on us the same attention. A child likes to play in the presence of its earthly parents, even though they take no notice of it, and is happy simply because it is with them. How much more ought we to be joyous in our heavenly Father's presence! We need not be always singing. The heart has a silent language. There is too little of adoration—simple worship—at the present time.

ANDREW A. BONAR.

Worship is a blessed privilege, not only because it brings supreme joy, but because it also brings likeness to God. It is by communion with God we are made like him. When Moses came down from beholding God, his own face shone with a strange and awful glory; and Paul says that "we all, reflecting as a mirror the glory of the Lord, are transformed into the same image from glory to glory." Our complete transformation into his likeness will come through the complete and undivided vision of himself. "We shall be like him; for we shall see him even as he is."

R. A. TORREY.

We talk about being "filled with the Spirit," yet
Paul goes beyond that in Ephesians iii. 14, where he
says, ."For this cause I bow my knees unto the
Father of our Lord Jesus Christ, . . . that ye,
being rooted and grounded in love, may be able to
comprehend with all saints what is the breadth, and
length, and depth, and height; and to know the love
of Christ, which passeth knowledge, that ye might
be"—filled with? No; "that ye might be *filled
into* all the fullness of God." Do you not see the
difference? Here are empty vessels. You say,
"First get yourself empty and then full." I may
dip out and fill these vessels; but put an empty vessel into the ocean, and it quickly fills itself. This
seems to be Paul's thought. Archbishop Leighton
makes a beautiful comment on the words of Christ,
"Enter thou into the joy of thy Lord." The archbishop, lifting up his eyes to heaven, said, "Lord
Jesus, it is only a little joy that now enters into us;
but by and by we shall enter into joy as vessels put
into a sea of happiness." Cast yourself into the
great deeps of the Spirit, then there will be no
trouble in getting filled.

A. J. GORDON.

The gift of Pentecost is for you; as you claimed
forgiveness from the hand of the dying Christ, you
must claim your Pentecost from the hand of the
risen Christ; and as you were forgiven in answer to
your faith, so you shall now be endued and filled
and glorified by the Holy Ghost according to your
faith. The same law applies inviolably.

F. B. MEYER.

 APRIL

God loveth a cheerful giver.—2 Cor. ix. 7.

In Herefordshire there was one very rich man in
my parish, who had a sudden paralytic stroke when
I was away from home for a holiday. He was a
common, ignorant farmer, and had come into eighty
thousand pounds through the death of a brother.
He had told me that he did not care for his brother's
money because he had as much as he wanted before,
and yet he had not given more than sixpence a year
for charity. As soon as I returned home I went
down to see him, and he said, "The Lord has
stricken me, and I am afraid I may die. I have sent
for you at once that I may do what I suppose is
right before God; I want to go to heaven, and I want
you to take a hundred pounds for the poor." I
looked him straight in the face, and said, "Do you
think you are going to buy your soul's way to glory
by a dirty hundred pounds! Give your money where
you like; I will not touch it!" That was rather
strong; but, blessed be God, the man lived seven
years, and was a very different man before he died.

H. W. WEBB-PEPLOE.

There is no happiness in having and getting, but
only in giving; half the world is on the wrong scent
in the pursuit of happiness.

HENRY DRUMMOND.

"Our citizenship is in heaven." Any Christian
who can realize the meaning of that text will be a
Christian wholly separated from the world. He will
pay taxes where his treasure is. Nine tenths of the
Christians are paying taxes down here in the world.

A. J. GORDON.

Month of May

And Elisha said, I pray thee, let a double portion [the first-born son's portion] of thy spirit be upon me. And he said, Thou hast asked a hard thing: nevertheless, if thou see me when I am taken from thee, it shall be so.—2 Kings ii. 9.

That was the condition of the coveted blessing— "if thou see me." Do you not think that Elisha kept a sharp watch on Elijah? Then suddenly there swept down that chariot of fire; Elijah stepped into his Father's carriage, which had come to take him home, and was swept away up to heaven. As Elisha watched him, Elijah seems to have suddenly thought he would not want the old mantle up there, that he would get a new white robe; so he threw the old one down at Elisha's feet. Then Elisha took it up reverently, and said to himself, "I have seen him go, and I have what he promised." I doubt not the devil said to him, "Ah, you are a fool! you have nothing but an old mantle that is not worth your carrying." "Yes," said Elisha, "I have something more than that—I have his power." "You do not feel it, do you?" "No; but that makes no difference; I have it for all that. I saw him go, and I have it though I do not feel it." When he reached the Jordan there were a number of young students watching him. I think the devil said, "Now see those shrewd young fellows looking at you; if you make a failure, they will never forget it; and you are bound to fail. Wait until they have gone home to supper, and when it is a bit dusk you can practise with your old mantle." "No," he said, "I am not going to practise with it; I do not need to; I have my master's power, and I am going to act in faith." And he struck the waters in faith; in the act of faith he found he received that for which he trusted God.

F. B. MEYER.

131

Would it not be better to leave to-morrow with God? That is what is troubling men; to-morrow's temptations, to-morrow's difficulties, to-morrow's burdens, to-morrow's duties. Martin Luther in his autobiography says, "I have one preacher that I love better than any other upon earth; it is my little tame robin, which preaches to me daily. I put his crumbs upon my window-sill, especially at night. He hops on to the sill when he wants his supply, and takes as much as he desires to satisfy his need. From thence he always hops on to a little tree close by, and lifts up his voice to God and sings his carol of praise and gratitude, tucks his little head under his wing and goes fast asleep, and leaves to-morrow to look after itself. He is the best preacher that I have on earth." H. W. WEBB-PEPLOE.

Moment by moment I'm kept in his love;
Moment by moment I've life from above;
Looking to Jesus till glory doth shine,
Moment by moment, O Lord, I am thine.
D. W. WHITTLE.

So many Christians want to walk by sight; they want to see how a thing is going to come out. Jacob walked by sight. He never could have gone through the temptations and trials that his son Joseph did. Joseph had more faith: he could walk in the dark. Lot was a weak character, and should have stayed with Abraham. A good many men, as long as they are bolstered up by some godly person, get along very well; but they can't stand alone. Have faith in God to guide you, even though you can't see. D. L. MOODY.

It is not strange when you have the Bible dealing with the physical world, and when physical science is dealing with the same facts, that you should have a double interpretation of the same phenomena. The double interpretation makes it all the stronger; we see that every day. I go early in the morning and make a very informal call upon a friend with whom I am very intimate. I walk in without knocking, it may be, and I say to the first one I meet, "Is So-and-so at home?" I say to myself, "Yes, he must be here; his hat and cane are here, and there is a favorite book he has left open; there are indications all around of his having been here within a short time." And, answering my question himself, he says, "Yes; I will be down in a minute." I have performed a rapid and unconscious induction, and then received the direct information from him. I go around this world and I investigate it; I interpret it and say, "Is God here?" And I perform an induction, which I call an argument, for the existence of God; and while I am going through that process of reasoning I get a message from God himself. He says, "In the beginning God created the heavens and the earth." Is there any trouble about my inference reached one way and God's information given me in another way? No; the Christian creed is strengthened by the double testimony of science and revelation.

FRANCIS L. PATTON.

No single fact in science has ever discredited a fact in religion.

HENRY DRUMMOND.

The authenticity of the Scriptures depends upon the truth of the facts contained in them, and not upon men's interpretation of those facts. Facts alone can authenticate anything. Leave the settlement to interpretation, and you have as many interpretations as you have interpreters. If a document is authentic its authenticity must be established by questions of fact, and when this is done no interpretation can set it aside. All the philosophies of man must fall when they come in contact with a single fact. The fall of an apple and the discovery of gravitation destroyed the philosophy that man had been building for six thousand years.

Suppose that I should attempt to do with the Constitution of the United States what the opposers of Christianity for eighteen hundred years have been trying to do with the Bible. They offer their own interpretations as proof that God is not the author of the Bible. I might offer my interpretation to prove that the fathers never made the Constitution.

If the Bible is ever authenticated, it must be done in the same way that any other document is authenticated—by a study of its facts. In no other way could a revelation be given than by supernatural acts attesting a divine mission, and then by monumental testimony, as "seals," putting these evidences in an imperishable form to transmit to future generations. The acts which Moses and Christ performed were the highest evidences that God could give that he had sent them. The national monuments are as good evidence to us as the acts were to those who saw them. Testimony, accompanied by proper "seals" and attestations, can lose none of its value by time.   I. D. DRIVER.

134

A Bible that man can comprehend, or anybody else can comprehend, is not very much of a Bible. Infinite things cannot be grasped by the human mind. The Bible opens with three great mysteries: the mystery of time, the mystery of being, and the mystery of creation. We cannot understand them; they are past our finding out.

ALEXANDER McKENZIE.

The great canon of interpretation, that spiritual things are spiritually discerned, cannot be too strongly insisted on. One cannot interpret Scripture by mere intellect any more than a mathematician can interpret the oratorio, "The Creation," by his multiplication table, or a shopkeeper can comprehend "Paradise Lost" with his yardstick. Only the Spirit that inspired the Word of God can give us the key to that Word. A. J. GORDON.

Did you ever notice the inspiration that is found in what is *not* said in the Bible? Swedenborg openly declares what the Bible leaves in mystery. Suppose that the Bible had pronounced on the age when we become morally responsible. Suppose the Bible had pronounced on science, and so diverted man's attention from spiritual things. We do not know what Paul's thorn in the flesh was; consequently we each think that our particular infirmity or trouble may be like Paul's. Nothing is said as to the limits of propriety in the matter of worldly amusements. Nothing is said of the personal features of the Lord Jesus Christ. These and many other matters are passed over in silence, and the wisdom of that silence is as great as the wisdom of speech.

A. T. PIERSON.

135

We find in Scripture the word "true" used with regard to a number of objects: the true bread, the true wine, the true manna, the true tabernacle. What is this intended to teach us? God could have made man to need no sleep, to need no food, as we have reason to suppose the angels were made; but had this been the case we should have known nothing of rest, as we now know it, nor could we have learned the spiritual truths revealed to us through the illustration of food and nourishment. So that the bread we eat is not true bread; but Christ is the true bread, of which it is merely a type. The earthly relationship of parent and child is only a type and dim reflection of the preëxisting relationship in the divine mind; and all that the bridegroom and bride bring before us of trust and of love are only intended to teach us the true relationship of the church to Christ, and of Christ to his church. We only rightly know him when we realize that to please God is to give God pleasure, as earthly parents receive pleasure when their children please them.   J. HUDSON TAYLOR.

There are seven marvelous truths contained in John iii. 16: 1. The greatest possible *gift:* God gave his Son; 2. For the greatest possible *number:* "the world;" 3. On the easiest possible *terms:* "whosoever believeth;" 4. For the most blessed *deliverance* from eternal perdition: "shall never perish;" 5. The greatest *blessing:* "everlasting life;" 6. On the highest possible security: on the witness of Christ himself; 7. From the highest possible *motive,* God's love: "God so loved the world."

   MARCUS RAINSFORD.

This little world was the altar of the universe on which lay the almighty Sacrifice. The incarnation was but the scaffolding for the atonement. It is the cross that shows us the love of God at white heat.

ANDREW A. BONAR.

God's Word teaches us two things about the cross of Christ: Christ died *for* sin and for me. But what gave his death such power to atone was the spirit in which he died. He died *unto* sin. Sin had tempted him in Gethsemane to say, "I cannot die." But, God be praised, he died unto sin, and in dying he conquered. He gave up his life rather than yield to sin. I cannot die *for* sin like Christ, but I can and must die *to* sin like Christ.

ANDREW MURRAY.

We are not pardoned on the ground of any compromise. God has not agreed to let us off for fifty cents on a dollar; he has not allowed us to go into bankruptcy and take a poor debtor's oath. We are forgiven on the ground of justice. "Justification" is Paul's word. God is just to you because in Christ you have died. So in Romans you read, "He that is dead is free from sin;" Revised Version, "He that hath died is justified from sin." A man was drafted in the war, and his substitute went to the field of battle and died. When the man was drafted again he pleaded that he was dead, and was justified by the courts. That point has been decided in court three times: once in America, once in France, and once in Germany.

A. J. GORDON.

137

It were easier to disprove the existence of George
Washington or Napoleon Bonaparte than that of
Jesus Christ, and to blot out Bunker Hill or Waterloo than Calvary.   Did George Washington live, and
do the 22d of February and the 4th of July prove
it?   How about that other anniversary, dear to
England and to America, and destined to be the
greatest day in all the earth, observed by gifts from
parents to children to commemorate God's gift to
man?   Why is that observed at all?   Because of
Christ.   Who is he?   Suppose that he were just
now to come—as come he will, we know not when
—and, making himself evident to us, should say,
"Who do men say that I, the Son of man, am?"
I would have to say, "Blessed Master, some say that
thou art a myth," unless my tongue should cleave
to the roof of my mouth so that I could not utter the
word.   "Some say that thou art a fancy portrait,
and that a picture has turned the world on its
hinges."   And then, should he go on to say, "Who
say ye that I am?" oh, now, on my bended knee and
with streaming tears, I would cry, "Thou art the
Christ, the Son of the living God."   For he has outlived himself, outlived death and the grave.

CYRUS D. FOSS.

Christ's character was prefigured by the national
tabernacle.   The Holy Ghost gave the tabernacle
three names: the tent of meeting, the tent of witness, and the dwelling-place of God.   Christ was
the meeting-place for God and man, a witness for
the Father, and there God dwelt.

M. E. BALDWIN.

In the first Adam I died to God; I died in sin.
When I was born I had the life of the fallen Adam.
The moment I am born again by believing in Jesus
I become united to Christ, the second Adam, and am
made partaker of the life of Christ—that life which
died unto sin and rose again. Therefore God tells
us, "Reckon yourselves indeed dead unto sin, and
alive unto God in Christ Jesus." As in the first
Adam you died in sin and unto God, so in the second
Adam you died in Christ and unto sin. Many Christians do not understand that they are dead to sin;
therefore Paul says, "How shall we, that are dead to
sin, live any longer therein? Know ye not, that so
many of us as were baptized into Jesus Christ were
baptized into his death?"

You must get hold of your union to Christ; believe
in the new nature within you, that spiritual life which
you have from Christ, a life that has died and has
been raised again. Every man acts according to
the idea he has of his state. A king acts like a
king if he is conscious of his kingship. So I cannot
live the life of a true believer unless I am conscious
every day that I am dead in Christ. He died unto
sin: I am united with him, and he lives in me, and I
am dead to sin. Adam lives in a natural man the
death-life, a life under the power of sin, a life of
death to God. Christ, the second Adam, has come
to me with a new life, and I now live in his life, the
death-life of Christ. ANDREW MURRAY.

The difference between the regenerate and the
unregenerate man is that the unregenerate man
lives in sin, and he loves it; but the regenerate man
lapses into sin, and he loathes it.

A. J. GORDON.

He that covereth his sins shall not prosper.—Prov. xxviii. 13.

Sins unconfessed and not set straight are hindering a mighty work of God in many a man and woman to-day. David tried not confessing his sins to God, and we know the misery he experienced. He says in the Thirty-second Psalm, "When I kept silence, my bones waxed old through my roaring all the day long. For day and night thy hand was heavy upon me." At last he came to his senses; he confessed his transgressions, and the Lord forgave the iniquity of his sin. Then God wrought mightily in David, and the Thirty-second Psalm and the Fifty-first Psalm, and many another psalm that has comforted and edified the children of God for nearly three thousand years, are the result.

R. A. TORREY.

Nine tenths of our prayers never go higher than the room they are uttered in. Why? Something is concealed. If I regard iniquity in my heart God will not hear, much less answer; and if our prayers are not answered let us not think the trouble is on God's side, for it is on ours. Isaiah lix. is quoted many times by men who stop in the wrong place. "Behold, the Lord's hand is not shortened, that it cannot save: but your iniquities have separated between you and your God, and your sins have hid his face from you, that he will not hear." As long as you have a bullet in your body you will never have a perfectly healthy body; and as long as you have a sin in your soul you will not have a healthy soul.

D. L. MOODY.

Let the redeemed of the Lord say so.—Ps. cvii. 2.

Run up the colors to the masthead. We must confess Christ. Some of us mean well, but a false discretion overtakes us. We are not unlike that soldier who was always discovered, in the shock of battle, betaking himself, without orders, to safe places. The captain at last accused him of having a cowardly heart. "Oh," said the soldier, "my heart is as brave as can be, but whenever danger comes I have a cowardly pair of legs that run off with my brave heart." Many of us are like that. Our convictions are right when confession is not needed, but in the shock of battle we fail.

JOHN MCNEILL.

I heard of a young man who went into the army. The first night in the barracks, with about fifteen men playing cards and gambling around him, he fell on his knees and prayed, and they began to curse and to throw boots at him. So it went on the next night and the next, and finally the young man told the chaplain what had taken place, and asked him what he should do. "Well," the chaplain said, "those soldiers have just as much right in the barracks as you have. It makes them angry to have you pray, and the Lord will hear you just as well in bed." Some weeks after that the chaplain met the young man and asked, "By the way, did you take my advice?" "I did for two or three nights; but I felt like a whipped hound, and the third night I knelt down and prayed." "Well," said the chaplain, "how did that work?" The young soldier answered, "We have a prayer-meeting there now every night; three have been converted, and we are praying for the rest."

D. L. MOODY.

141

Thomas said before Christ's death, "Let us go and die with him;" and Peter said, "Lord, I am ready to go with thee, both into prison, and to death." But the disciples all failed, and our Lord took a man, one of the offscouring of the earth, who hung beside him on Calvary, and through him shows us what it is to die with him. He shows us, first of all, the state of a heart prepared to die with Christ—a humble, whole-hearted confession of guilt. Here is one reason why the church enters so little into the death of Christ; men do not wish to believe that the curse of God is upon everything in them that has not died with Christ. The church suffers to-day from trusting in intellect and culture. Men rob the intellect of its crucifixion mark. Christ said to Paul, "Go, preach the gospel of the cross, but not with wisdom of words." The intellect, the affections, everything, must go into the grave with Christ. God will raise them from the dead again, sanctified and made alive unto God.

Then the penitent thief had faith in the almighty power of Christ; there is not a faith in the Bible like that. This cursed malefactor, hanging on the cross beside Jesus, dares to say, "I am dying under the just curse of my sins, but I believe that thou canst take me into thy heart. Remember me when thou comest into thy kingdom." Brother, you and I need a much deeper faith in the power of Christ to take us into his arms and carry us through this death-life. Would you, now that Christ is on the throne, be afraid of doing what the malefactor did when Christ was upon the cross—to trust yourself to him to live as one dead with him?

ANDREW MURRAY.

Have you ever noticed that people who flatter themselves that it is not foolish to live a kind of half-and-half life, sanctified so far as belonging to God is concerned, but living in the most perilous surroundings and dangerous habits, always think that they can escape the danger of corruption and influence others? Lot dwelt in Sodom with the expectation that he could affect the people around him for good. But be assured that the world will drag you down to their level; you will never bring them up to your level until you have taught them boldly to know Christ and to see the depravity of their nature and their ways.

H. W. WEBB-PEPLOE.

One backslider will do more harm than twenty Christian men can do good.

W. E. BLACKSTONE.

Many Christians believe in Christ without belonging to him; they give Christ their faith, and withhold from him their fealty; they own him, but shrink from being owned by him. We plead for a service of Christ which is entire, undivided, and wanting nothing. Therefore we urge upon Christians the duty of separation: separation from associations that are secret, that they may live an open life of devotion to Christ; separation from societies that assess a tax on time which is already mortgaged for its full value to the Lord; separation from bonds that hold men together by compacts and oaths, when they aught to be free to yield with their full force to the attractions of Christ—separation in order to concentration.   A. J. GORDON.

143

Let every one that nameth the name of Christ depart from iniquity.—2 Tim ii. 19.

Forsake dangerous associations. Health is not contagious, but sickness is. We quarantine yellow fever to keep it out of the country, but we do not bring in health or quarantine it. Sin is catching; holiness is not. Be very careful to whom you give the key of your heart. Look out! This association, with us imitative creatures, has a tremendous influence on a man's or a woman's Christian character. Lot bought real estate down near Sodom; pitched his tent over against Sodom; then he moved into Sodom; and pretty soon Sodom moved into him. The angel put a hand on his shoulder and said, "Escape for thy life, lest thou be consumed." That is the only way for any one to get out of dangerous associations in business, in politics, or anything else. Christians, the moment you find that you are in any associations that harm and poison your piety, escape out of that place as quickly as Lot hastened out of Sodom, for there is no safety in remaining there.

THEODORE L. CUYLER.

Christians call the Bible the only rule of faith and practice; but is it the only rule of practice? Do we take this Bible when any question of doubtful propriety comes up, and ask ourselves what the Bible says on that subject? Do we make the Bible the standard of our life? Do we take that Bible when difficulties arise, and say, "How does Paul's teaching or Jesus Christ's teaching bear upon this?" Nay; we are more apt to be governed by what people will say, by what they all do, and by what the law allows. FRANCIS L. PATTON.

144

Woe unto him that striveth with his Maker.—Isa. xlv. 9.

We may strive with our Maker in two ways: we may say to him, "What makest thou?" or we may say, "He hath no hands." We may quarrel with God as to the direction in which he is making us, and we may quarrel with God as to the method which he adopts.

What makest thou? "If thou wouldst make me a man of business I shouldn't mind, if I am successful; but I do not wish to be only a clerk. Why didst thou make me this way?" "If thou hadst only made me a Moody I should thank thee; but thou hast made me a working-man, to earn my bread by the sweat of my brow; I don't like this." What makest thou? "I am a young girl, and want to go to the zenanas in India; but I have a widowed mother, and sisters and brothers, and I must work for them. Make me something else, O God; I am tired of this. I will be good and obedient and loving and sweet if thou wilt let me have my way; but why didst thou make me this way? I don't like it." That is striving with your Maker.

Another man thinks that God is doing nothing. He says, "*He hath no hands.*" He thinks that he could do better for himself; as much as to say, "My God, thou dost not understand what thou art doing; thou hast no hands; thou dost not know how to deal with souls. Not this way; put me there, and I shall do better." That is the way in which people, who would not put their thoughts into those words, are nevertheless striving with their Maker.

F. B. Meyer.

145

We do not teach sinlessness; for when a man is living up to his loftiest ideal there will always be a chasm between God's ideal and man's loftiest living. The man who boasts about his sinlessness is the man who has not seen the perfect standard of God, and he usually calls infirmities what God calls sins. We do not teach sinlessness, but we do teach that God is able so to possess a soul that it shall not be constantly conscious of failure; and if there is any failure in your life it is because you have not apprehended God's deliverance. And why? Because there is some one thing in your life—there may be more than one—which has come between God and your soul and which has shut off God's helpful grace. You will never be happy and able to sing again until you are willing to renounce that thing and let God draw you closer to himself.

F. B. MEYER.

We often see a thing and yet do not possess it. You often see beautiful fruit displayed behind a plate-glass window or in some shop, and the hungry little boys look and long for it, but they cannot reach it. If you were to tell one of them who has never seen glass to take some, he might attempt it; but he finds something invisible between him and that fruit. Just so many Christians can see that God's gifts are beautiful, but they cannot take, because the self-life comes in between, even though they cannot see it. What glorious blessings we should have if we were only willing to give up the self-life and take what God has prepared for us—not only righteousness, not only peace, but the joy of the Holy Ghost!   ANDREW MURRAY.

146

In the fable of the magic skin it gave the wearer power to get anything he wanted; but every time he gratified his wishes the skin shrank and compressed him into smaller dimensions until, by and by, with the last wish life itself was crushed out. The magic skin is selfishness. It is a great thing to learn to say NO to one's self instead of indulging every whim and wish, even though there be nothing sinful in it. Moses renounced the pleasures and treasures of Egypt for the sake of a higher recompense of reward. There was no necessary wrong in his inheriting the royal treasures and enjoying the pleasures of Egypt, so far as they were not in themselves sinful; but Moses had a high vocation, and these would have been hindrances; so he renounced them.

ARTHUR T. PIERSON.

All that there has been and ever will be of sin and of darkness and of wretchedness and of misery will be nothing but the reign of self, the curse of self, separating man and turning him away from his God. If we are to understand fully what Christ is to do for us, and are to become partakers of a full salvation, we must learn to know and to hate and to give up entirely this cursed self.

ANDREW MURRAY.

You can't jump away from your shadow, but if you turn to the sun your shadow is behind you, and if you stand under the sun your shadow is beneath you. What we should try to do is to live under the meridian Sun, with our shadow, self, under our feet.

F. B. MEYER.

Under the Levitical law if a man came in contact with death he could only be cleansed from that contact by sacrifice. There is, perhaps, a danger in some quarters at the present day of the thought being accepted that certain things are right if we do not feel them to be wrong—that certain things are right if we are, so to speak, unavoidably thrown in contact with them. We must ever bear in mind that we have in God's will, as revealed in the Scriptures, an absolute standard of right and wrong; and no ignorance on our part, or want of opportunity on our part, can make the wrong to be right. If a person through ignorance does that which is contrary to God's revealed will, it may not at the time hinder communion; but as soon as it is revealed to him that the thing done is contrary to God's will it must be confessed, not as a misfortune, but as a sin, and the atoning blood must be upon it before communion can be fully and satisfactorily reëstablished.

J. HUDSON TAYLOR.

The glory of the Lord cannot stay in the house of man, because of sin. God wants a consecrated temple, a consecrated people. God is ready to consecrate you, but it will cost you something. Are you ready for any sacrifice?

H. W. WEBB-PEPLOE.

When a man finds out that he can't empty his own heart, what he wants to do is just to let the water in from above. Get under the fountain and stay there, and there will be no trouble about your being full to overflowing.   D. L. MOODY.

To give a *perfect* rule of life humanity needs many things besides laws; example, experience, mistakes, departures—all are needed. To safely navigate the seas the compass, quadrant, and chronometer are not sufficient. By the aid of these the mariner knows which way to go and where he is; but without the discoveries, mistakes, and disasters of those who have gone before him he is in constant danger. These mistakes and disasters are not put down on his chart for him to imitate and follow, but to show him where there is danger that he may avoid it; and every such place marked on his chart has been the scene of greater or less disaster, and its location on the chart is the highest evidence of honesty and wisdom. Viewed from this standpoint, the sins and mistakes of the patriarchs, related by inspiration, show a faithful record and point out to us the danger by showing the disastrous results and telling of the condemnation of God; yet all writers against Christianity have used these departures to disprove the inspiration of the Bible. As well might they use the past accidents and disasters on the seas against the art of navigation. They first ignore the Bible, then condemn Noah, David, and Solomon by the Bible.   I. D. DRIVER.

The Bible is the only book which shows us what we are—not only our needs, but our possibilities. Too many men are content to live in the valley or to roam about among the foot-hills, who might be climbing upon the peaks of the higher Christian experience.   JOHN R. MOTT.

Repent, and be baptized every one of you in the name of Jesus Christ for the remission of sins, and ye shall receive the gift of the Holy Ghost. For the promise is unto you, and to your children.—Acts ii. 38, 39.

What promise is here referred to? Ah, it refers to this glad news, the promise of the gift of the Holy Ghost, which is for every child of God in every age of the Christian church. What a wondrous truth, that there isn't a man or a woman or a child who has a living, saving faith in Jesus Christ that cannot have the baptism with the Spirit of God! But with the glorious privilege there is the deep responsibility. If I am not willing to pay the price and claim the blessing I am responsible before God for the work I might have done and did not do. I tremble for myself, and for my brethren in the ministry, and my brethren in Christian work in the larger ministry—not because they are preaching error; but because they are preaching the truth, but not preaching it in the power of the Holy Ghost. The most deadening thing on earth is the truth preached in the power of the flesh. "The letter killeth; it is the Spirit that giveth life."

R. A. TORREY.

We are told that John and Peter were filled in the second chapter, and again in the fourth. Now, they had either lost some of their power or had greater capacity. If Peter and John needed to be filled again so soon after Pentecost, don't you think you and I need to be filled again?

D. L. MOODY.

If ye then, being evil, know how to give good gifts unto your children, how much more shall your heavenly Father give the Holy Spirit to them that ask him?—Luke xi. 13.

There is no article "the" in that passage; the word is partitive, not personal; it is "Holy Spirit." There is no doubt that none of us have realized the fullness of the possibilities that might be expected concerning the gift or powers or qualities of this "Holy Ghost," and that the holiest of us will always be conscious of needing more. It is one thing for me to ask God to give me more of the Spirit in my own personal enjoyment; it is another thing to ask God to give his own perfect gift again from heaven as though he never had bestowed it. It is one thing to recognize that I have failed to take and to use what my Father has bestowed; it is another thing to charge my Father with not having bestowed what he says he has given.

H. W. WEBB-PEPLOE.

There is a difference between gifts and graces. The graces of the Spirit are humility and love, like the humility and love of Christ, and are to make a man free from self; the gift of the Spirit is to fit a man for work. We see this illustrated among the Corinthians. In the twelfth and fourteenth chapters we read that the gifts of prophecy and of working miracles were in great power among them; but the graces of the Spirit were noticeably absent.

ANDREW MURRAY.

We should abandon the idea that we are to use the Holy Ghost, and accept the thought that the Holy Ghost is to use us. There is a wide distinction between those two conceptions. I was in the Chicago World's Fair, and was attracted to a man dressed up in a very gaudy Oriental costume, who was turning with all his might a crank which was attached to a pump from which a great stream of water was pouring out. I said, "That man is working hard and producing splendid results." I came near, and, to my astonishment, found that the man, which was really only wooden, was not turning the crank, but the crank was turning him, and, instead of his making that stream of water go, it was making him go. Many people want the secret of power. They hear about Peter preaching that wonderful sermon, and of course they would give anything if they had the ability to preach one sermon and convert three thousand people. They say to Peter, "How did you get hold of the power?" "I didn't get hold of the power at all," he would say; "the power got hold of me." "We have preached the gospel unto you *with* "—no, not "with"; if it had been translated correctly we should learn that, instead of Peter using the Spirit, the Spirit used him. "We have preached the gospel unto you *in* the power of the Holy Ghost." As a wheel dips itself into the river and makes all the cotton factories whirl, so Peter dipped into the Spirit and was swept by the current.

A. J. GORDON.

The very power that raised Jesus from the dead, notwithstanding the host of devils that opposed him, and set him at the right hand of God is waiting to lift each one of us from the grave of sin and lust, above the heads of the devils that oppose us, and to set us in heavenly places in Christ. If man will only live in his Head, in Christ, the devil is always under his feet; but the mistake with so many of us is that we do not maintain our heavenly life, but by getting out of fellowship with Jesus we, as it were, get into the devil's power again. If you and I would always live in him we would always live above.

F. B. MEYER.

Our union with Christ is a real union. Everything that concerns me Christ is concerned in, and everything that concerns Christ I am concerned in. The Bible tells us from beginning to end that our salvation is not our own salvation merely, but that Jesus Christ may be glorified. Our pardon shows his grace; our sanctification shows his holiness; our resurrection shows his power; and our being glorified is to reflect his glory. It all concerns him, and because it concerns him it ought to concern us; and we ought to love—oh, how we ought to love!—his glorious appearing.

D. W. WHITTLE.

Count nothing small. The smallest thing may be a link in the golden chain which binds a man to the divine Master himself.

A. F. SCHAUFFLER.

153

Knowing this, that the trying of your faith worketh patience.
But let patience have her perfect work, that ye may be perfect
and entire, wanting nothing.—James i. 3, 4.

James actually declares that if a man has perfect
patience he has a perfect character. I wish I had
a voice that could ring over our run-mad country
in this end of the nineteenth century, when men are
tumbling over one another, rushing after nothing and
finding it. I would like to proclaim this lesson: who-
ever has perfect patience has a perfect character.

JOHN A. BROADUS.

A just man is a man who in society is most exact
in all the details of duty; honorable in his dealings;
he pays all his debts; he won't injure any one. Joseph
of Arimathea was also a " good man "; that is to say,
a kind man, a man of generous disposition. These
are the two characteristics of the natural man, in this
case at least; it is these which make a man liked by
his fellow-men. Joseph was all this and yet not a
Christian. A man in his natural state may be all
that Joseph was and yet be outside of the pale of
salvation. ANDREW A. BONAR.

A friend went one morning to Sir Robert Peel's
house and found him with a great bundle of letters
lying before him, bowed over it in prayer. The
friend retired, and came back in a short time and
said, "I beg your pardon for intruding upon your
private devotions." Sir Robert said, "No; those
were my public devotions. I was just giving the
affairs of state into the hands of God, for I could
not manage them." Try trusting the living God
with your letter-bag or your housekeeping.

H. W. WEBB-PEPLOE.

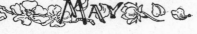
By faith Noah, being warned of God of things not seen as yet, moved with fear, prepared an ark to the saving of his house.—Heb. xi. 7.

The fear of God makes a hero; the fear of man makes a coward. Fear to do wrong makes the hero; fear to do right makes the coward. Noah was warned of things not seen as yet, and he believed God's warning. Such a thing as a flood the world had never known. It was out of the range of his experience; there were scores of arguments against it; but God's word with Noah was stronger than all arguments. The need of this day is a healthy fear: faith in Sinai with its thundering of judgment as strong as faith in Calvary with its whisperings of love; a belief in the words of Christ about the worm that dieth not as strong as a belief in the mansions which he is preparing for his people.

The fear of Noah moved him forward; the fear of the coward moves him backward. Wellington once commissioned two soldiers to go on a dangerous errand. As they galloped along, one looked at the other and said, "You are scared." "Yes," replied his comrade; "and if you were scared as badly as I am you would run." The brave man turned his horse, and, galloping back to the general's tent, said, "Sir, you have sent with me a coward. I left him trembling like a leaf." "Well," said Wellington, "unless you return pretty soon his mission will be performed." And, sure enough, as the brave man galloped back he met the coward returning, with the dangerous work already done. It is manly to fear to do wrong; it may not be unmanly to tremble in the presence of danger while we stand, in spite of our trembling, at the post of duty. A. C. Dixon.

Some people seem to think that Jerusalem was built by men who desired a city and said, "We will not build on a hill, because then it will be necessary to carry the stone and timber up. We will get a smooth, level country down in the valley, and there build a beautiful city, and we will have a temple in the midst of it, and then when it is done we will get together and pray, 'O Lord, we have built a city; we have built it in a plain, because it was easier; now, Lord, please lift up the ground and make a hill of it.'" So the Lord did it. Then they prayed, "Now, Lord, please pile the mountains around us for our defense." So the Lord did that also.

What are the facts? These people wanted a city, and they said, "It is best that this city should be on a hill. We will build where God has laid the foundation. It will be hard to get the stone up, hard to get the timber up; but we will do it." It makes all the difference in the world whether you lay your plans and ask God to prosper them, or give your life to God, and let him make the plans, and then carry out his own plans. I fear that quite a proportion of the prayers of good people is really, "O Lord, my will be done." Did you pray this morning that God would bless you in something that you had made up your mind to do? You ought to have said, "Here, Lord, lies before me this strange, new day; I never saw it—nobody ever saw it. Here am I; what wilt thou have me to do?" God will never move the mountains around a selfish man; you must put your house where God put the mountains before he put you into the world; put your life where God has put the plan and purpose of your life.

ALEXANDER MCKENZIE.

Christ died that he might make us a "peculiar people." A great many Christians are afraid that they will be peculiar. A few weeks before Enoch was translated his acquaintances would probably have said he was a little peculiar; they would have told you that when they had a progressive-euchre party and the whole country-side was invited, you wouldn't find Enoch or one of his family there. He was very peculiar, very. We are not told he was a warrior or a great scientist or a great scholar. In fact, we are not told he was anything that the world would call great, but he walked with God three hundred and sixty-five years, and he is the brightest star that shone in that dispensation. If he could walk with God, cannot you and I? As old Dr. Bonar has said, "He took a long walk one day, and has not come back yet. The Lord liked his company so well that he said, 'Enoch, come up higher.'" We shall find him up there some day.

I suppose that if you had asked the men in Elijah's time what kind of a man he was, they would have said, "He is very peculiar." The king would say, "I hate him." Jezebel didn't like him; the whole royal court didn't like him, and a great many of the nominal Christians didn't like him; he was too radical. I am glad the Lord had seven thousand that had not bowed the knee to Baal; but I would rather have Elijah's little finger than the whole seven thousand. I wouldn't give much for seven thousand Christians in hiding. They will just barely get into heaven; they won't have any crown. See that "no man take thy crown." Be willing to be one of Christ's peculiar people, no matter what men may say of you.   D. L. MOODY.

Thou, O Lord, art a shield for me; my glory, and the lifter up of mine head.—Ps. iii. 3.

I like that last expression—"Lifter up of my head." There is your child, my good mother, and your child has been bad, and you have chastised it. You have put the poor little bundle of wretchedness and crossness into a corner, and there it is standing soiling all its face with hot, scalding tears. Then your heart relents; the extreme of misery tells upon you, for you are its mother. And you come toward the little thing, and it creeps into the corner and hangs its head. And what do you do? Instead of chastising it any more, you come quite close, and with one hand on the little one's shoulder, you put the other hand below its chin, and literally you lift up the little face into the light of your own, and stoop down and kiss it. Did you ever think that that is what God wants to do with the poor weary sinner who has gone back and done shamefully? When fears are on every side, and awful voices in your heart speak ominously of eternal doom, God comes, and with his own gracious hand lifts up your head. He anoints and cheers your soiled face; he lifts up your head, and lets the light of his own reconciled countenance beam down upon you.

JOHN McNEILL.

If we were to believe in the survival of the fittest there would not be much chance for some of us. But the glory of the gospel is this, that God comes to the unfit, to the marred and spoiled, to those who have thwarted and resisted him, and that he is prepared to make them over again; and if you will let him he will make you too.   F. B. MEYER.

158

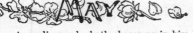
According as he hath chosen us in him before the foundation of the world, that we should be holy and without blame before him in love.—Eph. i. 4.

Christians, claim your full privileges. In temporal things men are beginning to do this. Suppose that the son and heir of some wealthy deceased man were told by certain trustees that he was left with only three or four hundred dollars a year, and that the rest was left in their hands in trust; he would go along on that three or four hundred dollars only so long as he was obliged to. Some one tells him that the whole fortune is left to him, and he goes to some lawyer's office and asks to see his father's will. As he reads the will the whole truth comes out, and he says, "I have been living on three hundred dollars a year when I have a hundred thousand. I am going to come into possession of what I have, and live proportionately to my wealth." Thousands of us are yet living on two or three hundred dollars that might live on the exceeding riches of God's glory. M. E. BALDWIN.

The beautiful trees and green grass and the bright sun God created that they might show forth his beauty and wisdom and glory. When that tree, one hundred years old, was planted, God did not give it a stock of life in which it could carry on its existence. Nay, verily. God clothes the lilies every year afresh with their beauty; every year he clothes the tree with its foliage and its fruit; every day and every hour it is God who maintains the life of all nature. God created us that we might be the empty vessels in which he could work out his beauty, his will, his love, and the likeness of his blessed Son. ANDREW MURRAY.

159

The accidental miracles of our Lord are among
the most remarkable—those that, as it were, he
spilled over by the way. While he was on his way
to do one miracle he dropped another, almost as if
he didn't intend it. He was going to heal the
daughter of Jairus when the woman with an issue
of blood reached out her hand, touched the hem of
his garment, and was healed. When an electric jar
is filled, only a touch will unload it. So it might be
in the experience of every believer. I do not know
but that, if we were fully the Lord's, the greater
part of the good we did would be that of which we
were not cognizant. Service would overflow from us.

A. J. GORDON.

If you are abiding in Christ you are reproducing
yourself in thousands of instances when you are
wholly unaware of it. Out of the personal relationship between the soul and Christ come the fruits of
holy living. The vine does not bear fruit of itself;
it bears its fruit through the branches. Our unconscious influence thus becomes far more fruitful
than our conscious influence. In the last great day
many will bewail that they have accomplished so
little, and, looking at the scanty results, will say,
"When saw we thee hungry, and fed thee? or athirst,
and gave thee drink?" to find that unconsciously
their lives had abounded in fruits well pleasing in
the Master's sight. It is from such holy lives as
this that is derived our Master's highest joy. It is
when the whole body of Christ becomes instinct with
his spirit that the world is made conscious of his
divine headship over the church.

BISHOP HENDRIX.

160

If you go into a dark room filled with vermin you cannot see anything; but if you light a match, you see some crawling creatures; if you light a lamp you see more; and if you turn on an electric light it reveals the good and the evil in sharp contrast. "That which doth make manifest is light," and Christians are to be lights in the world. When the Christian holds up his light, men are able to see good and evil. The church establishes the moral standard for men who never go near it and for communities who reject it.

CHARLES A. BLANCHARD.

A candle that won't shine in one room is very unlikely to shine in another. If you do not shine at home, if your father and mother, your sister and brother, if the very cat and dog in the house are not the better and happier for your being a Christian, it is a question whether you really are one.

J. HUDSON TAYLOR.

Whatever rest is provided by Christianity for the children of God, it is certainly never contemplated that it should supersede personal effort. And any rest which ministers to indifference is immoral and unreal—it makes parasites, and not men.

HENRY DRUMMOND.

Let the engineer pull out the throttle and play cards, let the pilot of a steamer in a hurricane immerse himself in a novel, but let not the watchman of the Lord be anything but awake and in dead earnest, when all around immortal souls are in death-grapple with their great enemy. CYRUS D. FOSS.

Dying with Jesus, his death reckoned mine;
Living with Jesus, a new life divine;
Looking to Jesus till glory doth shine,
Moment by moment, O Lord, I am thine.

Moment by moment I'm kept in his love;
Moment by moment I've life from above;
Looking to Jesus till glory doth shine,
Moment by moment, O Lord, I am thine.

Never a trial that he is not there,
Never a burden that he doth not bear,
Never a sorrow that he doth not share;
Moment by moment I'm under his care.

Never a heartache and never a groan,
Never a tear-drop and never a moan,
Never a danger, but there on the throne
Moment by moment he thinks of his own.

Never a weakness that he doth not feel,
Never a sickness that he cannot heal;
Moment by moment, in woe or in weal,
Jesus, my Saviour, abides with me still.

D. W. WHITTLE.

Month of June

Bias of mind has a great deal to do with the conclusion which a man reaches; we have to recognize this sometimes to explain men's manner of dealing with gospel evidence. It is exactly as our Saviour said: "If they hear not Moses and the prophets, neither will they be persuaded, though one rose from the dead." If the trouble had been a lack of evidence, then more evidence would have helped them. But there was a lack of something else. And when that is the case more evidence does no good. You cannot cure a man's eyes by operating on his ears. We understand that. Here is a president of a bank; he has his books and his securities, and he locks up his safe and sets the time-lock for ten o'clock in the forenoon of the next day. He goes home and thinks of something he would like to get out of the vault. He goes down to the bank, but he cannot open the vault. He has the combination; he may be president and cashier and stock-holder and director all in one, but he cannot open that vault until ten o'clock next day. If he could only get inside, or if there were only somebody inside that he could talk to and tell him to change the adjustment, all that he would want then would be knowledge of the combination. But he cannot open it. That is what I think is really needed in men. They need some one to change them within —what we call regeneration. We may accumulate argument, and pound at men with the presentation of the truth objectively; but we won't do very much until the hour strikes for the soul's release, and when the Spirit does his work then the combination comes into play, and men yield to the power of entreaty and respond to the presentation of evidence and argument.   FRANCIS L. PATTON.

163

Have ye received the Holy Ghost since ye believed?—Acts xix. 2.

Evidently there is a reception of the Holy Ghost over and beyond that which first brings us to believe in Jesus. Therefore I put it to you, in all earnestness, hast thou received thy share in thy Father's gift? If not, it is waiting for thee to-day in the hands of the living Saviour, and thou hast but to claim it and it will be thine.

F. B. MEYER.

The filling with the Holy Spirit is the Spirit of God coming upon the believer, taking possession of his faculties, imparting to him gifts not naturally his own, but which qualify him for the service to which God has called him.

R. A. TORREY.

What, then, shall we do to be filled? What did they do in the days of Hezekiah, when the temple had had all kinds of iniquity and filth brought into it? The priests came and purged out all the filth that they found, and cast it into the brook Kidron. What did they do in Nehemiah's day, when Tobiah had filled God's chambers with household stuff? The prophet cast it all forth out of the Lord's house. What did the Lord Jesus do when the temple was filled with money-changers and sellers of merchandise? He made a scourge of small cords and drove them all out.

H. W. WEBB-PEPLOE.

A revelation of Christ by the Spirit to our souls must precede our being filled by Christ with the Spirit.

D. W. WHITTLE.

He that believeth on me, as the Scripture hath said, out of his belly shall flow rivers of living water.—John vii. 38.

There is a promise to test. Do you believe on the Lord Jesus Christ as the giver of this full blessing? It does not mean, "He that believeth on me for the pardon of his sins," because there are many persons who are pardoned and who have not this fullness of blessing—you can see that rivers of living water do not rush out from them. But it is, "He that believeth on me as the giver of the fullness of the Spirit." Look also at that other passage, "Whosoever drinketh of the water that I shall give him shall never thirst." I accept that promise. I do believe that I shall never thirst again. I do believe that from me—poor little me—rivers shall flow, rivers of living water; and God shall be glorified.

J. HUDSON TAYLOR.

Since it pleased the Father that in Jesus all fullness should dwell, and it pleases Jesus and the Father, and the Spirit too, that all poor sinners who believe in Jesus shall be branches in him, incorporated into him—since he assumed the connection and the position of a root to his branches, God has no chance to show himself out if it be not through his people. Oh, think what a glorious company we shall be by and by, when all the fullness in Jesus Christ shall be expressed. Then again, just as if you take away the branches from the root it cannot express itself, so if you take away the root from the branches they must wither and die. The branches depend on the root for their very life, and without the branches the root cannot be manifested—there can be no expression of its nature but through the branches.

MARCUS RAINSFORD.

Our Lord's great lesson in John xv. is about the vine and its branches. He says, "I am the vine, ye are the branches." If you look at the branches of a vine, you observe that the bark is the same, the leaves are the same, and the fruit is the same. There is the closest resemblance between the branches and the vine. Some Christians reduce your spiritual temperature to zero. They have comparatively little or no spirituality, and, worse, they are worldly. If I brought you a slip of a log, and said I had found it growing on a vine, you would say, "I think there is a mistake; this is oak, the leaves are ragged like those of an oak. We are not accustomed to see that kind of branch on a vine." I can believe that that oak grew on a vine before I can believe that some men and women that I have met grow on Jesus Christ.

M. E. BALDWIN.

A man standing erect on the earth breathes air of a purer quality than that breathed by the insects that crawl at his feet; so the man risen with Christ should stand erect, as a new man in Christ Jesus, and breathe the air of heaven.

D. W. WHITTLE.

Make Christ your most constant companion. Be more under his influence than under any other influence. Ten minutes spent in his society every day— aye, two minutes, if it be face to face and heart to heart—will make the whole day different. Every character has an inward spring; let Christ be that spring. Every action has a key-note; let Christ be that note to which your whole life is attuned.

HENRY DRUMMOND.

Israel passed through two stages—two parts of God's work of redemption: God brought them out from Egypt that he might bring them into Canaan. This is applicable to every believer. At conversion God brought you out of Egypt; and the same Almighty God is longing to bring you into the Canaan life. God brought the Israelites out, but they would not let him bring them in; so they were obliged to wander for forty years in the wilderness—the type, alas! of so many Christians. The wilderness life is wandering backward and forward; going after the world, and coming back and repenting; led astray by temptation, and returning, only to go off again—a life of ups and downs. In Canaan, on the other hand, is a life of rest, because the soul has learned to trust. A second difference is that one was a life of want, the other a life of plenty. In the wilderness God graciously supplied their wants by the manna and the water from the rock. But alas! they were not content, and their life was one of want and of murmuring. But in Canaan God gave them a land flowing with milk and honey, a land nourished by the rain of heaven, and which had the very care of God himself. Oh, believe that there is a possibility of such a change for you, a way out of that life of spiritual want and complaining, into the land of supply of every want! A third difference is that in the wilderness there was no lasting victory. In Canaan they conquered every enemy. So God waits to give, not freedom from temptation, but victory every day. You desire an entrance into the life of rest and victory; then in the stillness of your heart say, "My God, I believe there is such a life prepared for me and within my reach."   ANDREW MURRAY.

There are many, very many, Christians who are afraid of making an unreserved surrender to God. They are afraid that God will ask some hard thing of them, or some absurd thing. They fear sometimes that it will upset all their life-plans. In a word, they are afraid to surrender unreservedly to the will of God, for him to do all he wishes to for them and whatsoever he wills with them. Friends, the will of God concerning us is not only the wisest and best thing in the world; it is also the tenderest and sweetest. God's will for us is not only more loving than a father's; it is more tender than a mother's. It is true that God does oftentimes revolutionize utterly our life-plans when we surrender ourselves to his will. It is true that he does require of us things that to others seem hard. But when the will is once surrendered the revolutionized life-plans become just the plans that are most pleasant, and the things that to others seem hard are just the things that are easiest and most delightful. Do not let Satan deceive you into being afraid of God's plans for your life.

R. A. TORREY.

When a ship is moored at a dock and is ready to start, the order is given, "Let go!" Then the last rope is loosened and the steamer moves. There are things that tie us to earth and to the self-life; but to-day the message comes, "If thou wouldst die with Jesus, let go!" Jesus carried the penitent thief through death to life. The thief knew not where he was going, but Jesus, the mighty conqueror, took him in his arms and landed him in Paradise in his ignorance. If you cannot understand all about this crucifixion with Christ, never mind; trust the Lord's promise. ANDREW MURRAY.

When a heavy morning mist veils the beautiful valley and hills, the landscape is shut out from our vision. But suddenly there comes a breath, or the sun's rays; the mist parts, and the magnificent scenery stands unveiled. So God often parts the mist that hides the future, and shows what a man may be. Young people especially, seek from God the vision of what your life may be, and then follow out that revelation, because when you catch God's vision you will always find him responsible for the outworking of it.

F. B. MEYER.

A sculptor has many models from which he chisels various statues, though one may be his masterpiece. But when I come into the Lord's studio I find only one design: that we should be made in the likeness of Jesus Christ. "Whom he did foreknow, he also did predestinate to be conformed to the image of his Son." If you should go to the kingdom of glory to-day, and open the great book of God, and should find your own name there, after that name you would find written these words: "To be conformed to the image of my dear Son." Not the image of Paul, however grand; not that of any sanctified man that we may meet in our pilgrimage here; but that of the dear Lord, that Holy One. You may say that the materials of your heart are vicious,—and they are not single in that,—but be assured that, if Thorwaldsen could not make a masterpiece of art out of loose sandstone, God can make a being that will shine like a star before his throne out of the poor, weary, burdened sinners that his grace calls to the hallowed feet of Jesus Christ. The materials form no obstruction to that heavenly architect.

M. E. BALDWIN.

169

For what are you living? Are your pursuits
bounded by the narrow horizon of earth and limited
to the fleeting moments of time? Are you constantly
engaged in lining as warmly as possible the nest in
which you hope to spend old age and die? Are you
perpetually seeking to make the best of this world?
I fear that these are the real aims of many professing Christians; and if so, it is simply useless for them
to claim kinship with that stream of pilgrims which
is constantly pouring through the earth, bound to
the city which hath foundations, their home and
mother city. F. B. MEYER.

Our choice in life must be a cubic choice. It must
have three dimensions. First, it must be very high
—as high as I can reach with my life. Next, it
must be very broad, covering all the powers of my
life—mind, voice, hands, feet. And then it must be
very long—run out seventy years, if that be the sum
of my days on earth. I cannot afford to swap horses
in the middle of the stream. I cannot afford to change
my choice at thirty or forty. We are to make our
choice the highest, the broadest, and the longest
possible. This is to be our aim: that the life of
Christ in us shall be and do what the life of Christ
was and did in himself. We are so to live that our
life shall repeat the life of Jesus of Nazareth.
ALEXANDER MCKENZIE.

Some of the maxims of the ungodly are very good
when they are properly interpreted. An example
may be found in the maxim, "Take care of number
one." Who is number one? The ungodly man says,
"I am number one." But God is number one. Take
care of God's interests first, and he will look after
yours. J. HUDSON TAYLOR.

A soldier was once posted in a forest to watch for the approach of Indians. It was a position of peculiar danger, three different men having been surprised and killed at this post without having had time to fire a shot. The soldier was left with strict orders to observe the utmost vigilance. In a short time an object moving among the trees at some distance caught his eye. He watched it attentively, with gun ready, until, as it came a little nearer, he saw it to be a wild hog. Another came in sight. He satisfied himself it *was* a wild hog, rooting under the leaves. Presently in another direction the leaves were rustled, and a third wild hog appeared. Being now used to these creatures, he paid but little attention. The movements of the last animal, however, soon engaged the man's thoughts. He observed a slight awkwardness in the movements of this one, and thought that possibly an Indian might be approaching him covered with a hog's skin. If it *was* an Indian the safest thing was to shoot. If it was not an Indian, and he should shoot, he would run no risk. He raised his rifle and fired. With a bound and a yell, an Indian leaped to his feet and fell back dead. The man had saved his life, and prevented the surprise of the garrison, by his watchfulness. So the child of God must be ever on the alert and guarded against the approaches of the Evil One. Draw the Word of God upon every object that approaches you in this dark world of sin. If the devil is in it, you may be sure the Word will expose him. Stripped of his disguise, he will howl and will leave you. In the name of Christ we can ever have the victory. Without Christ, and in our own strength or wisdom, we shall suffer defeat. D. W. WHITTLE.

171

Did you ever notice that when some of the strongest men in the Bible failed they almost always failed on the strongest point of their character? Elijah was noted for his boldness, and Jezebel scared him out of his wits. Moses was renowned for his meekness, humility, and gentleness; yet he became angry and killed that Egyptian; he was angry and said, "Must I bring water out of this rock, ye rebels?" God kept him out of the Promised Land because he lost his temper. If you think you are meek, it is a good sign that you are not. Peter was one of the boldest of all the disciples, but when one little maid looked at him and said, "You are one of his disciples," he began to curse and to swear and to say that he was not, and down he fell. John and James were noted for their meekness and gentleness, and yet they wanted to call fire down from heaven to consume a town in Samaria. Do you not see that man is a complete failure away from God? But he that is in you is greater than he that is in the world. When Jesus Christ on the cross said, "It is finished," it was the shout of a conqueror. He had fought and overcome the world. Now if I have Christ in me, I will overcome the world, and if I have not it is the height of madness for me to undertake to overcome.

D. L. MOODY.

The men that have redeemed human history, and stood like lighthouses on the dark and stormy promontories of life, casting out healing rays and saving beams through the dark waters, have been men that got their enthusiasm for humanity out of the cross —men whose motto was, "The love of Christ constraineth me." M. D. HOGE.

172

Christians do not know how much they rob Christ by reading what literature they choose. Bring your mind to the feet of Jesus. Then there is the whole outer life: your relation to society, your home life, your money, your time, and your business. Put everything in the hands of Jesus.

ANDREW MURRAY.

You never can drive out the uncleanness of evil thoughts except by pouring in the clean wholesomeness of the thoughts of Christ. Have you made Christ for any length of time the one object of your thought? Try it, you men who want to break loose from the shackles that you know are keeping you away from the great blessing of God and from the pure sweetness of his free and holy life. What else is there to think about that is worth anything, compared with him? All treasures of wisdom and knowledge are hidden in him. How it must grieve him, who, though he was rich, yet for our sakes became poor, to see us filling our minds with passing things, worthless things, dying after the fashion of the world, while Christ is crowded away into some bare and paltry place in our lives! Oh, that we might learn to make Jesus, and Jesus only, the object of all our thinking! If we did, how we would lose taste for much that pleases us now! How music, that perhaps takes a large place in our hearts now, would be put into a subordinate place! How the taste for certain classes of books or of studies or certain lines of thought would vanish into an insignificant place the moment we gave to Jesus Christ the place to which he is entitled in our thinking!

ROBERT E. SPEER.

Walk in the Spirit, and ye shall not fulfil the lust of the flesh.
—Gal. v. 16.

I do not believe that that passage is meant to be
done away with by the Christian. I have heard it
said, "I pity St. Paul when he wrote that; he was in
a low, groveling experience." Nay, brethren; the
lust of the flesh is in all men to the last. If a man
says that he is delivered from the flesh so that it
has no longer any existence in his experience, he is
contradicting God's holy Word. The flesh is there,
and what is the Christian to do? "Walk in the Spirit,
and ye shall not fulfil the lust of the flesh." The
flesh is lusting against the Spirit, and the Spirit
against the flesh, and you are between the two. The
question is, To which are you going to yield? Walk
in the Spirit because willingly led of the Spirit, and
stay there all the days of your life; if you do, you
will never fulfil the lust of the flesh.

H. W. WEBB-PEPLOE.

A saint without the help of the Holy Spirit can no
more walk in the light as God is in the light than a
sinner can be justified apart from the shedding of
the blood without which there is no remission.

ANDREW BONAR.

A good many are trying to work with the anointing they got three years ago.

D. L. MOODY.

174

And Jesus being full of the Holy Ghost returned from Jordan, and was led by the Spirit into the wilderness, being forty days tempted of the devil. And in those days he did eat nothing: and when they were ended, he afterward hungered.—Luke iv. 1, 2.

Jesus was full of the Holy Ghost, and yet he was tempted. Temptation often comes upon a man with its strongest power when he is nearest to God. As some one has said, the devil aims high. He got one apostle to curse and swear and say he didn't know Christ. Very few men have such conflicts with the devil as Martin Luther had. Why? Because he was going to shake the very kingdom of hell. Oh, what conflicts John Bunyan had! If a man has much of the Spirit of God he will have great conflicts with the tempter.

D. L. MOODY.

Our Lord's temptation came right after his baptism and right before his ministry, as soon as the heavens had been opened above him, and the Spirit of God was seen descending and resting upon him; immediately the Spirit leadeth him—more, *driveth* him—into the wilderness to be tempted of the devil. Ah, my friends, after feelings have been stirred, after resolutions have been made, after means of grace have been received, then we should look for temptations. Those things are not to keep temptation at arm's-length; they are to prepare us to meet temptation, to stand in the evil day, to stand by our promise, to be true to God's voice that has been heard, to claim, aye, to appropriate and really make our own, the grace that has been bestowed.

A. C. A. HALL.

But truly I am full of power by the Spirit of the Lord.—Micah iii. 8.

There is a great difference between strength and power. Strength implies ability; but power implies activity and efficiency. A man may be a strong man, even a giant, and yet be powerless because he is bound by fetters—unable to exercise his strength. The great lack in our entire spiritual life is a lack of power. We cannot do the things that we would. Romans vii. 19 is too often the experience not only of the Christian, but of every man: "The good that I would, I do not: but the evil which I would not, that I do." Ovid said, "I see and approve the right, but I follow and practise the wrong." Therefore the great requirement of man is power—power in two directions: power to overcome evil; power to help others to effect the same thing.

ARTHUR T. PIERSON.

Christ said that the works that he did we should do, "and greater works than these." He turns us from the miracles unto higher things which are within our reach as his disciples. He might have given to us the power to lay our fingers upon benighted eyes and give them sight, to put our hands upon crooked ankle-bones and give them strength, to speak to the sick and bring them back to health, and to summon the dead to life again. Greater works than these are ours. If you open the eyes of a man so that he sees God, if you touch his ankle-bones so that he walks with God, if you bring healing to his spirit and he is made holy, if you shall call the dead to the life of a child of God, your greater work is done.

ALEXANDER MCKENZIE.

176

Son, go work to-day in my vineyard.—Matt. xxi. 28.

Let us put out of our minds forever the thought that thirty years from now we are going to do something. You will not, unless you do it now. There is more time wasted, more sin committed, waiting for a more propitious opportunity than from any other one cause. "Behold, *now*"—not thirty minutes from now, not ten seconds ahead, but *now;* the "now" of Scripture has not the duration of a thousandth part of a second. "Now is the accepted time," not only to believe on Jesus Christ, but to *serve* him.

H. C. MABIE.

A religion of effortless adoration may be a religion for an angel, but never for a man. Not in the contemplative, but in the active, lies true hope; not in rapture, but in reality, lies true life; not in the realm of ideals, but among tangible things, is man's sanctification wrought.

HENRY DRUMMOND.

Don't wait for something to turn up, but go and turn up something.

D. L. MOODY.

We are not responsible for results. What is success in our estimation may be failure from God's standpoint. Peter was filled with the Holy Ghost and lifted three thousand people into the kingdom. Stephen was filled with the Holy Ghost and was stoned to death. One was as great a triumph as the other in the thought of God.

J. WILBUR CHAPMAN.

177

In many theological treatises the definition of the church is, "A body of believers voluntarily associated together for the purpose of worship and edification." As well say that my body is a voluntary association of hands and feet and ears and eyes, for the purpose of work and locomotion! The fact is that, as my body was formed out of a germ and all stands together in the head, so the church is formed out of Christ. As Eve was taken out of Adam, so the church, the bride of Christ, is taken out of Christ; and when he rises and ascends to the Father, then the Holy Ghost comes down, and as the Word is preached he begins to gather about himself those who are to constitute the church of Christ.

It is very instructive to notice the "additions" named in the Acts of the Apostles. As soon as Peter finished his first sermon "they that gladly received his word were baptized: and the same day there were added unto them about three thousand souls." The words "unto them" do not belong there; all that is said is that believers were "added." If we are anxious to know to what they were added, read Acts v. 14: "And believers were the more *added to the Lord*, multitudes both of men and women."

Ah! that is it. If you put a slip down into the earth, there will be an addition of branch after branch growing out of it. Jesus Christ came down in the person of the Holy Ghost to constitute the center for the church, and as soon as believers were regenerated they became added to him.

A. J. GORDON.

Let the blessed Lord come, step aboard our poor fishing-boats, take charge, order us to the right and left, make the biggest of us mere deck-hands. Let the great Master's voice ring from stem to stern on every ship: "Launch out into the deep, and let down your nets for a draft." No masters, no lieutenants, no officers, no "orders of clergy"; everybody just a deck-hand to pull ropes and shoot nets when he comes. When the Lord is away, oh, we play fine games! We divide the boat into the officers' quarters and the forecastle, and we walk majestically on the poop, some of us, and spend a great deal of time discussing the different places and positions, and the rules and regulations—how far my command is to go, and where it is to stop, and on what chalk-line your command begins. Just let the Lord come and take command, and you will not be splitting hairs as to your position in the church.

JOHN McNEILL.

There is a familiar story about John Wesley and others going to the river that bounds the Holy City, and finding, to their astonishment, that they had to drop their cloaks and garments in which they approached. One drops his cloak, another his robe, another his surplice, and they come out on the other side astonished to find that they are all in the same white, beautiful robe, the robe of righteousness, which is Christ Jesus, our Lord. Cannot we gain a little more of heaven upon earth by handing out more of the right hand of fellowship? "Stand fast in one spirit, with one mind."

H. W. WEBB-PEPLOE.

We very often see people who say that they do
not believe in foreign missions, but believe in home
missions. They are very largely like the man in one
of our Western States who, when a subscription was
presented to him for foreign missions, said, "I don't
know anything about them, and I do not want to give
my money to the work." They let him rest, but when
they had an urgent appeal to help a needy church
in Minnesota, they went to him, hoping to get his
subscription; but he said, "I do not know anything
about Minnesota; that is too far away. I want to
give my money right here at home, where I can see
what it does." Then, when they found that the fence
around the graveyard needed to be repaired, they
said, "Well, we have him now sure." And so they
presented the subscription for the fence around the
graveyard, and the good brother looked at it and said
very solemnly, "I don't see the use of that; for those
that are in there can't get out, and those who are out
don't want to get in." That is my belief in regard
to people professing to be Christians who have no
interest in foreign missions. I do not think they have
any interest in any mission; for when they have the
interest which the divine teaching brings they will
want to have the gospel preached to every creature.

S. L. BALDWIN.

I do not imagine that an Anglo-Saxon is any dearer
to God than a Mongolian or an African. My plea is
not, save America for America's sake, but, save
America for the world's sake.

JOSIAH STRONG.

Five hundred years before Christ India was groaning under Brahmanical sacerdotalism, priestcraft, polytheism, idolatry, and caste. Buddha arose as a reformer, teaching them that there was one God, that no human mediation was necessary between God and man, that all men constituted one brotherhood. He fired his disciples with zeal, and they went forth with him to conquer India to their new-found faith. Kings became the nursing fathers of the new religion. A prince crossed to Ceylon, and that island was converted to Buddhism. They penetrated the jungles and climbed the mountains, and Siam and its monarch embraced the faith. They climbed the Himalayas, and the Nepaulese became Buddhists. They climbed over into Tibet, and that land is to-day their stronghold. They passed on into Siberia and into China, and that mighty empire embraced their faith. They crossed over to Japan, and the standard of Buddha was planted there.

Let this history be a prophecy and an inspiration to us. We may, by God's blessing, bring India to Christ within our generation. The Hindu converts, touched by the divine fire, inspired by the love of Christ, will repeat the history of the past, but with new zeal, aided by a power that Buddha's disciples knew not. The nations of Asia will be conquered for Christ, and will together plant the royal standard of King Immanuel, and from those united hosts will go up the shout, "Halleluiah: for the Lord God omnipotent reigneth." Brothers, be it ours, each one, to own a share in that halleluiah shout of victory.

JACOB CHAMBERLAIN.

There is none other name under heaven given among men, whereby we must be saved.—Acts iv. 12.

Apart from Christianity we have nothing to depend upon. Without stopping to decide the question whether your Christian experiences have been genuine or not,—you need not go into the rubbish of the past,—if you give up Christianity you are gone.

JOHN A. BROADUS.

If Christianity were a mere philosophy, you would spin it out of your own brain, and then you would write articles and defend your positions against others, and they would defend theirs against you, and when you got through it would make very little difference whether you or they came out ahead. A great deal of philosophical discussion consists in a trial of wits, in sword-play. If it were a matter of science, you would scrutinize the facts and by a process of induction generalize the laws that express the order of sequence in which these facts occur. Christianity is neither philosophy nor science. A circumstance occurred last night outside of your knowledge, except as somebody conversant with the facts comes to you and tells you the facts. And, upon the assumption that men generally speak the truth, you believe your informant, and you call the recital of the facts "a piece of information." Now the Christian religion is a piece of information about something that happened outside of your knowledge, and that you never could have known under any circumstances, and that no process of thinking could have ever educed, induced, or deduced; it is a piece of information given to us on the part of God.

FRANCIS L. PATTON.

182

If any of you lack wisdom, let him ask of God, that giveth to all men liberally, and upbraideth not; and it shall be given him. —James i. 5.

The truth of a personal God is the great and fundamental need of philosophy and of human life, the one profoundest want of man's brain and of his heart. The great masters of skeptical thought, after the profoundest investigations into the science of the known and the probable, come back with the awe-struck air of men who have heard footsteps which they cannot trace, and the rustle of royal robes whose wearer is unknown to them. Thus they go a step further than Athens, which worshiped the "unknown God," while they recognize merely the "unknown." I am reminded of some doubters by the royal psalmist: "The fool hath said in his heart, There is no God"—as though only a fool could say it, and he only in his heart. Lord Bacon, great in logic and not mean in philosophy, said, "I would rather believe all the fables of the Talmud and the Koran than that this universal frame is without a mind." The great want of philosophy is God; and if of philosophy, how much more of the great, aching brain and heart of the world, which in every age has cried out, "As the hart panteth after the water-brooks, so panteth my soul after thee, O God." CYRUS D. FOSS.

No man of the human race has been in circumstances to become absolutely wise; but every one of the human family possessed of sufficient wisdom to be responsible can be good; and Jesus did not say, "Blessed are the wise in head," but, "The pure in heart shall see God." I. D. DRIVER.

183

What is called "metaphysics" is often only a beclouding of a hearer's mind by subtleties that are meant to confuse and bewilder.

A certain case at law turned on the resemblance between two car-wheels, and Webster and Choate were the opposing counsel. To a common eye the wheels looked as if made from the same model, but Choate, by a train of hair-splitting reasoning and a profound discourse on the "fixation of points," tried to overwhelm the jury with metaphysics, and to compel them to conclude, against the evidence of their eyes, that there was really hardly a shadow of essential resemblance. Webster rose to reply. "Gentlemen of the jury," said he, as he opened wide his great black eyes and stared at the big twin wheels before him, "there they are—look at 'em!" As he thundered out these words it was as though one of Jupiter's bolts had struck the earth.

That one sentence and look shattered Choate's subtle argument to atoms, and the cunning sophistry on the "fixation of points" dissolved as into air. I have great confidence in the strong common sense of an honest mind feeling the utter worthlessness of an argument even when unable to tell the reason why.

ARTHUR T. PIERSON.

The alternatives of the intellectual life are Christianity or agnosticism. The agnostic is right when he trumpets his incompleteness. He who is not complete in Him must be forever incomplete.

HENRY DRUMMOND.

Faith has done many things in this world besides the bringing down of the walls of Jericho. Men sometimes laugh at faith as though it were a feeble thing, when, in fact, it is one of the great forces of the world.

If we were to use scriptural language with regard to all the things that faith has accomplished, we might speak as follows: By faith Columbus crossed the ocean, not knowing whither he went. By faith Cyrus Field planned and perfected the Atlantic cable, while all men laughed at him and called him visionary. By faith our forefathers crossed the deep, seeking a country where they could freely worship their God. By faith Edison toiled on, seeking new discoveries in his science, not sure of the issue of his efforts. All these wrought with faith, and so worked wonders. The fact is that without faith the world would come to a standstill.

This same faith applied to spiritual things has done wonders for the world. Faith in the word and promises of God has led to the establishment of missionary work all over the world. Faith leads men and women to go far from home and friends to preach the truth to those in darkest Africa. Faith leads the city missionary to go to the plague-spots in darkest New York or London, and to believe that he can bring light and purity there. And God rewards this faith, so that the modern miracles are not so much those of the healing of the bodies of men as of their spirits. If ever this old and sinful world is to be made over, so that it shall be full of righteousness, it will only be when men act more by faith and less by sight, and dare and do great things for God and their fellow-men.   A. F. SCHAUFFLER.

Sell that ye have, and give alms; provide yourselves bags which wax not old, a treasure in the heavens that faileth not.—Luke xii. 33.

A bag that does not wax old is one that will never fail to be sending in an income. There are men in heaven, saved by grace (as all are), who were rich while on earth. But all their money was invested in fine mansions and gardens and railroads and bank shares. When they had possession of them they failed to convert any part of them into the exchange of heaven, and now they get no more good from them. Ask him, "O saint, are you getting in anything now from your investments down there?" He will tell you, "Nothing whatever; the interest is all paid in the coin of earth, and that is not transmissible. I ought to have seen to that when I had a chance; I cannot do it now." Very different is it with the saints who have given money to help save men from death, whether the amounts be large or small. Look, for example, at those who in some wise way have invested their property with a view to results in another world. Ask them, "Are you getting any income from your investments down there?" "Oh yes, a wonderful income. There is a continual stream of persons coming in here who were started heavenward or were helped on their way by those investments. They are beginning to come up out of all lands and tribes and kindreds and tongues." These earthly investments pay dividends in heaven. WILLIAM ASHMORE.

Christianity removes the attraction of the earth; and this is one way in which it diminishes men's burden. It makes them citizens of another world.
HENRY DRUMMOND.

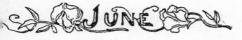

Once in the end of the world hath he appeared to put away sin by the sacrifice of himself.—Heb. ix. 26.

When sin entered into the world, and long before sin entered into the world, the God of all grace had provided a remedy. The Lamb of God was slain from the foundation of the world. But Adam was not created from the foundation of the world. Then God had provided that *when* man sinned, and entailed death upon himself, he might die by proxy. That was what the great heart of God proposed and provided, determined and arranged. And many a picture was hung out before the world to set it forth. When Adam's nakedness was discovered to him, and he tried to make himself clothes of fig-leaves, God provided him with better clothes; he clothed him and he clothed Eve with the skins of beasts. The life of the animal that provided the clothing of course was forfeited. It was the first illustration of the great substitution that the Lord in his love had provided. Ages rolled on and animals were sacrificed. There was the morning lamb, and there was the evening lamb, telling of the blood that was to be the substitute for the life of man (for the blood is the life), until at last the Lamb himself came—the Lamb of God, that taketh away the sin of the world. As it was "appointed unto men once to die,"—the great emphasis is upon the "once,"—so Christ was once offered. And oh, "if the blood of bulls and of goats, and the ashes of a heifer sprinkling the unclean, sanctifieth to the purifying of the flesh; how much more shall the blood of Christ . . . purge your conscience from dead works to serve the living God?"

MARCUS RAINSFORD.

187

A man is not converted without first having conviction of sin. When that conviction of sin comes and his eyes are opened, he learns to be afraid of his sin and to flee from it to Christ. But a man needs a second conviction of sin; a believer must be convicted of his peculiar sin. The sins of an unconverted man are different from the sins of a believer. An unconverted man, for instance, is not ordinarily convicted of the corruption of his nature; he thinks principally about external sins: "I have taken God's name in vain, been a liar, and I am on the way to hell." He is then convicted for conversion. But the believer is in quite a different condition. His sins are far more blamable, for he has had the light and the love and the Spirit of God given to him. He has striven to conquer his sins, and has grown to see that his nature is utterly corrupt, that the carnal mind, the flesh within him, was making his whole state utterly wretched. When a believer is thus convicted by the Holy Spirit, it is specially his life of unbelief that condemns him; he sees that, because of the great guilt connected with this, he has been kept from receiving the full gift of God's Holy Spirit; he is brought down in shame and confusion of face, and he begins to cry, "Woe is me, for I am undone. I have heard of God by the hearing of the ear; I have known a great deal of him, and preached about him, but now my eye seeth him." God comes near him, and Job, the righteous man whom God had trusted, sees in himself the deep sin of self and its righteousness that he had never seen before.

ANDREW MURRAY.

In these days there is a great deal of lowering the standards. Business men tell me that business standards have been lowered, and now a good deal of business runs into gambling. In politics the standards have been lowered. There has been a lowering of standards in theology, and in reference to the supreme authority of God's blessed Book. We must keep the standard up to the very tiptop peak of God's flagstaff. Be careful, my brother, about lowering your standard of right, obedience, and holiness. You remember, perhaps, that scene in the days of conflict, when a color-sergeant had carried the colors so near to the enemy's redoubt that the regiment shouted to him to bring them back or they would be captured. The color-sergeant said, "No, no; bring your men up to the colors!" With a magnificent dash, they carried the colors themselves into the rampart. The commandment of the Captain of our salvation to us ministers is, "Bring my church up to my colors, and then we will go forward and capture the enemy."   THEODORE L. CUYLER.

One in twelve of the ancient apostles was a Judas. I don't believe that one in twelve of the modern apostles is a Judas. Nevertheless, there is this difference between the ancient and the modern: the ancient Judas carried the bag, and when he betrayed his Master he had the grace to go and hang himself. In our modern church system, when the man who carries the bag proves dishonest he shows no sorrow; and, what is worse, the churches have such lax ideas of discipline that they do not even turn him out of office.   JOSEPH COOK.

I cried unto the Lord with my voice, and he heard me out of his holy hill.—Ps. iii. 4.

What a grand philosophy of prayer we get in God's Book! Down here in darkness, with trouble closing upon me like wolves upon the belated traveler, I cried; and One as loving and human and personal as myself heard me. My Father, God up yonder in heaven, heard me. When I, his child, fell down here on the earth, I tried to get up and began to cry. He knew the cry of his bairn, and, quicker than I can tell it, flew to my relief. "That's my David," said God, as he rose and came to the front door of heaven to listen, when they were badgering him and the hounds of hell were upon him. "I knew my David's voice among ten thousand voices." And God came out and scattered the foe right and left, and set him on high from all his enemies.   JOHN McNEILL.

If we had prayed more we need not have worked so hard. We have too little praying face to face with God every day. Looking back at the end, I suspect there will be great grief for our sins of omission—omission to get from God what we might have got by praying.   ANDREW A. BONAR.

Jesus never taught his disciples how to preach, but he did teach them how to pray. I would rather be able to pray like Daniel than to preach like Gabriel. If men know how to pray they know how to work for God.   D. L. MOODY.

You may work without praying, but you can't pray without working.   J. HUDSON TAYLOR.

190

Pray without ceasing.—1 Thess. v. 17.

We prove the value which we attach to things by the time we devote to them. The kingdom of God asks our time, and it is only by giving it that the kingdom can be kept in its true place, first every day, and all day. God has broken up our lifetime into day and night. One object of that is that we may learn to live a day at a time, and should thus have a time every morning, after having been raised out of sleep in which we were utterly helpless, when we should begin afresh with our God. Begin the day with God, and God will maintain his kingdom in your heart. ANDREW MURRAY.

Men do not excel to-day, because, after their conversion, they do not go apart, like Moses and Paul, into Horeb or Arabia for a season. Young Christians must go into Arabia. Book-learning will never make preachers. You must but get away alone with God and his holy Word, and let God speak to you until you can see God. Then you will see the burning bush, the majesty of God, and it will make you take off your shoes, for you will see that the ground whereon you stand is holy. Then only will God call you to be delivered and a deliverer.

H. W. WEBB-PEPLOE.

He who rushes into the presence of God and hurriedly whispers a few petitions and rushes out again never, perhaps, *sees* God there at all. He can no more get a vision than a disquieted lake can mirror the stars. We must stay long enough to become calm, for it is only the peaceful soul in which eternal things are reflected as in a placid water.

ARTHUR T. PIERSON.

191

There is no warrant for carelessness or self-sufficiency in the smallest thing we may be called upon to do for God. A young divinity student in Ireland was preaching for the Bishop of Cashel. As they went into the pulpit the good bishop asked the young student what he would preach about. He replied that he had made no preparation, and that he was quite uncertain, but was confident that he could occupy the time, as he was just from the university. After two or three minutes of labor over a text glibly given out, he broke down in confusion, and the bishop was obliged to finish the sermon. When they came back to the vestry the young man buried his face in his hands and groaned in shame and humiliation. "My young brother," said the bishop, "if you had gone up as you came down, you would have come down as you went up."

D. W. WHITTLE.

May we always have grace to take our proper place under the Master's table and plead for the crumbs. God says you have sinned and come short of his glory. Let us reply, "Truth, Lord; yet thou receivest sinners and eatest with them." God says, "Ye are weakness itself." "Truth, Lord; yet in our weakness thou dost delight to show forth thy strength." God says, "Your wisdom is folly." "Truth, Lord; yet thou hast promised to give wisdom to them that ask it of thee." We receive God's favors only as we thus accept the positions of unworthiness and weakness to which we are assigned in his Word.

A. C. DIXON.

Month of July

Concerning the work of my hands command ye me.—Isa. xlv. 11.

In nature we find great universal forces—light, heat, gravity, cohesion, magnetism, electricity, chemical affinity, life. We have only to understand the laws or conditions within which they act, and we may command them: obey the law of the power, and the power obeys you. Thus we command light, and it becomes our artist; heat, and it becomes our refiner and purifier; gravity, and it becomes our giant mechanic; magnetism, our pilot; electricity, our motor, messenger, illuminator. The Holy Spirit is the all-subduing power of the spiritual realm. Obey the laws of the Spirit, and all his power is at your disposal. In the work of God the believer may command him.

ARTHUR T. PIERSON,

Imagine one without genius, and devoid of the artist's training, sitting down before Raphael's famous picture of the "Transfiguration" and attempting to reproduce it! How crude and mechanical and lifeless his work would be! But if such a thing were possible that the spirit of Raphael should enter into the man, and obtain the mastery of his mind and eye and hand, it would be entirely possible that he should reproduce this masterpiece; for it would simply be Raphael reproducing Raphael. For this purpose have we been filled with the Spirit of God, that we might do the very things which he would do if he were here. "The works that I do shall ye do also; and greater works than these shall ye do; because I go unto my Father."

A. J. GORDON.

193

God never alters his law. The two visits of Moses up the mount were different, yet they ended in the same way. Moses broke the first tables of stone, but made the new exactly the same. It is as impossible to alter God's law as to alter his throne. You cannot get above the law. Then get deeper and deeper in sympathy with it, because that law is the mind of God.   ANDREW A. BONAR.

In our estimate of the decalogue we have made too much of the *law* element, and too little of the element of *love*. As a consequence, it has not been easy for us to see how it is that God's law is love, and that love is the fulfilling of God's law. But the ten commandments are a simple record of God's loving covenant with his people, and they are not the arbitrary commandings of God to his subjects. They indicate the inevitable limits within which God and his people can be in loving union rather than declare the limits of dutiful obedience on the part of those who would be God's faithful subjects.
                    HENRY CLAY TRUMBULL.

The law is used by God as the means of putting an end to man's boasting; it stops every man's mouth. A man who is trying to measure himself by the law is pretty small; but if he measures himself by his neighbors he thinks that he is about two inches taller than any one else. Under the old dispensation the prodigal would have been turned out and stoned. The law says, "Smite him;" grace says, "Forgive him." The law says, "Cast him out;" grace says, "Bring him in."   D. L. MOODY.

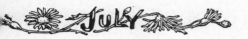
God does not want any further expiation for sin than that which has already been so blessedly accepted. Christ's resurrection is receipt in full for all the law's just claim upon us; and the Holy Ghost has come down to give us a blank draft upon God's fullness. He writes his name—I AM; and you put in what you want, send it, backed by faith and prayer, and God will honor it. Do you want strength? "I am strength." Do you want salvation? "I am salvation." Do you want peace? "I am that peace." It is all for Jesus, and all for you; for, as it has pleased God that in Christ all fullness should dwell, so he is pleased that of his fullness all we should receive, and grace for grace. There is no fountain on this earth to slake a poor sinner's thirst. If you do not get a drink from the living water you will never be satisfied. All the kingdoms of the earth are vanity and vexation of spirit.

MARCUS RAINSFORD.

The love of God is as universal now as in the day when Jesus Christ said it included every man; the needs of the world are as intense to-day as when they pierced the very heart of God and drew his only Son down to earth to die for the sins of men. The pathetic appeal of the poor lost world, as it staggers, blindfold, around the great altar, is the more pitiable because it does not know it is blind, and calls us to an immediate and undaunted effort to at once undertake operations which shall secure, before we die, the evangelization of this world.

ROBERT E. SPEER.

The Lord's portion is his people.—Deut. xxxii. 9.

We should be solicitous not only as to what we have in God, but what God has in us. We are God's heritage; we are his property, which he has reclaimed from the waste wilderness of the world, which he has fertilized with his own blood, which he has fenced in by his cross, in which he has erected his dwelling-place, and which he has brought under his own cultivation. O soul, conceive of thyself as an estate which has come into the possession of the eternal God. Some time ago, in Scotland, I gained new light upon this thought, as I noticed the amount of care which Scotch people take of very poor land. Some of us have been barren land, just reclaimed from the ocean of barrenness and waste, and we have come beneath the cultivation of God, and, if we will only let him, God is prepared to bring under his care every faculty, every quality of our nature, leaving no part untouched, but raising crop after crop out of us—his estate. In earlier life we are all inclined to do the best we can with our powers for God, till repeated failure convinces us how little we can make of ourselves; and when the sun is reaching its zenith, when we have despaired of getting any more crops out of the soil that seems hopelessly impoverished, we are led to fall back upon God and say to him, "My God, this estate is thine; rear from the spirit, from the imagination, from the will, from the affections, from all the powers that thou hast given me, some fruit which shall bring glory to thee and shall keep my life from having been wasted."

F. B. MEYER.

196

Christ Jesus: whom God hath set forth . . . to declare his righteousness [justification] for the remission of sins that are past, through the forebearance of God; to declare, I say, at this time his righteousness: that he might be just, and the justifier of him which believeth in Jesus.—Rom. iii. 24, 26.

Righteousness, or justification, means, therefore, not only the sinner's vindication, but God's vindication. It is the divine scheme of mercy and love whereby God can acquit and justify a transgressor, and yet acquit and justify himself, as having no complicity with guilt or sin or laxity as to his inviolable law.

This side of justification is habitually overlooked. In pardoning sin the perfection of God is in danger of compromise. In the loose notions of forgiveness now prevalent, there is a tendency to magnify *love* at the expense of belittling *law*. Perfect government demands perfect law, and perfect law demands perfect sanctions of reward and penalty. The certainty that every transgression and disobedience receives its just recompense of reward is part of the perfection of God and his government. Laxity of administration imperils the foundations of society. Hence, if God forgives and justifies the sinner, it must be in such a way as to justify himself. His law must be kept intact and his justice must not suffer for the sake of his mercy.

Here lies the glory of God's justification. It is so provided for as that law and justice and government and the character of God are absolutely safe. Penalty is borne by the innocent Substitute, so that the law is magnified; the hatred of sin is as manifest in the sacrifice of God's dear Son as though all transgressors received their full recompense. ARTHUR T. PIERSON.

197

By faith Abel offered unto God a more excellent sacrifice than Cain.—Heb. xi. 4.

Abel's offering was such as God could accept. His first thought was to get rid of sin; he came with the blood. Cain, like the Pharisee who "prayed with himself," offered unto himself. He came with the fruits of his field as the result of his industry and intelligence. There was no mysticism about him; in his own opinion, he had no sin needing atonement; if, indeed, there was sin, he thought that his industry and other good qualities made amends for it, so that God would accept his fruits as an atonement for his faults. He presented the fruit of prayer with the serpent of sin coiled in it. Abel heroically saw himself as he was; Cain looked at himself as he wished to be. Sinner that he was, Abel presented the offering of blood; self-complacent as he was, Cain refused to confess his sin, which, unconfessed, soon developed into crime.

A. C. DIXON.

Men will never find salvation until they give up all efforts to save themselves. Some one asked an Indian how he got converted. He built a fire in a circle round a worm, and then, after the worm had crawled round every way and then lay down to die, he reached over and took him out. That is the way in which God saves us.

D. L. MOODY.

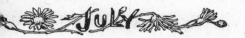
That which is born of the flesh is flesh; and that which is born of the Spirit is spirit.—John iii. 6.

Spiritual things may be imitated by the flesh but cannot be produced from it. It would be folly to look for anything but crab-apples from a crab-apple tree, if no better fruit had been grafted in upon its stem. So it is useless to exhort a piety that does not exist, and fruitless to teach an unregenerate man to cultivate an unrenewed heart.

D. W. WHITTLE.

The Spirit must convict before you can convert.

A. J. GORDON.

Not more certain is it that it is something outside the thermometer that produces a change in the thermometer than it is something outside the soul of man that produces a moral change upon him. That he must be susceptible to that change, that he must be a party to it, goes without saying; but that neither his aptitude nor his will can produce it is equally certain.

HENRY DRUMMOND.

He who would be most like Christ must pay the cost. As God reckons jewelry, there is no gem that shines with more brilliancy than the tear of true penitence; yet God only knoweth what heart-pressure and what crushing of wilful pride may have been necessary to force the tear to the cheek of a stubborn sinner.

THEODORE L. CUYLER.

199

There is no joy like hearing the joy-song of a new-born soul. Yes, another joy may be as deep— the joy of sympathy with Jesus in his rejected life, and the assurance that the Father looks on me with pleasure. Think of the number of Christians in the world, and then of the unsaved millions of heathendom, and then ask, Are we true followers of Christ, who went all the way to Calvary to give his blood for man? Remember, the joy of the Holy Ghost is the joy of working for God. Most of us look at all our facilities for work and say that we will try to manage these things better. Oh, if we had a sense of the state of the millions around us, we should fall on our faces before God and say, "God help us to something new. Oh, that every fiber of my being may be taken possession of for this great work with God!" ANDREW MURRAY.

If I had the choice of preaching like Gabriel, swaying men at my will, without winning them to Christ, or taking them one by one in private and leading them to the truth, how gladly would I choose the latter! Men ought to prize the reputation of knowing how to win young men and clear away their troubles. It is the greatest honor you and I can enjoy. D. L. MOODY.

Personal work means helpful contact with another so as to awaken or promote in him the Christ-life. Aim to put yourself in his place, and in Christ's place in relation to him. Seek to learn what is his real difficulty, the truth he needs to realize; how to win an entrance for truth into his heart, and to find a parallel case in Scripture.

JAMES McCONAUGHY.

The atonement of Christ reveals the great heart
of the Almighty beating with love and compassion
for men; and to attempt to reduce it to any theory
is simply presumptuous and hopeless. "The good
Shepherd giveth his life for the sheep." There are
the sheep, and there are the wolves, and here is the
good Shepherd. I understand thus much thoroughly,
that I should have died from the wolves if Jesus
Christ had not died for me. But I bless God that
the atonement is so great I cannot measure it, that
the heart of the Eternal is so deep I cannot sound
it. There is such a vastness in atoning love, there
is such fullness in it, that it cannot be reduced to
any form of speech, and the reverent heart comes
at last to see this great, burning, loving heart of
the Eternal and to be quiet in adoring love and trust.

ALEXANDER MCKENZIE.

What could the world give Christ that was not
already his? What could it add to the position of
one of whom it was said, "By him were all things
made, and without him was not anything made that
was made"? What could the world add to the glory
of him who had been by the Father seated at his
own right hand, far above principalities and powers
and thrones and dominions, with a name above every
name? There was but one new glory Christ could
acquire—that of service and sacrifice. All crowns
were already his, save one—the crown of thorns.
His whole life was a ministry of love, of instruction
to the ignorant, pardon to the penitent, healing to
the sick, and comfort to the sorrowing.

M. D. HOGE.

201

If any man sin, we have an Advocate with the Father, Jesus Christ the righteous.—1 John ii. 1.

I will pray the Father, and he shall give you another Advocate. —John xiv. 16.

After the day of Pentecost this promise of another Advocate was fulfilled, and now what do we have? One Advocate on the throne; another Advocate here; just as, sometimes, there is a law firm in which there are two partners. One of them is the pleader, and the other is the counselor. The one goes into court; the other occupies the office, and gives advice and counsel to the clients. So to-day there are two partners in the divine Trinity. One has gone into court; he is the Advocate to plead for us there; the other is down here, and he is the Counselor. Whatever Jesus Christ, the Advocate, does for us up there, the other Advocate does in us down here.

A. J. GORDON.

There is a great difference between possessing the Spirit and being possessed by the Spirit. Was there not a difference between the apostles before and after Pentecost? Before, they were full of rivalry and jealousy, weak in confessing their Master, and quick to misunderstand him; but after, they were bold as lions, intelligent, loving, spiritual. Chronologically we are living on this side of Pentecost; but experimentally many are living upon the other side. F. B. MEYER.

We know not what we should pray for as we ought: but the Spirit himself maketh intercession for us.—Rom. viii. 26.

The Greek or Roman advocate helped his client in two different ways. Sometimes he spoke for the client before the tribunal, as our advocates do, and it is in this sense that Christ is called our Advocate, pleading for us before the throne. But in other cases the ancient advocate merely prepared a speech which the client might speak for himself. It is in this sense that the Holy Spirit is our Advocate. He teaches us what to pray for. The desires which the Spirit works in the heart will often be too deep to find adequate expression in human language; and so the Spirit is said to intercede with groanings which cannot be uttered. But their meaning is fully known to God, and the prayer which the Spirit works in us is sure to be according to the will of God, and it is as sure to be answered.

JOHN A. BROADUS.

When, in Christ's name, we come to God, not we, but *he is the suppliant*. Hence he is said to offer the prayers of God's saints at the golden altar which is before the throne, and even to pray the Father for us. More than this, he hints that it is not needful that he should thus pray the Father for us, for the Father himself loves us because we have believed in Jesus and are thus one with him, whom the Father heareth always.

ARTHUR T. PIERSON.

It is not God who has not given; it is we who have not taken. We have filled the temple of God with our household stuff, and have put the money-changers and divers kinds of folly into the Father's house; therefore we are not filled with the Holy Ghost. Let a man, let the church, go down before God and say, "Search me, O God." When he has searched you, he will show you things you never knew. You can only get rid of what you find; and God gives no further than man can take; and man can take only what he knows. Let us go to God and tell him all our sin and folly, and the pride that has prevented us from confessing the evil things of which we knew.

H. W. WEBB-PEPLOE.

An old man once said to me, "Do you think that it is right, when paying money that has been taken wrongly, to give your name at the same time?" I asked what he meant, and he replied, "I took thirty pounds' worth of coal that did not belong to me, and I feel miserable. When I try to speak for God, it seems as if something choked me. I have put ten pounds in the letter-box, but that didn't make me any happier, and so I went and put in another ten pounds. I thought I would put in another ten to make it thirty, but do you think I ought to confess it?" I said, "Certainly; you must be a man; you must own up to it." The man did confess, and his employer was so struck with it that he told his manager they would break off a practice that was not perfectly honest, because he was not quite easy in his conscience. That old man, after he had done his duty, shot right up into the sunlight!

F. B. MEYER.

A rough sailor once stood alone before Munkaczsy's great picture of "Christ before Pilate." As he looked, he could not turn away, but stood there with his eyes fixed on that central figure of majesty and love. In a few moments he took off his hat and let it fall to the floor. Then a little later he sat down and picked up a book that described the picture, and began to read; every few seconds his eyes would turn toward the canvas and toward the figure of Christ. The doorkeeper saw him lift up his hand and wipe away some tears. Still he sat there—five, ten, fifteen, sixty minutes—as though he could not stir. At last he arose, and, coming softly and reverently toward the door, he hesitated, to take one last look, and said to the woman who sat there, "Madam, I am a rough, wicked sailor. I have never believed in Christ; I have never used his name, except in an oath. But I have a Christian mother, who begged me to-day, before I went to sea, to come and look at this picture of the Christ. To oblige her I have come. I did not think that anybody believed in Christ; but as I have looked at that form and that face I have thought that some man must have believed in him, and it has touched me, and I have come to believe in him too." Oh, beloved, if a poor, weak man, living in a godless land, could take his brush and preach on canvas, and cause our Christ to glow upon it, until a rude, licentious man was won to believe in him, what might not our God do if he might paint Christ in us—nay, if he might reproduce Christ in a human life, that the life might be Christ's, and that men might come to believe on him! B. FAY MILLS.

That Christ may dwell in your hearts by faith; that ye, being rooted and grounded in love, may be able to comprehend with all saints what is the breadth, and length, and depth, and height; and to know the love of Christ, which passeth knowledge, that ye might be filled with all the fullness of God.—Eph. iii. 17–19.

Oh, may God point out more to us of the heights and depths and lengths and breadths of the believer's position in Christ, that we may know the love of Christ, which passeth knowledge, and that we may be filled with all the fullness of God! I do not know what the breadth is or what the length is, but I think I know what the height is. I am in Christ— there is nothing higher. And I think I know what the depth is; that is, Christ in me—and God knows I know nothing lower.   MARCUS RAINSFORD.

If we are like Christ, there will be about us the savor of his name. We are to be chosen witnesses to his resurrection. Men can believe that there is a God up in heaven if they can see a God dwelling in our hearts. The greatest evidence of the spiritual religion is a holy life. A man that will be pure in the midst of impurity, that will be loving in the midst of the bitter sarcasms of a cruel world, that will reproduce the lowly character of the dear Saviour in a polluted, sinful world, is the most clear and irrefragable argument that God is true and that his Word is true.   M. E. BALDWIN.

God does not ask to have us hide Christ away in our impure hearts; he wants Christ so formed in me that Christ and I are one, and that the image of his blessed Son may be manifest in my thoughts and heart and life.   ANDREW MURRAY.

206

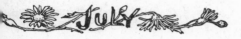
Ye are dead, and your life is hid with Christ in God.—Col. iii. 3.

If this is true of me, then one thing is very clear: if my life is hid with Christ, I haven't it; and if I haven't it, I can't lose it. Is not that plain? Some people think they will lose it. Blessings on his holy name, no! It is hid in the safest place in all the universe, is the life of a Christian. It was too dearly purchased for God to leave it for us to keep. Why, if he did that, the devil would soon get hold of it. God gave life to Adam to keep, and how long did he keep it? If he had given me my life to keep, oh, what neglect there would be! I thank God that I have not the keeping of it.

MARCUS RAINSFORD.

I never saw a long-faced Christian that amounted to anything. It is worse to meet such a man than to face an east wind in March. What we want is the spirit and confidence of the old martyr who said to a king who threatened to banish him because he would not give up testifying for Christ, "I am not afraid of that, for you cannot banish me from where Christ is." The king said, "Well, I will take away your property." The man replied, "No, you can't; my treasure is laid up in heaven; it is hid with Christ in God." The king said hotly, "I will kill you, then." "You can't do that, either; I have been dead these forty years!" exclaimed the martyr. "What are you going to do with such a fanatic?" asked the king. You can't do anything with him; he has a security and peace which all the kings on earth cannot disturb.

D. L. MOODY.

However distasteful a service may be, or however disagreeable the person to whom it must be rendered, God is back of it all, and loved that person well enough to give his Son to die for him. Dr. Guthrie was walking along the streets of Edinburgh, when he overtook a little girl carrying a child much too heavy for her. In a very gentle way Dr. Guthrie said, "My child, the baby is too heavy for you, isn't he?" With a shining face, she made quick response, "No, sir; he's my *brother*." It makes a difference that one for whom I must toil and wait, whose burden I must bear, was one for whom Jesus died, and thus is bound to me with the chord of divine love.   J. WILBUR CHAPMAN.

Humanity loves to be loved for itself, and under the ragged shirts and soiled dresses of poor outcast men and women there is a heart that wants love just as much as you want love, and a good deal more, because they haven't had it and you have.
                              S. H. HADLEY.

Where is the secret of power? In my college days the professor of natural philosophy used to exhibit his great horseshoe magnet, wound about with coils of wire. He hung it up, charged the wire with a galvanic current, and it caught up and held four thousand pounds. He signaled to his assistant to draw off the current, and the power was gone. My brother, encircle your soul with faith and let the divine electricity of the love of Jesus Christ charge it. Then you can lift anything; you can do anything that God wants you to do. Draw it off, and you are a shorn Samson, a weakling.
                              THEODORE L. CUYLER.

Many a man seeks to excuse himself for his sinful
habits by saying, "If God wants me to be good and
happy, why doesn't he *make* me good?" We cannot really be good unless we *might* be evil. We are
endowed by Almighty God with the awful but blessed
prerogative of free will, and God will not ignore that
feature of his image with which he has endowed us.
He would not have us serve him with a merely
mechanical obedience; from us he looks for a moral
obedience, and that involves preference. The heavenly bodies serve God with an undeviating obedience; to them he has given a law which cannot be
broken. But the obedience of a little child in
some trifling matter is something infinitely higher,
because it is a moral act of surrender of will to
will. We can only become pure by choosing purity
when we might choose self-indulgence. We can
only become loving when we sacrifice ourselves in
one way or another for others when we might cling
to our own self-interest. We can only become really
true and brave when we stand by honor and truth
when we might gain some advantage by swerving
from truth, by compromise or concession. Temptation is necessary for the moral development of
a moral being.   A. C. A. HALL.

God permits temptation because it does for us
what the storms do for the oaks—it roots us; and
what the fire does for the painting on porcelain—it
makes us permanent. You never know that you
have a grip on Christ or that he has a grip on you
so well as when the devil is using all his force to
attract you from him; then you feel the pull of
Christ's right hand.   F. B. MEYER.

And the Lord said, Simon, Simon, behold, Satan hath desired to have you, that he may sift you as wheat: but I have prayed for thee, that thy faith fail not.—Luke xxii. 31, 32.

And Satan was permitted to have Peter—not to enter and possess him, as he did Judas, who never was a child of God, but to have him in the sense of being let loose upon him to tempt him and to overcome him, for the humbling of Peter's pride and for sifting out his self-confidence, God overruling all that Satan did for Peter's spiritual good and God's own glory.

Peter's experience is a type of the experience of the whole church, and of the individuals of the church. In each generation of its history the church has been sifted by Satan. He changes from age to age the agencies employed, but his malice is unchanged, and the results are still the same. Persecution at one period; prosperity at another. Truth without the Holy Spirit in one age; false doctrine following. Contempt from the world in this generation; world conformity in the next. Zeal without knowledge, breaking out into fanaticism and dividing the church; knowledge without zeal, ending in materialism and paralyzing the church. Ecclesiasticism and spiritual oppression dwarfing the church; lawless liberty, with no recognition of scriptural authority, scattering the church. Thus the body of Christ has been, and is being, sifted, and will continue to be sifted unto the end. What the Holy Ghost has recorded of its early history, he has prophesied should be its experience until Satan should be bound.

D. W. WHITTLE.

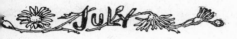

The devil . . . is a liar, and the father of it.—John viii. 44.

The great tempter of men has two lies with which he plies us at two different stages: Before we have fallen he tells us that one fall does not matter; it is a trifle; we can easily recover ourselves again. After we have fallen he tells us that it is hopeless; we are given over to sin, and need not attempt to rise.

It is a terrible falsehood to say that to fall once does not matter. Even by one fall there is something lost that can never be recovered again. It is like the breaking of an infinitely precious vessel, which may be mended, but will never be again as if it had not been broken. Again, one fall leads to others; it is like going upon very slippery ice on the face of a hill; even in the attempt to rise we are carried away again farther than ever. Moreover, we give others a hold over us. If we have not sinned alone, to have sinned once involves a tacit pledge that we will sin again, and it is often almost impossible to get out of such a false position. God keep us from believing the devil's lie, that to fall once does not matter.

But then, if we have fallen, Satan plies us with the other lie: it is of no use to attempt to rise; you cannot overcome your besetting sin. This is falser still. You may rise. If we could ascend to heaven to-day, and scan the ranks of the blessed, should we not find multitudes among them who were once sunk low as man can fall? But they are washed, they are justified, they are sanctified through the blood of our Lord Jesus Christ, and by the Spirit of our God. And so may we be.

JAMES STALKER.

Put ye on the Lord Jesus Christ, and make not provision for the flesh, to fulfil the lusts thereof.—Rom. xiii. 14.

Self-indulgence is the besetting sin of the times; but if you long to be a strong, athletic Christian, you must count the cost and renounce the things of the flesh. It will cost you the cutting up of some old favorite sins by the roots, and the cutting loose from some entangling alliances, and some sharp conflicts with the tempter; it will cost you the submitting of your will to the will of Christ; but you will gain more than you ever gave up.

THEODORE L. CUYLER.

Every permitted sin incrusts the windows of the soul and blinds our vision, and every victory over evil clears the vision of the soul, so that we can see God a little plainer. The unholy man could not see God if he were set down in the midst of heaven; but men and women whose hearts are pure see him in the very commonest walks of life.

J. WILBUR CHAPMAN.

If I have not victory over myself, I am the last man to help somebody else. Appetite is very good in its place, but out of its place it becomes my foe. Fire is a very good friend to man if it is his servant, but when it becomes his master it is his enemy. Water is very good—you cannot live without it—when it is under your control, but when it controls you it is your ruin. The lust of the flesh will either conquer me, or I must conquer lust.

D. L. MOODY.

Be not conformed to this world: but be ye transformed by the renewing of your mind, that ye may prove what is that good, and acceptable, and perfect will of God.—Rom. xii. 2.

Offer yourselves to the Lord, and keep offering, and you will find that you are delivered out of the hand of your enemy, both the attacking enemy and the seductive enemy. The world says, "Come and have a little dance, a little gambling, a little pleasure. We will not gamble for dollars, but let us put up a few cents on a game of whist." What we must say is, "I am doing a great work, and I cannot go down. I am building the walls of Jerusalem." You need not ask whether it is wrong to go to a ball or the theater. Preach Christ, live for Christ, look for Christ, and walk with Christ, and the world will very soon drop you. Faith in a living Christ will keep us from the world.

H. W. WEBB-PEPLOE.

You will notice that in the placid waters of a lake everything which is highest in reality is lowest in the reflection. The higher the trees, the lower their image. That is the picture of this world; what is highest in this world is lowest in the other, and what is highest in that world is lowest in this. Gold is on top here; they pave the streets with it there. To serve is looked upon as ignoble here; there those that serve reign, and the last are first. Any girl is willing to fling away paste diamonds for the real stones; when a man understands what God can be to the soul, he loses his taste for things he used to care for most.

F. B. MEYER.

There are two marks of a little child. One is that a little child cannot help himself, but is always keeping others occupied to serve him. What a little tyrant a baby often is! The mother cannot go out; there must be a servant to nurse it; it needs to be cared for constantly. God made a man to care for others, but the baby was made to be cared for and to be helped. So there are Christians who always want help. Their pastor and their Christian friends must always be teaching and comforting them. They go to church and to prayer-meetings and to conventions, always wanting to be helped—a sign of spiritual infancy.

The other sign of an infant is this: he can do nothing to help his fellow-man. Every man is expected to contribute something to the welfare of society; every one has a place to fill, and a work to do; but the babe can do nothing for the common weal. It is just so with Christians. How little some can do! They take a part in so-called work, but how little sign there is that they are exercising spiritual power and carrying a real blessing!

ANDREW MURRAY.

There are hundreds of members in our churches who injure the cause of Christ every time they get up to speak in meetings, because they are jealous, unforgiving, and backsliding, and live too much like the world. What we want in our churches are members who are filled with grace and who live up to what they preach.

D. L. MOODY.

214

A young girl who had been born blind was utterly
ignorant of the fact that she was blind until she was
eight or ten years of age. All her training had in
view the concealment of the fact that she was different from other children, and, as she had never *seen*,
she did not know what it was to see or not to see.
She used freely the language of sight with her own
ideas of that language. She spoke of being glad to
see those whom she met, and of being pleased with
their looks; of enjoying the sunlight and the clear
sky and the fine scenery after a storm had passed
away. So little thought had she that she was walking in darkness that, on one occasion, when a stranger
spoke out pityingly in her hearing of her misfortune,
she ran merrily to her parents and said, "There's a
little girl over there who says I am blind. I think
I can see as well as *she* can." There is a great deal
of such training in the world of morals.

Orientals are taught from infancy that lying to an
enemy, or where anything can be made by lying, is
a duty, and they try to attend to *that* duty. Ameri-
can Indians are taught that a man's character is best
rated by the scalps he can show, so they risk their
lives for scalps. The Dyaks of Borneo are taught
that skulls are worthier trophies than scalps, and
they "hunt heads" accordingly. Our fathers were
taught that human slavery was a divine institution,
and that rum was to be swallowed gratefully as a
"gift of God," and they lived up to those teachings.
How can men's consciences discern truth from
error on points where their instruction from the
beginning has been as much at fault as in these instances? We all are sadly in need of being taught
of God.   HENRY CLAY TRUMBULL.

215

There are many Christians who seem to think, "How little can I do, and yet keep up a respectable appearance in the community, and finally be saved?" Perhaps some one of you says, "Well, I hope I was converted several years ago. I joined the church, I come to the sacrament, I never brought any scandal on religion—never; I lead a respectable life. If, at the last, saved by grace, I can get through the door into heaven, I shall be satisfied." Do you think you will? No! you never will be—*never!* If, by the grace of God, you are, as the saying goes, "saved by the skin of your teeth," and once get inside of the pearly gates, and look up and see Paul and all the apostles and martyrs and prophets and evangelists, Luther and Calvin and the Wesleys and Spurgeon, and all that glorious array; and not only these, but some poor, hard-working washerwoman that, at the end of a day's toil, dragged herself away to a prayer-meeting, and at the end of the week carried her little pile of rags to a mission school—when you look at these, you will be so ashamed of yourself that you will ask God to let you come back and work out your salvation. Satisfied? God have mercy on any one who is satisfied with himself or herself! May the Holy Spirit give us all a holy dissatisfaction with our condition, and a desire to rise and go forward.

THEODORE L. CUYLER.

If you do not indulge in godly sorrow, is it not likely you are losing a good deal of sanctification? Have we nothing to repent of? No wasted hours? How little we have done for God! Ah, that we had prayed more!

ANDREW BONAR.

Archbishop Ussher, in his declining years, had a room built with windows facing the east, south, and west, so that he could warm himself by the rays of the sun. In the morning he stationed himself at the east window, at noon at the south window, and in the evening at the west window, where he could watch the setting of the sun. The west window was at that time symbolical of the setting of his sun of life. But sunrise follows the setting of the sun, and the sunset of life is the sunrise of immortality.

ARTHUR T. PIERSON.

What was the outlook for the child of God? Ask Paul as he sits in the Mamertine prison, a deep dungeon with only a ray of light. He stood or lay there for three years, most of the time with a chain on his hand and a soldier watching by his side. I notice that his face glows with rapture, and, as he writes, his pen almost catches fire in the speed of its flight. "Blessed apostle, what of the outcome?" "That is just what I am writing: 'I have fought the good fight, I have finished my course, my departure is at hand: henceforth a crown.'" "Is that all you see—a crown? For I see a man waiting with a sword just outside the city gate to take off your head. Do you hear anything in particular, Paul? For I hear the crunching of bones and groans in that den of beasts." "Since you speak of it, I do hear the welcome of innumerable harpers, harping to welcome me home." That was the salvation which Paul had, and in the joy and light of which he steadily lived, and which, in God's name, I commend to you.

CYRUS D. FOSS.

217

Our Saviour Jesus Christ, who hath abolished death, and hath brought life and immortality to light through the gospel.—2 Tim. i. 10.

How can Christ have abolished death? Christians die as really as others. We know of but two persons of all the race of Adam who have been exempted from dying.

The English Parliament decreed, August 1, 1836, to abolish slavery in the West Indies, but the decree did not go into effect until one year later. During that year the slave was still under the whip of his master, and all went on as in the old slavery days. But on July 31, 1837, twenty thousand slaves met together in Jamaica. They put on white robes, and at eleven o'clock they knelt down and waited for one hour with upturned faces. When the clock struck twelve these white-robed slaves rose up and shouted, "We are free! we are free!" Slavery was abolished by enactment a year before, but now it was abolished in fact. In Revelation vi. 9, 10, we read, "I saw underneath the altar the souls of them that had been slain for the Word of God: . . . and they cried with a great voice, saying, How long, O Master, the holy and true, dost thou not judge and avenge our blood on them that dwell on the earth?" They wanted the resurrection bodies. They were tired of waiting, though they were in Paradise beholding his face in glory. "And white robes were given unto every one of them; and it was said unto them, that they should rest yet for a little season, until their fellow-servants also and their brethren, that should be killed as they were, should be fulfilled." O ye martyrs, be not impatient; there is another company of martyrs coming on; wait for them!   A. J. GORDON.

He that overcometh shall inherit all things; and I will be his God, and he shall be my son.—Rev. xxi. 7.

Perhaps you didn't know that I was a millionaire. I don't know how many millions I own. They say the Rothschilds can't tell within millions how much they are worth. That is just my condition. All the wealth of this world and all the planets—everything—is mine; I am joint-heir with Jesus Christ. Find out what Jesus Christ is worth, and I will tell you what I am worth. "He that overcometh shall inherit all things; and I will be his God, and he shall be my son." Think of that—the son of God!

D. L. MOODY.

Battles are not won by lectures on gunpowder. It is no holiday work to which we are called, no dress-parade service. It cost the Son of God his life to witness for his Father here in this sinful world, and he says, "Whosoever doth not bear his cross, and come after me, cannot be my disciple." Spirit-filled men and women have always been, and always will be, cross-bearing men and women. When Paul was called to service, he was told of a great work which God would do through him, and there was added to the message, "I will show him how great things he must suffer for my name's sake." Before Stephen received his crown he had to bear the cross. We are quite willing to share his crown, but how about his cross?

D. W. WHITTLE.

You must take possession of Christ for salvation, but to win a crown Christ must take possession of you.

H. W. WEBB-PEPLOE.

There are resources at God's command which men
nowadays seldom take into account. One can hardly
speak in the nineteenth century about angels, we
have become so materialistic—we have got so "ad-
vanced." "Oh, supernatural stories!" Men come
to us with hypocritical faces and say, "If you would
suppress all this about angels and heavenly powers,
and interference with the natural order of things,
and reduce your Book to what undoubtedly is in it,
a very valuable collection of ethical maxims, well,
then we might accept it." Thank you, sir, for nothing. If we could take all the bones out of it, what
a beautiful jellyfish it would be! No; we keep in the
miraculous; it is the very strength and mainstay of
revelation; it is all miraculous. The angels are here
still, although we do not see them. Although they
do not come into actual contact with us, and with
gracious violence smite our sides, and wake us up,
and lead us forth past all peril into safety, still unseen they stand about us, and still God has a thousand thousand resources at his hand for the marvelous preservation of his people. "We are immortal
till our work is done."

JOHN McNEILL.

God does not work miracles, and God does not send
angels to do that for which he has already provided
means. He will not send his angel to snatch us from
some temptation into which we deliberately run any
more than he will send his angel to avert the pesti-
lence or the scarlet fever if we neglect to keep our
sanitary conditions pure.

A. C. A. HALL.

It is not enough that we shall know what the Bible says, but we want to know that the Bible has a right to be respected when it speaks; we want to know how it came into existence, and by what right it holds its present position in our thought. Of course apostolic Christianity has been supernatural Christianity, and prayer-meeting Christianity has been supernatural Christianity, and ecclesiastical Christianity has been supernatural Christianity, and martyr Christianity has been supernatural Christianity; and the Christianity that is robbed of its supernaturalness will be a Christianity for which the world will have very little use after a short time. The question which men are raising, therefore, involves the inquiry whether the Christian world has been the victim of a great delusion.

FRANCIS L. PATTON.

If apostolic Christianity were to die, it would have died long ago. It has had many good chances to die—better chances than it will ever have again. It would have been bound to the stake with the early martyrs, have expired in their ashes, and have been entombed in the graves of her first and last apostles. But "all true work," as Carlyle has said, "hang the author of it on what gibbet you like, must and will accomplish itself."

L. T. TOWNSEND.

Religion is not a strange or added thing, but the inspiration of the secular life, the breathing of an eternal spirit through this temporal world.

HENRY DRUMMOND.
221

People read infidel books and wonder why they are unbelievers. Why do they read such books? They say that to form an unprejudiced opinion they must read both sides. If a book is a lie, how can it be one side? Infidel books are not one side.

D. L. MOODY.

Agnosticism is simply not believing; it is denial, negation, darkness. There is only one cure for darkness, and that is coming to the light. If you will persist in putting your eyes out or in barring God's daylight out, there is no help for you; you must die in the dark. Sin has made your soul sick, and if you will not even try Christ's medicine, then the blood-poisoning of infidelity will run its fatal course. Neither skepticism nor agnosticism ever won a victory, ever slew a sin, ever healed a heartache, ever produced a ray of sunshine, ever saved an immortal soul. Unbelief is foredoomed to defeat; do not risk your eternity on that spider's web.

THEODORE L. CUYLER.

The torrent of the love of God is pouring into your human nature, and there is an incarnation begun in your home by the love of God. You know that God is love when you begin to live a life of love. But, on the other hand, I often find that people who doubt that the nature of God is love are the people who are unmerciful, untender, austere, and harsh. Men throw on God the hues of their own characters. Oh, that God may make us godlike, that we may know God!

F. B. MEYER.

God has made us with two eyes, both intended to be used so as to see one object. Binocular vision is the perfection of sight. There is a corresponding truth in the spiritual sphere. We have two faculties for the apprehension of spiritual truth—*reason* and *faith;* the former intellectual, the latter largely intuitive, emotional. Reason asks, How? wherefore? Faith accepts testimony and rests upon the person who bears witness.

Now reason and faith often seem in conflict, but are not. Reason prepares the way for faith, and then both act jointly. We are not called to exercise blind faith, but to be ready always to give answer to every man who asks a reason.

There are three questions which belong to reason to answer: First, is the Bible the Book of God? Second, what does it teach? Third, what relation has its teaching to my duty? When these are settled, faith accepts the Word as authoritative, and no longer stumbles at its mysteries, but, rather, expects that God's thoughts will be above our thoughts. Thus, where reason's province ends faith's begins.

ARTHUR T. PIERSON.

Verily, theology without the Holy Ghost is poison; there have been more men ruined by handling the deep things of God without the Spirit of God to help them than by any other process that I am aware of. The light is made for the eye; but if the eye is diseased, the light becomes intolerably painful; it torments the eye. So the truth is made for the soul; but if our soul is unsanctified, that which ought to come to it as its own native air hurts, injures, destroys.   A. J. GORDON.

Take time to be holy,
  Speak oft with thy Lord;
Abide in him always,
  And feed on his Word;
Make friends of God's children,
  Help those who are weak,
Forgetting in nothing
  His blessing to seek.

Take time to be holy,
  The world rushes on;
Spend much time in secret
  With Jesus alone;
By looking to Jesus,
  Like him thou shalt be;
Thy friends in thy conduct
  His likeness shall see.

Take time to be holy,
  Let him be thy Guide,
And run not before him,
  Whatever betide;
In joy or in sorrow,
  Still follow thy Lord,
And, looking to Jesus,
  Still trust in his word.

Take time to be holy,
  Be calm in thy soul,
Each thought and each motive
  Beneath his control;
Thus led by his Spirit
  To fountains of love,
Thou soon shalt be fitted
  For service above.

                    W. D. LONGSTAFF.

Month of August

Be ye therefore perfect, even as your Father which is in heaven is perfect.—Matt. v. 48.

A man is called into existence to enjoy fellowship and union with God; to know God until he becomes in some sense the representative of God. Should there, then, not always be present to man's mind this one thought: "I am created for God; I am to represent God to the things below me; I am to walk in oneness with God; the ambition of my soul is so to be the very reflector of God that I become one with him, and yet remain a creature to the end of eternity"? If that be the standard it is evident that something must be done to meet man's present circumstances and to bring them into accord with what God requires, which is nothing less than perfection. Our holiness is the extent to which we carry out that perfection.

H. W. WEBB-PEPLOE.

Many souls are being exercised about holiness, but not equally about righteousness. Holiness is the hidden thing we cannot see; righteousness is the manifestation of holiness in act and life.

ANDREW A. BONAR.

It is the law of influence that we become like those whom we habitually admire. . . . Through all the range of literature, of history, and of biography this law presides. Men are all mosaics of other men. There was a savor of David about Jonathan, and a savor of Jonathan about David. Jean Valjean, in the masterpiece of Victor Hugo, is Bishop Bienvenu risen from the dead. Metempsychosis is a fact.

HENRY DRUMMOND.

225

Difficulties are the parents of all progress. Things "hard to be understood" is the price paid for all wisdom. A religion without difficulties never came from the Author of nature. For the last three thousand years no pagan worship has contained anything "hard to be understood." The regions of the dead have made as much mental progress as the generations of the living. Twenty-five hundred years before Christ China made gunpowder, and yet has gone no further than to blaze it away in fire-crackers. Two thousand years before the Christian era she had the magnet, and yet a Chinese junk never crossed the ocean unless she was towed by a Christian ship. Show us one step in mental or moral progress for two thousand years outside of where the Bible circulates. It contains the germs of all natural and scientific progress.

I. D. DRIVER.

There are certain immutable elements in the primitive Christian faith, as there are in nature, which never have changed, and never can change, and which will never outgrow the passions and loves of the human soul. The beauty of a mild sunset, the sublimity of a midnight heaven, the dazzle of lightnings playing across the sky, the repose and beauty of a lily clad in raiment surpassing that of any present or future Solomon in all his glory, will not be outgrown, though society should exist in a state of constant progress for ten thousand years.

L. T. TOWNSEND.

226

It is sometimes said to us, in the name of science,
"Let us distribute the territory in which science and
religion claim undivided interests. You religious
people may take your part, and we scientific people
will take our share. We will be generous with you:
we will let you have the unexplored dark continent
of don't-knowdom, and we will keep the little island
of ascertained fact." But Christian apologists very
properly decline the offer. They say, "We are
going to take possession of the entire continent of
thought, in the name of the Father and of the Son
and of the Holy Ghost." Let us understand it; religion is not afraid; she does not ask for any specific
arithmetic or grammar or exceptional canons of
evidence; all she needs, as Chief Justice Gibson
once said, is a common-law trial and a fair jury.

FRANCIS L. PATTON.

Paul was a great man of logic. He was a wonderful man to argue. This is true, but never, never
think of the great apostle as one of those poor ped-
dling creatures called "logicians." Logic is a very
shriveling science when there is nothing but itself.
Never dream of Paul as being simply one of your
argumentative, dry logicians. Paul was a volcano
in a perpetual state of activity. Logic? Aye; but
logic set on fire with love to Christ and with love to
the souls of men.

JOHN McNEILL.

227

See then that ye walk circumspectly, not as fools, but as wise,
redeeming the time, because the days are evil.—Eph. v. 15, 16.

The words, "redeeming the time," are not fairly
translated. They mean "buying up the opportunity."
Be on the lookout for opportunities. The saddest
part of our record, I fear, is that we have let precious
opportunities flow by us, never to be recalled. Think
of the opportunities you have had to say a word to
an impenitent soul, or some word of comfort to a
friend, or to testify for Christ. The specter I most
fear is the ghost of lost opportunities. Be on the
lookout for opportunities, and you will never know
just what blessing is going to burst on you. A poor
itinerant Methodist minister went to Colchester to
preach. It was a cold day, and he found only fifteen
or twenty people in that primitive little chapel. He
went up into the pulpit and took for his text, "Look
unto me, and be ye saved." The whole sermon was
only a repetition of the one thought, look to Christ.
"A young lad up in the gallery looks very sad. He
will never get any comfort until he looks to Christ."
Heaven knows who that boy in the gallery was; the
world knows; but from that day Charles H. Spurgeon
never saw that preacher again. He went his way.
He did his work. Spurgeon has already met him in
heaven, I doubt not. Oh, would not life be worth living if a stray shot of ours should bring a Spurgeon
to the Saviour? Who knows! Who knows! If you
have consecrated yourself to the work of lifting up
the Saviour, how do you know who is to look to him
and be saved?

THEODORE L. CUYLER.

Lord, increase our faith.—Luke xvii. 5.

All faith which has Christ for its object is the right kind of faith.

If you want your faith to grow there are four rules that you must adopt: First, be willing to have a great faith. When men say they cannot believe, ask, "Are you willing to believe?" because if the will is toward faith the Holy Ghost will produce a great faith. Second, use the faith you have; the child's arm, with its slender muscles, will not be able to wield the sledge-hammer unless he begins step by step to use it. Do not, therefore, stand on the boat's edge and wait to be able to swim a mile, but throw yourself out from its side into the water and swim a yard or two; for it is in these smaller efforts that you are to be prepared for the greater and mightier exploits. Third, be sure to put God between yourself and circumstances. Everything depends on where you put God. There are three matters to consider in the case—yourself, your own position, and God's position and the position of the circumstances with which you have to deal. Most men put circumstances between themselves and God so much that they can hardly see God at all, or if they do see him it is like looking at a landscape through a reversed telescope, which makes it seem at a great distance. But there are other wiser and happier souls who put God between themselves and circumstances, and at once, when one looks out through God upon circumstances, that which before had almost paralyzed him becomes infinitesimal and unworthy of his dread. Fourth, live a life of daily obedience to God's will. Observe these rules and your faith will grow.   F. B. MEYER.

229

Many there be who say of my soul, There is no help for him in God.—Ps. iii. 2.

That is the last and deadliest arrow in Satan's quiver; when that thought comes then the old guard of hell has burst upon your soul. That shot goes home all the more, proves itself to be all the more deadly, if there is something in your own heart that only too sadly inclines to say the same thing as the voices from without. But wait a minute and think of it. What an awful silence comes into one's heart! What a midnight this day would be if it were true! But it is not. David does not argue; he ignores it and goes on, "But thou, O Lord, art a shield for me; my glory, and the lifter up of mine head." There is no use trying to argue down some thoughts and temptations. If this desertion and abandonment by God is true then hell has come. There is no time to argue; I must instantly destroy it. So David meets a very positive statement by another equally positive. When any thought comes to you and says, "There is no help for you even in God," that messenger has shown the cloven hoof. He has not only done it, but he has overdone it. It is not true. Then let these voices be the voices of so many liars unto you. When they say, "There is no help in Absalom," quite right; when they say, "Ahithophel has turned treacherous," I do not doubt it; "Shimei is cursing you," perfectly true; when they say, "You are an old hypocrite," quite right; but when they say, "God has cast you off," get thee behind me, Satan! Liar! Worse than I am is the voice that would dare to speak against the faithfulness of my Redeemer, God. "He abideth faithful."   JOHN McNEILL.

230

Who is among you . . . that walketh in darkness, and hath no
light? let him trust in the name of the Lord, and stay upon his
God.—Isa. l. 10.

If we can put our trust in God when we are in
total darkness, when may we not trust him? Sometimes we are called upon to trust in God when he
seems to go right back against all his promises.
That is trusting him in the darkness. Weak faith
will judge God's promises by one's feelings, by one's
evidences, when we ought to judge the feelings and
the evidences by the promises. As long as I have
the promises, God give me grace to trust in him,
whatever befall, and bid my soul keep still, knowing
that he will never fail.

MARCUS RAINSFORD.

Faith is the soul's organ of vision and hearing and
touch. By faith we behold and hear and take hold
on God. Hence the reality and power of all communion with God depend on how far we believe his
own word of promise.

ARTHUR T. PIERSON.

I use my Bible as I use my check-book in the bank,
only with this difference: I have to tear a leaf out
every time I cash a check, and can't use it a second
time; but in taking from this book I can leave the
leaf in and use it again and again. It is a sort of
circulating letter; you never come to the end of it.

J. HUDSON TAYLOR.

Going through the magnificent Rocky Mountain scenery some time ago, we plunged into the Royal Gorge, and later swung into the Grand Cañon, and it seemed to me that scenery more sublime could not be found in all the world. If I had never been impressed before with the existence of God, I should have cried out unto him in the midst of those mountain-peaks. Every one in the car, with one single exception, was gazing in rapt admiration. This one woman was intently reading a book, and did not lift her eyes once from the printed page while we were passing through that wonderful scenery. When we had swung out into the great table-land I overheard her say to a friend, "This is the thirteenth time I have crossed the mountains. The first time I could not keep the tears from rolling down my cheeks, so impressed was I; but now I know it so well that I frequently go through the whole range with scarcely a glance cast out the window." It is thus, alas! that we too often read God's Word; that which furnishes the angels a theme for never-ending praise we read with indifference, or fail to read at all.

J. WILBUR CHAPMAN.

When people have lost all enjoyment in the Word of God, this is no reason why they should relinquish its study. They may lose all enjoyment in their morning ablutions, but that is no reason why they should not bathe. A man should go on reading because of the almost unconscious effect the Bible may have upon his inner life, and because he may thereby learn to love it.

F. B. MEYER.

232

If we want to live more than ordinary spiritual lives as Christian men, it is necessary that we be great feeders upon the Word of God, which is not only quick, but powerful. De Quincey divided all literature into the literature of knowledge and the literature of power; this is preëminently the literature of power. "If ye abide in me, and my words abide in you, ye shall ask what ye will, and it shall be done unto you." And still further, we might make this additional statement: that without spiritual Bible study other spiritual helps may often lead us in danger, and ultimately they may be abandoned. Take the matter of meditation; without the Bible meditation may lead a man to morbid introspection. Secret prayer is not a monologue, but is a dialogue.

JOHN R. MOTT.

The study of Christ in the Old Testament is exceedingly profitable. In Genesis he is described as the seed of the woman; in Exodus as the "Passover lamb"; in Leviticus the high priest; in Numbers the smitten rock and the uplifted serpent; and in Deuteronomy the person of Moses. All of these typify and set forth the person and work of the Lord Jesus Christ. The Psalms also are full of references to him. All the prophets, either in type or in prediction, "testified beforehand of his sufferings, and the glory that should follow." The gospels record his life, death, resurrection, and ascension; the Acts the establishment of his church; the epistles the development of his doctrines; and the Apocalypse the revelation of his coming glory. The great work of the Holy Spirit is to testify. W. W. CLARK.

233

The bane of humanity is bad heredity. We cannot get rid of it. "The fathers have eaten sour grapes, and the children's teeth are set on edge," say the Scriptures. The fathers have drunk the cup of sinful pleasure, and the children have drunk the dregs. The wondrous thing about the gospel is that it gives us a new heredity. I count that the very highest and sublimest statement of the doctrine of regeneration. A man grafting trees saws off a limb to put in the scion. If the limb is rotten he has to saw it off nearer to the trunk. We were grafted in Adam, but it was discovered that the branch was rotten, and then God began at the very beginning, and grafted us into Jesus Christ, the divine Son of God. Dr. Williams, of Boston, was asked, "How early do you think the training of a child ought to begin?" He replied instantly, "A hundred years before the child's birth." When God would build up a child holy in all things he goes back to the very beginning and gives us our birth in God himself: "Which were born, not of blood, nor of the will of the flesh, nor of the will of man, but of God." The river of life has its sources in the very throne of God, and when we get that life we have something in us which tends to make us do well instead of doing ill. As from Adam we had this hereditary tendency to do wrong, so when we are grafted into Jesus Christ, and given the eternal life, we have that influence impelling us to holiness: "Whosoever is born of God doth not commit sin; for his seed remaineth in him: and he cannot sin, because he is born of God."

A. J. GORDON.

A call to be a disciple is one thing, and a call to be a clergyman is another. A good many people make a mistake because they haven't made that distinction. Peter, James, and John were called to be disciples. They wouldn't have left their nets and their fishing-smacks and followed Christ if they had not been called. Afterward they were called to be apostles. I believe no man ought to go into the ministry unless he is forced into it by the Spirit of God. Many men nowadays think if they can't do anything else they will turn their hand to the ministry. They might better be hammering iron, or making clothes, or sowing wheat. I'd rather plow or saw wood than be in a work to which God hadn't sent me. If a man runs before he is sent he will be a miserable failure; he'll break down. But if a man waits till he gets his commission he is going to bear good testimony, and God will bless his testimony. One way to tell whether you have been called is to look at the results of your work. If you preach because you can't help it, and your whole soul is in it, and souls are won to Christ, that is a pretty good sign that you have been called of God.

D. L. Moody.

If you desire to know God's will first pray to him for guidance. The man who neglects this sins. But no less is it important to use all the facts within our reach, and our faculties of judgment and decision, and then our full power of locomotion.

John N. Forman.

Epaphras, who is one of you, a servant of Christ, saluteth you, always laboring fervently for you in prayers, that ye may stand perfect and complete in all the will of God.—Col. iv. 12.

The prayer of Epaphras for the Colossians should be our prayer for ourselves and others. We do sometimes bow down and say, "Thy will be done." Men put up the whites of their eyes and roll their heads about as if with agony at the thought that the will of God is to be done. One would think the will of God was the most terrible infliction that the Almighty could lay upon his creatures. But the will of God is the joy of Christ Jesus. It is the one joy of a sanctified soul that it is permitted and enabled to do the will of God; so that when a person prays for me that I may "stand perfect and complete in all the will of God," it is the most blessed prayer that can be offered for me.

H. W. WEBB-PEPLOE.

Our first parents forfeited Eden by their disobedience, and Christ, the second Adam, takes up the battle in the wilderness and fights his way back to Paradise. We have to do the same. We have forfeited our Eden of innocence and peace with God by disobedience to some higher law. We have lost our Eden, and we find ourselves in the wilderness, and we have got to take up the battle and, under Christ's leadership and relying on his sympathy and help, to fight our way back again to Paradise. "To him that overcometh will I give to eat of the tree of life, which is in the midst of the Paradise of God."

A. C. A. HALL.

In whom we have redemption through his blood, the forgiveness of sins, according to the riches of his grace.—Eph. i. 7.

There is the riches of God's grace. Ephesians i. 18 tells us of the riches of his glory: "The eyes of your understanding being enlightened; that ye may know what is the hope of his calling, and what the riches of the glory of his inheritance in the saints." What is the riches of his glory? It is unfolded further on, in Ephesians iii. 16: "That he would grant you, according to the riches of his glory, to be strengthened with might by his Spirit in the inner man." Contrast these two things, and you find this: the riches of his grace is that which we get from the cross; the riches of his glory is that which we get from the throne. Forgiveness is of grace; the enduement of the Spirit is of glory.

A. J. GORDON.

There are different ways of coming to fortune. You may inherit it, or you may achieve it, or you may come to it as Ruth did. Like her, although at first only a poor gleaner, you may marry the Laird! And that is the only way to true possession. Faith marries us to the Lord of all.

JOHN McNEILL.

Gleaning is a poor trade; it is hard work, with comparatively little result. There are so many Christians who have never been taught anything better than to go into the field and labor hard and carry away as much as they could carry. But that never makes a home, that never makes full provision.

H. W. WEBB-PEPLOE.

237

The one lesson that God has taught me, if he ever has taught me anything in connection with the grace of God, is that there is such a thing as a divine plan in a man's life, and that the only wisdom in this world is to find out what that plan is, and to be led into it step by step, and not to mind what is the end of it. There is much said about the divine call, little said about the end of it. Why? Because no tongue, not even the divine tongue, will attempt to tell what is the outcome of a life that is led of God. Even the Bible, with all its majesty and divinity, does not undertake to tell how great that life is which takes its way into the life of God; it only gives a clue by which we can find the way step by step.

Only two patterns are possible. The Bible does not present a third. Every man must live the life of Cain, the first rejecter of the gospel, or the life of Abel, the first believer. Cain was the first unbeliever. He rejected God's testimony, and murder was incidental to it. It was the fruit, not the root. A man must live the life of Jacob, the supplanter, or of Israel, the prince of God. He must live the life of Saul, the persecutor of the church and of the Lord Jesus Christ himself, or the life of Paul, apostolic in its tone and spirit and temper and outcome. He must live the life of the old man, or the life of the new man.

H. C. MABIE.

Where a foundation has been laid anybody can build, but only God can build on nothing.

A. J. GORDON.

A dear companion of mine, for three years a true
yoke-fellow in evangelistic work, one extremely cold
winter evening, as he joined me in a railway-train
to take his last journey on earth in the service of
his Master, said pleasantly, "I got a good illustration
from the man at the gate as I came on to the train.
It is very cold, and every one was grumbling, and
some abusing him as he made them all get their
tickets out and show them before they could get past.
I said to him, 'You don't seem to be very popular
around here.' 'If I am popular with the man that
put me here it is all that I want,' was his reply.
Ah," said this dear friend, "if we could go through
this world keeping the same thought toward Christ,
what a straight path we should make!" May this
be our ambition, the only ambition the gospel enjoins.
"Wherefore also we are *ambitious*, whether at home
or absent, to be well pleasing unto *him*."

D. W. WHITTLE.

What we want to-day is men of one idea. Men
said that Paul was a narrow-minded man, a man of
one idea. If you have one idea that covers everything—the one idea of Christ crucified—you can
afford to be called fanatical.

D. L. MOODY.

There is no vital connection between merely having the ideal and being conformed to it. Thousands
admire Christ who never become Christians.

HENRY DRUMMOND.

Be not overcome of evil, but overcome evil with good.—Rom. xii. 21.

Simple resistance is not enough; we need to be aggressive, not defensive only. To stand against evil is a great thing, but to compel evil to withdraw before us and drive it away is greater. He who is *not* overcome is not conquered, but he who overcomes is a conqueror. In one case he is not defeated; in the other case his foe is defeated and driven from the field. If the former is conquest the latter is more than conquest. And the secret of it is not to stand on the defensive, but in the power of the truth and goodness carry on the war in the confidence of faith, with the sword of the Spirit, in the power of prayer.

ARTHUR T. PIERSON.

The Bible is positive and negative; it requires and forbids; it points out evils and prescribes the remedies. Some say that the way to destroy evil is to proclaim the good. God does not do this. It is necessary both to root out the evil and to establish the good. God commands us not to profane his name, not to steal, or kill, or commit adultery, and then gives positive commands to honor our fathers and mothers, to remember the Sabbath, and to love God and man. No farmer is fool enough to try to kill weeds by planting good corn. He relies upon the plow and the hoe. No brier patch was ever brought into subjection by sowing good wheat upon it. Evil must be eradicated and good must be implanted.

CHARLES A. BLANCHARD.

Every time we overcome one temptation we gain strength to overcome another.

D. L. MOODY

Fight the good fight of faith.—1 Tim. vi. 12.

The fight of faith is a "good fight" because it is for the best objects; it insures a clean heart, a pure conscience, and God's approval. It is a good fight because God supplies us with weapons. It is a winning fight because the omnipotent Christ takes us into his own keeping, and neither man nor devils can pluck us out of his hand. When the Son of God is conquered we will be conquered, and not before.

THEODORE L. CUYLER.

A merchant in Glasgow used to preach wherever he thought he could do good. One day he was talking about Shamgar. "Over the hill," he said, "there came a man. He came near Shamgar and said, 'Shamgar, Shamgar, run for your life! Six hundred Philistines are coming over the hill after you.' But Shamgar said, 'They are four hundred short. I'll take care of them.' He believed in Scripture, you see—that one should chase a thousand."

D. L. MOODY.

Never dare to fight God's battles with the devil's weapons, whatever they may be, and never dare do evil that good may come. The end never justifies the means. Never compromise with the world's laxity, and never snatch in your own way at what God will give you with a blessing in his own way.

A. C. A. HALL.

How can we get spiritual power? *We cannot get it.* No man ever possessed it; no man ever owned it; no man ever used it. It is a question, not of our getting power, but of God getting us; not of our using God, but of God using us. The disciples were not told to pray for power nor to seek for power. They were told to wait for the Holy Ghost. A wind always blows *toward* a vacuum. In that upper chamber the disciples were being emptied and a vacuum was being made. The son of thunder was emptied of the thunder that he might be filled with love. The doubting Thomas was emptied of his doubt that he might be filled with light. Peter was emptied of his presumption and his fickleness that he might be filled with all the power of God. Then there came the sound as of a mighty rushing wind, and God came upon them and used them.

A great mesmerist told me that the one qualification under which he could mesmerize people was that they should have vacant minds. If a man might pour his mind into the vacant mind of another creature until he should think his thought and do his will, what might not God do if only he could have vacant spirits into which he could pour himself? The great condition of power is to be emptied of self and to be filled with God; to renounce self and to appropriate God; to be dead unto self, but to be alive unto God by the power of the Holy Ghost.

B. FAY MILLS.

If the incense of prayer is rising steadily and fervently from our souls, the Spirit of God will blow upon us stronger and stronger.

W. W. MOORE.

What saves men? Not the blood of Christ alone, not the gospel message alone, not the work of the Holy Ghost alone; not all of these alone. Some believer is the link to connect with that atoning blood, that witnessing gospel, and that comforting Spirit. There is almost always a human agent somewhere; it may be only in the giving of a tract, the asking of a question; it may be a parent, a Sunday-school teacher, a minister of Christ; but there is some human link that comes between the soul and the gospel, and so men are saved. So Paul said, "I fill up that which is behind of the afflictions of Christ." Until the believer falls into line something is missing. Christ on the cross is to be brought to the knowledge of men. The gospel of the printed page is to be brought to the knowledge of men. The Holy Ghost is an invisible personality, unknown and unrecognized by the world. How is the world to be saved? The believing child of God lifts up the cross, tells the gospel story to the unsaved, becomes the dwelling-place of the Holy Spirit, and out of him flows the water of life. Paul counted mission work a sublime privilege: "Unto me, who am less than the least of all saints, is *this grace* given, that I should preach among the Gentiles the unsearchable riches of Christ."

ARTHUR T. PIERSON.

He who is not a missionary Christian will be a missing Christian when the great day comes for bestowing the rewards of service.

A. J. GORDON.

243

Therefore, my beloved brethren, be ye steadfast, unmovable, always abounding in the work of the Lord, forasmuch as ye know that your labor is not in vain in the Lord.—1 Cor. xv. 58.

Only fixed convictions will produce permanent Christian activity, and only those who are actively at work will maintain fixed convictions. The two may stand together; either attempted alone will fail.

JOHN A. BROADUS.

God can take the devilment, the meanness, and the skill that a man had in serving the devil and that he learned in serving the devil and make them useful in his own work. Oh, I think that is great, that the dear Lord Jesus Christ can turn the guns on the devil. S. H. HADLEY.

The honest service of Jesus Christ pays the soul a rich dividend of solid satisfaction. There is no wretchedness in a true Christian's trials; his bruised flowers emit sweet fragrance. The fruits of the Holy Spirit are love, joy, and peace; the promise of the Lord Jesus is that his joy shall be full. The sweetest honey is gathered out of the hive of a busy, unselfish, useful, and holy life.

THEODORE L. CUYLER.

I shall pass through this world but once. Any good thing, therefore, that I can do, or any kindness that I can show to any human being, let me do it now. Let me not defer it or neglect it, for I shall not pass this way again.

HENRY DRUMMOND.

244

We are laborers together with God.—1 Cor. iii. 9.

Too many men say, "My God, I am going to work in such and such a part of the vineyard to-day; please come and help me." Our true prayer should be, "Lord, where are you working to-day? Let me come and work along with you." We want God to help us carry out our little plans; God wants us to help him accomplish his great plan. We would be much happier if, instead of trying to fit God into our scheme, we would fit ourselves into his and be workers together with God. That is the secret of George Müller's work; he took for his motto, "Our fellowship [our partnership] is with the Father." Our partnership is with the Father, and with the Son, and with the Holy Ghost, and we become very humble members of the very great firm which never suspends payment. We are workers together with God. F. B. MEYER.

Let us do what we can. Let us not be seeking some high position, but let us get down at the feet of the Master and be willing to let God use us—to let him breathe his Spirit upon us and send us out to his work. If you can't be a lighthouse you can be a tallow candle.

We want to get possession of power and use it. God wants the power to get possession of us and use us. If we give ourselves to the power to rule in us the power will give itself to us to rule through us. ANDREW MURRAY.

One ought to talk only as loud as he lives—a rule which would deprive some people of the privilege of shouting.

J. WILBUR CHAPMAN.

245

God does not want us to withdraw from the world
as recluses, but he wants us to mingle with our
fellow-men, and to seek in all ways to lead them
Godward. We are to own the ties of family and of
country, and to have sympathy for all humanity,
even as we have Christ for our example. He was a
familiar guest in the homes of the people. He took
the little children up in his arms and blessed them.
He was present at the marriage feast and in the
house of mourning. He went regularly to the feasts
at Jerusalem, and in all places and at all times was
ever accessible to and in sympathy with man. But
in doing this he ever retained his character as a
heavenly man. In the home he spoke of God. We
cannot conceive that he ever occupied his precious
time in talking with Martha and Mary about Herod's
last ball or the theatrical entertainments at the
Jerusalem theater, or gossiped with them about the
latest Roman fashions or the last scandal at Herod's
palace. Nor would Jesus be led by Simon and the
Pharisees to spend the dinner hour in discussing
ecclesiastical politics and criticizing the latest
speeches in the sanhedrim; nor by Zaccheus into
a calculation as to the future course of the stock
market and the movements in the commercial world.

Filled with love and benevolence, a citizen of
heaven, Christ moved here a man among men; but
a heavenly-minded man—never allowing himself to
be dragged down to a *worldly* level, but ever seeking
to lift up the men of the world to the plane of
heavenly things where he abode.

D. W. WHITTLE.

Has a Christian concern with any other conversation than Christ? This whole land would be swept with the Christian life as no section of the world has ever been swept with it if men made it their business to talk Christ; if, when they walked with one another, they talked him; if, when they sat down for a conversation, they talked him; if they came to know Christ as the object of their speech. Mr. Ruskin gathers up what the conviction of all of us must be, in his "Notes on the Construction of Sheepfolds," when he says that it is the business of every Christian man, whether he be a minister or layman, to be constantly and incessantly talking Christ, not only indirectly but directly; to the servants in his home, to the men he meets on railway-trains, to that man with whom he is thrown in touch in his work in life; it is his one business as a Christian man to talk Jesus Christ. Oh, the glory of the lives who have learned that lesson!

ROBERT E. SPEER.

You never can tell when God will take a little word you may drop, like an arrow shot at a venture, and cause it to strike some hearer between the joints of the harness and bring him down. Therefore let no opportunity slip for speaking a word for Christ.

A. F. SCHAUFFLER.

Do you want to be like Christ? Go and find some one who has fallen, and get your arm under him and lift him up toward heaven, and the Lord will bless you in the very act. May God help us to act like the good Samaritan.

D. L. MOODY.

247

He giveth power to the faint; and to them that have no might he increaseth strength.—Isa. xl. 29.

God gives power to them that have no might; he increases their strength so that they mount up with wings as eagles. Notice the great contrast between the arrow and the eagle. The arrow shot from the bow always slackens in its pace with every inch of space over which it flies, because of the friction with which it meets; but the eagle's flight is ever swifter and higher because its speed is not derived from the impetus with which it is launched into space, but it is fed by the inherent fountain of vitality and strength within. Thus the believer does not know the slackening speed of the arrow, but the ever-soaring and quickening speed of the eagle, because his strength is fed from within, where God, the untired, is ever maintaining his energy.

F. B. MEYER.

Demonstrate in your own experience that God is teaching you to win souls for Christ here and now before you cross the Atlantic or Pacific. Has there been a revival in your town since you were called? You will never find men laughing at the idea of your being a missionary if you can wake up your native town. That is what we want for men who are to labor in China, in Japan, in India, where the most colossal difficulties have to be met; we want not an army so much as an elect company who have proved their power on their native sod before they encounter those bulwarks of Satan in pagan fields.

H. C. MABIE.

248

He that winneth souls is wise.—Prov. xi. 30.

I don't know the prominent business men of Babylon. I couldn't tell who the sharpest politicians were, the leading philosophers or astronomers; could you? But I know Daniel pretty well; his spotless life is still resplendent as the day, and the good he did to those about him is still recorded to perpetuate his name. Oh, it's true that he that winneth souls is wise!   D. L. MOODY.

By far the best way to help men with their temptations is to bring them to Christ. It may be of some service to a man if, in the time of trial, I put round him the sympathetic arm of a brother; but it is infinitely better if I can get him to allow Christ to put round him his strong arm. This is the effectual defense, and no other can be really depended on.

JAMES STALKER.

We can serve God acceptably in any sphere; every calling may be made a divine vocation. The great mistake of many is that they feel they must leave the carpenter's plane, give up the trowel, and enter some learned profession. God says, "What's that in your hand?" In Moses' hand was the shepherd's crook, in Solomon's the scepter, in David's the sling or the harp, and in Dorcas's the needle. The Bible is God's tool-chest. It is one of these patent tool-chests which contains every kind of tool. The Word of God is adapted to every purpose.

ARTHUR T. PIERSON.

249

No obstacles in the way of the Christian pulpit
and Christian work ought to be named as an apology
for omitting to do that work except the obstacles
within the church itself. As well might General
Grant have complained of the cannon and sharp-
shooting of Lee's army; but for them there would
have been no use for him. We are to go on with
the conquest set before us.   CYRUS D. FOSS.

To a very large extent preaching in the pulpit
to-day is preaching in defense of the Bible rather
than preaching the content of the Bible. We spend
a great deal of time in making clear and clean the
approaches to the temple, and a great many of us
never get any farther than the vestibule door, and
we spend so much time in this way that we do not
have time to go inside and worship.
                              FRANCIS L. PATTON.

Christ sends us into all the world to preach the
gospel; and every time we preach the Holy Ghost is
present to bring home the message to men's hearts.
I confess that I am not sure if I preach on politics
or on the strikes that the Holy Ghost will bear witness to that teaching. These may be important
matters, but the Spirit has been given to bear testimony to Jesus Christ. I have not the sense of his
presence in handling these themes, if I ever venture
on them; but I often do have it when preaching
Christ, even in the simplest way—the Holy Ghost
co-witnessing and bearing the message home to the
hearts and consciences of men.
                              A. J. GORDON.

The work of the world's evangelization is a matter
not of option but of obligation. Christianity is not
worth keeping unless we take for granted that what
makes Christianity worth having is that it brings
to us the message of life found nowhere else. If
that is so, then this places us under obligation to
give the message to all the world. The moment a
man says that his Christianity does not require him
to give the gospel to the world, then he hasn't a
Christianity at all. We believe that God sent his
Son from heaven, and that the Son gave his life for
the world's life upon the cross; that he came not to
judge, but to save the world; that God was in him
reconciling the world to himself; that he told his
disciples to give the message of his life and his death
and his blood to every creature; that you and I are
his disciples; and that apart from his name there is
"no name under heaven given among men, whereby
we must be saved." Does not this belief carry with
it the obligation to spread the knowledge of these
facts around the world? Yet here we sit. Imagine
Simon Peter standing on the shores running up from
the Sea of Galilee, with a loaf in one hand and a fish
in the other, while five thousand poor starving people
lie about on the grass, and saying, "What a pity it
is that these poor people are not given something to
eat! What a nice thing it would be if some one
went out and fed them!" Would Christ have
allowed him to go about with a misty sort of sympathy for a world that was dying for a practical
knowledge of Christ? No; he said, "Give *ye* them
to eat." The work of evangelizing this world, for
every man, is a matter of personal, inalienable
obligation. ROBERT E. SPEER.

If you find, by the Bible teachings, that one tenth
of your income and one seventh of your time belong
to the Lord absolutely and outright to begin with,
and that your hold on the other nine tenths of your
income and six sevenths of your time is not that of
unconditional ownership, but of conditioned Christian stewardship, then see whether your conscience-
chronometer does not run pretty slow in that latitude.
A rating up of Christian consciences generally, by
this standard, would add ciphers pretty fast at the
right hand of benevolent contributions. There would
be little trouble then about the support of missionaries or the building of new churches.

HENRY CLAY TRUMBULL.

I go to Christians of wealth and ask for money,
and they say, "My money is so tied up that I cannot
spare it." I want to see the church of God able to
say, "My money is so tied up that I cannot spare it
for the theater and ball-room; it is tied up for Jesus
Christ, it is under consecration."

A. J. GORDON.

God Almighty will take your poor gift with delight, even though it is not worth anything whatever. Only give him what you have, and you will
find that the joy of the Lord comes back to you
moment by moment, until at last you can say, "My
soul is satisfied with marrow and fatness," while
God is well pleased for his righteousness' sake.

H. W. WEBB-PEPLOE.

252

How are we to attain to the blessed position in which the kingdom of God shall fill our hearts with such enthusiasm that it will spontaneously be first every day? We must be willing to give up everything for it. You have often seen in history how soldiers and men who were not soldiers could give up their lives in sacrifice for king or country. In South Africa, not many years ago, the war for liberty was fought. They said, "We must have our liberty." They bound themselves together to fight for it, and went home to prepare for the struggle. Such a thrill of enthusiasm passed through that country that women whose husbands were exempt from service said, "No; go, even though you have not been commanded." Mothers, when one son was called to the front, said, "Take two, take three." Every man and woman was ready to die. It was in very deed, "Our country first, before everything." So, if you desire to have this wonderful kingdom of God take possession of you, I beseech you, give up everything for it.   ANDREW MURRAY.

If it costs much to be a zealous and successful Christian, it will cost infinitely more to live and die an impenitent sinner. Bible religion costs self-denial; sin costs self-destruction. To be a sober man costs self-restraint and the scoff of fools. To be a tippler costs a ruined purse, a ruined body, and a lost soul. The sensualist pays for his vices a tremendous toll. The swearer must pay for his oaths, and the Sabbath-breaker for his breach of God's law.

THEODORE L. CUYLER.

A holy life is made up of a number of small
things; little words, not eloquent speeches or sermons; little deeds, not miracles of battle nor one
great heroic act of mighty martyrdom, make up the
true Christian life. The little constant sunbeam,
not the lightning; the waters of Siloam that "go
softly" in the meek mission of refreshment, not the
"waters of the river, great and many," rushing down
in noisy torrents, are the true symbols of a holy life.
The avoidance of little evils, little sins, little inconsistencies, little weaknesses, little follies, indiscre-
tions, and imprudences, little foibles, little indul-
gences of the flesh; the avoidance of such little things
as these goes far to make up at least the negative
beauty of a holy life.   ANDREW A. BONAR.

Any man who persists in living in known sin or
indulging in questionable practices, entertaining
doubts about things that he would be certain about
if he woke up, is not in a position to be used by God.
We must live near to God that we may hear his
voice. His voice was not in the great wind nor in
the earthquake, nor yet in the fire, but in the still,
small voice, or, as the Revised Version puts it, the
"sound of gentle stillness." We hear the noise
of rumbling, the voice of birds, and other voices of
nature; if we shut these out, we listen to the voice
of man; if we shut this out, we hear the voice of
selfish ambition. How hard it is to get down to
that point where we hear the voice which the sheep
always know! I beseech you, be not content until
you have heard that voice. Keep near to God.
                              JOHN R. MOTT.

Where the devil cannot rob us of our salvation he often very easily robs us of our expectation. Your ability to exhibit better, brighter, more powerful, and more beautiful lives in future than you dreamed possible in the past depends upon your conception of God. If we could only comprehend God we should live a perfect life, because "this is life eternal, that they might know thee the only true God, and Jesus Christ, whom thou hast sent." It is for want of knowledge of God that our lives are such failures.

H. W. WEBB-PEPLOE.

Surely it is the marvel of angels how near we stand to God and spend so much of our life in carrying burdens that he would bear and in not seeking by fellowship with him that grace which we need for his work and for daily duty. Probably the reason why we pray so little is because we understand so slightly the philosophy of prayer. The key to the philosophy of prayer lies in the general conception that true prayer is the reflection of the thought and mind of God, and that just as the fountain, rising day and night, seeks the level from which it came, so the prayer of the believer comes from God and returns to God.

F. B. MEYER.

Some men tell us that they don't have time to pray; but if any man has God's work lying deep in his heart, he *will* have time to pray.

D. L. MOODY.

Blessed assurance, Jesus is mine!
Oh, what a foretaste of glory divine!
Heir of salvation, purchase of God,
Born of his Spirit, washed in his blood.

This is my story, this is my song,
Praising my Saviour all the day long.

Perfect submission, perfect delight,
Visions of rapture now burst on my sight;
Angels descending bring from above
Echoes of mercy, whispers of love.

Perfect submission, all is at rest,
I in my Saviour am happy and blest,
Watching and waiting, looking above,
Filled with his goodness, lost in his love.

FANNY J. CROSBY.

Month of September

I will pour water upon him that is thirsty, and floods upon the dry ground.—Isa. xliv. 3.

Do you know what it means to be thirsty? Ah, when a man is thirsty it seems as if every pore in his body cried one thing: "Water, water, water!" When a man is thirsty for the baptism with the Holy Ghost all the longings of his soul seem to be concentrated in one cry: "The Holy Ghost, the Holy Ghost, the Holy Ghost!" Just so long as a man is trying to find some way of accomplishing his work without the Holy Spirit, and believes that he can get along without this baptism, he is not going to receive it.

R. A. TORREY.

I wish that we were so thirsty to-day that the flood-gates would be lifted up and the tide from heaven come in upon us. What does the hungry man want? Money? Not at all. Fame? Not a bit. Good clothes? Not a bit. Good reputation? No; that isn't it. He wants *food*. What does the thirsty man want? Bonds and stocks? No; he wants *water*. When we are in dead earnest, and want the bread of heaven and the water of life with all our souls, we are going to get it. You may be as dry as tinder, but, thank God, you can have all this living water if you come boldly before the throne of grace and present your case.

D. L. MOODY.

We are sawing off the branch that we are sitting on when we resist the Spirit of God.

JOHN MCNEILL.

257

And when he is come, he will reprove the world of sin, and of righteousness, and of judgment: of sin, because they believe not on me; of righteousness, because I go to my Father, and ye see me no more; of judgment, because the prince of this world is judged.—John xvi. 8.

The Spirit has been sent *to* the church to bear witness *of* Christ in order to bring conviction *to* the world. Jesus Christ performs three offices in his work of redemption, as prophet, priest, and King. The Holy Spirit has also a corresponding threefold conviction to bring home to men's hearts. He convinces, first, concerning Christ who was crucified; second, concerning Christ who has been glorified; third, concerning Christ who is to come again and judge the world.

Conscience bears witness to the law; the Comforter bears witness to Christ. Conscience brings legal conviction; the Comforter brings evangelical conviction. Conscience brings conviction unto condemnation, and the Comforter brings conviction unto justification. "He shall convince the world of sin, *because they believe not on me.*" The coming of the Son of God made a sin possible that was not possible before; light reveals darkness. There are negroes in central Africa who never dreamed that they were black until they saw the face of a white man; and there are people who never knew they were sinful until they saw the face of Jesus Christ in all its whiteness and purity.

Conscience convicts of sin committed, of righteousness impossible, and of judgment impending. The Comforter convicts of sin committed, of righteousness imputed, and of judgment past.

A. J. GORDON.

He . . . commanded them that they should not depart from Jerusalem, but wait for the promise of the Father.—Acts i. 4.

If the apostles, who had been associated with Christ, who had heard all his sermons and seen all his miracles, needed to wait for power, do you not think that we need to wait upon God for power before we undertake service for him? Suppose that Peter had said, "Lord, you don't mean that we should wait here while men are perishing all the time; hadn't we better go to them now?" "No, no; go back and wait until the power comes, and greater works than I have done shall ye do." I used to think the greatest work in this wide world was the miracle of raising Lazarus from the dead; but the longer I work the more I am convinced that the greatest miracle the world has ever known was on the day of Pentecost, when three thousand Jews were converted by an unlettered fisherman from Galilee, in one sermon. Some one has said that now it takes three thousand sermons to convert one Jew. I believe that if these men had gone to preaching before they had received power they would have been swept from the face of the earth. They waited ten days, and then the power came. Oh, how refreshing it must have been! I suppose there were more converted at that one sermon of Peter than during all the three years of Christ's ministry.

D. L. MOODY.

Peter, when asked how the work of Pentecost was done, said, "With the Holy Ghost." The greatest works for God have been wrought with such power of the Holy Ghost that there has been no consciousness of forth-putting of human energy.

A. J. GORDON.

259

Ye shall be witnesses unto me both in Jerusalem, and in all Judea, and in Samaria, and unto the uttermost part of the earth. —Acts i. 8.

I venture to say the hardest place for those disciples to begin to preach was in their own city, Jerusalem. Then Judea was the next hardest place and Samaria was the next hardest. The hardest place to begin is at home, in your own church, your own family; but that is what God wants us to do.

D. L. MOODY.

God calls us to be witnesses. What does it require for you to be a witness? First you must know something, and then tell it. Is there any one who cannot do that? Have Jesus Christ in your soul and a tongue to tell it. Belief in the heart and confession with the mouth—that makes a witness.

ARTHUR T. PIERSON.

You must teach what the Spirit of God has brought home and wrought into your own experience, not what you gain from any one else. You must be able to say, "I not only know *whom* I have believed, but I know *what* I believe; I know the dangers against which I warn men; the means of grace— prayer, Scripture, and the sacrament—to which I point them; I lead them along paths which I have trodden; I teach them to value what I have come to prize."

A. C. A. HALL.

A man is never safe in rebuking another if it does not cost him something to have to do it.

ANDREW A. BONAR.

Follow me, and I will make you fishers of men.—Matt. iv. 19.

It is a simple thing to be a fisher. Fishing does not mean a gaily painted boat and a swallowtail coat. You want to set your heart on the fish and not on yourself. Too many regard the world as a place for boat-riding. Go where the fish are and do not be afraid to fish. Go into partnership with Christ, and you will find that you will have many miraculous drafts.

ARTHUR T. PIERSON.

There are lots of nets that will never catch any fish unless they are first washed and mended. It is always well when you are going to fish to go where the fish are; nowadays we have a fashion of building a big fish-house on a hill, and expecting the fish to come up out of the water to be caught.

H. L. HASTINGS.

The first thing we must do if we want to win sinners is to get down to a level with them. Don't go under the supposition that you are a great deal better than they. When Christ wanted to save the poor Samaritan woman he traveled forty miles to meet her, and in order to gain her confidence and reach her sympathies he asked her for water.

MARCUS RAINSFORD.

When a man gets up so high that he can't reach down and save poor sinners, there is something wrong. D. L. MOODY.

261

One great difference between the Christian and the non-Christian worker is this: non-Christian workers say that there is a certain proportion of men who cannot be reached anyway. As a modern English author has said, "There is no substitute for a good heart, and no remedy for a bad one." Oh, frightful gospel that some of the philanthropists of our day are preaching! Is that all the message they have to the world—no remedy for a bad heart? What means the parable of the lost coin if, though lost, there was no gleam of its original luster? What means the parable of the lost sheep if there was not some dumb, inarticulate longing for the shelter of the fold? And what means the parable of the lost son if there was not in those distant fields a cry of longing for the father's home and heart? The Christian worker holds on to the promise of God in Isaiah: "Though your sins be as scarlet, they shall be as white as snow; though they be red like crimson, they shall be as wool." There is no man so low that the gospel of Christ cannot reach him; there is no people gone so far astray, no slum in the great city, which the grace of God cannot redeem; there is no field so dry and barren and desolate that when God works with us it may not become the kingdom of our Lord and Saviour Jesus Christ.

W. H. P. FAUNCE.

"Son of man, prophesy to the bones." God says, "Do what you can; bare, white, and glistening though they be, preach; roll away the stone of do-nothingism and mere lamentation, and then trust me for the quickening breath."

JOHN MCNEILL.

Twelve men were Christ's guests at his own table. Their feet were dusty from the road, and it was the business of the servant to wash them. But Jesus never kept any servants, and these men were not willing to pour water on one another's feet. Peter thought, "It is just as much John's business to wash my feet as it is my business to wash John's." They said, "After all, our feet are not very dusty, and if they should be washed now they would be dusty again the minute we go out." Then Jesus gave Christianity its badge—a basin and a towel. The world has seldom seen a stranger thing than Jesus washing the feet of Judas. When he came to Peter, Peter said, "Lord, dost thou wash my feet?" Jesus said, "What I do thou knowest not now, but thou shalt understand hereáfter." "Thou shalt never wash my feet." "If I wash thee not, thou hast no part with me." "Lord, not my feet only, but my hands and my head." Be willing that God should give you just as much as he wants to give. Are you? It is a serious thing. He may say, "You want me to give you a very great blessing; very well; I will let you help bring China to Christ." Then you say, "I did not mean as much as that; I meant a *little* blessing." Ah, be willing that God should choose the blessing and give more than you ask. Do not shrink back as Peter did. Just take what he gives; God knows best. There is in this world a great deal that passes for humility which is pride. Humility says, "I am not worthy," but to that sense of unworthiness comes the blessing that mercy and grace bestow.

ALEXANDER McKENZIE.

263

Why call ye me, Lord, Lord, and do not the things which I say?
—Luke vi. 46.

Christ feels that he has a right to command us,
not only as one who possesses us, but also as one
who has absolute, unquestionable authority over us,
as absolute as the potter's authority over his clay.
We sing to this day of the glory of the "Charge of
the Light Brigade." They knew perfectly well that
no one was justified in giving them the order to ride
to needless annihilation. No one would have blamed
their refusal to obey that order. But without questioning the order they rode straight into the jaws
of death, into the mouth of hell.

If men in war will obey commands which they
know to be unreasonable simply because given by
those in authority, what shall be said of us who call
Jesus Christ "Lord," who know it is impossible for
him to give us anything but loving and reasonable
commands, and who still allow these commands to
go unheeded and disobeyed? It is not our place to
raise objections or postpone obedience by excuses.
The Master will take care of things if we obey him.
But if we disobey him the laws which govern us
carry with them curses to men and women who call
him "Master," but fail to do his bidding. Can any
one for one moment think that we are exempt from
this curse? Why is it that Satan's influence is so
strong? Why is it that all Christian effort finds so
many almost insuperable obstacles in its path of
progress? Simply because generation after generation of those who have called Christ "Master"
have failed to do his bidding, his will.

ROBERT E. SPEER.

Go ye therefore, and make disciples of all the nations, baptizing them into the name of the Father and of the Son and of the Holy Ghost.—Matt. xxviii. 19, R. V.

Do not wait for a *special* call to the foreign field. Do not wait for an avalanche to strike you or for a sheet to be let down from heaven. When Jehovah addressed Elijah, was it through the strong wind? Was the Lord in the earthquake or in the fire? Listen to the "still, small voice." It floats across the ocean. The millions of India, China, Japan, and Africa are crying, "Come over and help us." Who are under more obligation to go than we?

ROBERT P. WILDER.

We who have gone to the front send back an appealing voice to our home churches in all the lands that support us, asking them to hasten on the reinforcements, that the final assault may now be made. We strain our ears to catch the reply. What is it that we hear? "Hold on! you are going too fast. The church at home cannot afford to let you advance any further. Hold what you have gained if you can; but the church of Christ is too poor to let you go on to the final assault for victory." O merciful Jesus! is it thus that we, redeemed by thy precious blood—we for whom on Calvary thou didst cry in agony, "My God, why hast thou forsaken me?"—we, bought by the blood-sweat drops in Gethsemane—is it thus that we show the measure of our love to thee?

JACOB CHAMBERLAIN.

Good impulses are abundant and cheap. They
will never hold you in a sharp fight unless you have
the staying power which Christ imparts. To stand
the sneers of scoffers, to resist the sudden rush for
wealth, to conquer fleshly appetites, to hold an un-
ruly temper under control, to keep base passions
subdued, and to direct all your plans and purposes
straight toward the highest mark require a power
above your own. Christ's mastery of you will give
you self-mastery; yes, and mastery over the powers
of darkness and of hell. Faith will fire the last
shot, and when the battle of life ends you will stand
among the crowned conquerors in glory.

THEODORE L. CUYLER.

It may be a difficult task which is before us, but
we must not be discouraged. Difficulties are what
make character; men who can go into a hard field
and succeed—they are the men we want. Any
quantity of men are looking for easy places, but the
world will never hear of them. We want men who
are looking for hard places, who are willing to go
into the darkest corners of the earth and make those
dark places bloom like gardens. They can do it if
the Lord is with them.

D. L. MOODY.

Many church-members turn up in Sunday clothing at popular conventions and for all dress-parade
occasions, but when there is a real battle with evil
to be fought they are missing. As one has well said,
"The tendency in our day is to take our religion with
too many trimmings."

D. W. WHITTLE.

We need, above all things, more faith in God. You
may say that we cannot have too much of that. Yes,
we can. When Jesus was tempted of the devil he
was taken up on a pinnacle of the temple, and the
devil said, "Jump down." Our Lord replied, "Why
should I jump down?" "Why, simply because the
Bible says that God will give his angels charge over
thee, and they shall bear thee up in their hands,
lest thou dash thy foot against a stone. Now your
Father in heaven will not allow you to dash your
foot against a stone, so you just jump over and trust
to him." Jesus answered, "Thou shalt not tempt
the Lord thy God." You shall not jump off the
pinnacle of any temple unless you are called to do
it in the service of God and for his glory; you shall
not do it simply for the purpose of testing whether
God will keep his promise or not. There is the great
weakness of our Christian life and faith. We ask
God for something very earnestly, but without a
thought as to whether we are tempting God or
whether we are showing faith in him.

Faith in God leaves off and insanity and tempting
and recklessness begin at the moment when we ask
for more power and greater faith, while we intend
to use them for any other purpose than for his own
divine glory. If God had said to Jesus, "Jump off
the pinnacle of the temple, for it will be to my
glory," he would have leaped off. But when it was
only bringing God's power and providence to bear
upon his life with no advantage to the kingdom of
God, he said, "That is tempting God." You have
no right to exercise faith in getting from God that
which does not add to his glory.

RUSSELL H. CONWELL.

If thou canst believe, all things are possible to him that be-
lieveth.—Mark ix. 23.

Why is there no water in the pipes of some of
our houses in winter? It is not because the city
has no water-supply; it is not because the streets
are not threaded all through their length from the
great reservoirs with a perfect system of piping; it
is not that the system of piping does not go into
every house. Then why do we turn the tap in vain
in our houses? Because there is a block of ice in
the pipes. Why is the blessing not leaping and
laughing like bubbling water through humanity?
It is not because the great ocean and fountain of
fullness is not there; it is not because the links of
communication between divine fullness and our
emptiness are not formed. Christ is there and his
church is here, and all the channels and tubes and
pipes of prayer and promise and supplication are
there. What is wrong? There is ice in the pipe;
that is the trouble. The frost has come on our
hearts—we are frozen, and need to be thawed out
by the fire of the Holy Spirit.   JOHN MCNEILL.

Men tell me that the day of miracles has passed,
but I answer no. Miracles have not ceased. *Faith
has ceased.* God offers all things to him who has the
faith to claim them. When he said, "Be filled with the
Spirit," he simply declared that this was possible.
When the will is surrendered he in whose dispensation we live will come in and fill us. And the result
is a kind of passive activity, as if one were wrought
upon and controlled by some power outside of himself.   J. WILBUR CHAPMAN.

268

The Holy Ghost was not yet given; because that Jesus was not yet glorified.—John vii. 39.

What was true in the objective life of Christ must be true of the subjective life of the Christian. Only when Christ is King in your heart will you have the fullness of the Holy Ghost.

F. B. MEYER.

The Holy Spirit is given to make the presence of Jesus an abiding reality, a continual experience. The joy unspeakable, the joy that nothing can take away, the joy of the nearness and friendship and love of Jesus, fills our hearts. This alone will enable us to live in the rest of God. There is only one hindrance: God's people do not know their Saviour. They have no conception of Jesus as an ever-present, all-pervading, indwelling Christ, who longs to take charge of our whole life. Why can we not trust our glorious, exalted, almighty, ever-present Christ perfectly to do his work and bring us into the rest of God? A man can endure almost anything for the hope of joy; Jesus himself, "for the joy that was set before him, endured the cross." A sighing and a trembling and a doubting life is not right. Believe that the joy of the Holy Ghost is meant for you. Do you not believe that this adorable Son of God, who shed his blood for you, could fill your heart with delight day and night, if he were always present? He is longing for you, because he needs you to satisfy his heart of love. Let him have your whole heart, and the joy of the Holy Ghost shall be your portion.

ANDREW MURRAY.

All day long I have stretched forth my hands unto a disobedi-
ent and gainsaying people.—Rom. x. 21.

Have we ever thought of those "hands stretched
forth" from heaven to this world, draining themselves
of love, if it were possible, toward "disobedient and
gainsaying people"? "*All day long* I have stretched
forth my hands," saith the Lord. Is not this wonderful—wonderful? Men have to run away from the
love of God if they are ever without it. They must
get somewhere—I know not where; some strange
cell of their own invention must be found by men
who would escape the love of God; for God's hands
are stretched out, and they drip with riches of mercy.
Yet drops would not suffice, for, as we sing:

> "Mercy-drops round us are falling,
> But for the showers we plead."

And these showers of blessing are really falling upon
us all.   H. W. WEBB-PEPLOE.

This poor lost world that has swung out into the
cold and the dark doesn't know anything about the
love of God, and if we do not love men with the
same kind of love that Jesus had for this lost world,
we are not going to reach them. I wish we could
rise to a higher plane of duty and let love be the
motive power. How easy it is to work for God if
the heart is filled with love! and if it is not filled
with love let us pray God to fill it with love. What
we want is to be baptized with the love of Christ
for this world, and if we are full of love for the
perishing, we are sure to succeed.

                         D. L. MOODY.

In this the children of God are manifest, and the children of the devil: whosoever doeth not righteousness is not of God, neither he that loveth not his brother.—1 John iii. 10.

One of the greatest services of Jesus to the world was to harmonize religion and morality. He would not allow neglect of man to be covered by zeal for God, but ever taught that he only loves God who loves his brother also.

JAMES STALKER.

Tell me to love an unlovely person or one I have never seen,—some heathen in Africa or China,—and I cannot do it unless God puts the love for them in my heart. But when the Holy Ghost sheds abroad the love of God in our hearts, we shall have the same kind of love that Jesus Christ had. What we want is to be baptized with the Spirit of Calvary. Mr. Spurgeon, a few years before he died, went to visit a friend who had built a new barn, on which was a weather-vane, and on that weather-vane the text, "God is love." Mr. Spurgeon said, "Do you mean that God's love is as changeable as the wind?" "No," said his friend; "I mean to say that God is love whichever way the wind blows." So if a man is filled with the Spirit, he will be filled with love whichever way the wind blows.

D. L. MOODY.

The only greatness is unselfish love. . . . There is a great difference between *trying to please* and *giving pleasure*.

HENRY DRUMMOND.

Two Germans wanted to climb the Matterhorn, near which they were staying. They took three guides, and began to climb the mountain in its steepest and most slippery part. When traveling thus they rope themselves together; there was first a guide, next a traveler, then another guide, then the second traveler, and finally a guide—five men in all. When they had been ascending for a short time the guide at the bottom began to slip, but was held up by the other four, whose feet rested in niches cut in the rock; but the last pulled down the man just above him, and these two dislodged the next, and the three the one above them. The only man who kept his footing was the first, who drove his ax with all his might into the ice before him and clung to it; and as he stood, the man beneath regained his footing, and so the next and the next and the next, and the whole party were saved because the first man stood his ground.

I am one of those men that slipped, but, thank God, I am bound in living partnership to Christ in glory, and because he stands, I can never be cast away.　　　　　　　　　　　　F. B. MEYER.

The penitent thief turned to Jesus when of the whole world he alone was praying to Christ. Do not wait to see what others do. There must be personal intrustment of the soul to Jesus' death to sin; personal acceptance of Jesus to do the mighty work.
　　　　　　　　　　　　ANDREW MURRAY.

The gospels nowhere describe Christ's character. They nowhere tell us that he was dignified under insult, calm before opposition, submissive under suffering, indignant at the sight of hypocrisy, sympathetic with sorrow. These characteristics are manifested by him, but never affirmed of him. They appear only in his words and acts. The writers of the first three gospels make no attempt at delineation; they are apparently quite unconscious that they are giving to the world a portrait; they make Christ speak and act before us, and we form our judgment of his character independently, as if we had seen and heard him ourselves. Whatever feelings may spring from reading the gospels, they are never the result of sympathy with the writers. One could not be sure, judging simply from their style, that the synoptic evangelists were not indifferent spectators of what they recorded. There is no writing for effect, no exhibition of their own opinions, but an unadorned narrative which simply recounts the words and works of Christ. From these we get a distinct conception of this divine-human character. JOSIAH STRONG.

Many Christs are now preached, but we know only one—*Jesus*. To some, alas! he is a myth or fabled god; to others merely a hero, philosopher, or poet. Alas for such as are swept down the rapid current of humanitarianism, or are swallowed in the vortex of religious infidelity! Better believe in no Christ than be guilty of acknowledging a perverted or mutilated Christ. Better renounce all belief in the supernatural and spiritual if to us Christ is not verily divine, if Jesus is not God manifest in flesh. GEORGE C. NEEDHAM.

When I see the blood, I will pass over you.—Exod. xii. 13.

God did not say to Israel, and he does not say to us, "When I see your good works, your good intentions, your righteousness," but "When I see *the blood*, I will pass over you." What made those Israelites safe in Goshen when the Egyptians were all exposed to death? It was not their righteousness, but it was an act of obedience; it was putting the blood upon their homes. Some people say that it is not the death of Christ that atones for sin and that is going to help men, but that it is the life and teaching of Christ, the moral example, that it is preaching his character, that will reform the world. God didn't say, "When I see a live lamb tied at your door-post, I will pass over you." If some Israelite had tried that, death would have laid his hand on the first-born in that house. But it was the *death* of the lamb. Many men seem to think that if they were only as good as Moses or Aaron or Caleb or Joshua, they would be perfectly safe. But the babe in his mother's arms was just as safe as Moses or Caleb or Aaron, or any other of the Israelites. It was the blood that made them safe; it was not their own righteousness. If you are sheltered behind the blood, you are as safe as if you were in heaven to-day. Some one has said that a little fly in Noah's ark was as safe as the elephant. It was not the strength of the elephant that made him safe, but it was the ark that saved the elephant as well as the fly; so it is the blood of Christ that saves us.

D. L. MOODY.

We also joy in God through our Lord Jesus Christ, by whom we have now received the atonement.—Rom. v. 11.

Sin and guilt produced entire and hopeless alienation between God and man. The effect of Christ's work is *twofold*: first, it makes possible in God the reconciliation with man by the satisfaction made to a broken law and a dishonored government; and second, it makes possible man's reconciliation with God by the regeneration of his sinful nature. As alienation is *mutual*, so reconciliation must be mutual. Paul represents the reconciliation between man and God as already partial; i. e., on God's side, in Christ, the attitude of reconciliation has been taken. "God was in Christ, reconciling the world unto himself." And so all that remains is for man to turn toward God. He therefore adds, "We pray you in Christ's stead, be ye reconciled to God."

ARTHUR T. PIERSON.

The details of the atonement are questions which concern the government of God. If we choose to pry into them we shall find we are undertaking a very difficult task. The attempts to explain the process of salvation simply lead people into confusion. I think that emphasis ought to be placed upon the whole work of Christ more than it has ever been. The atonement is a question of status, man's standing in God's sight. Christ would also have us concerned about reproducing his life among men.

HENRY DRUMMOND.

There is a popular impression abroad that repentance is simply sorrow for sin. A man may be sorry for sin simply because of the consequences of sin which he has experienced, or because of the consequences which some other person whom he loves has experienced; and yet he may not be so sorry for sin but that, as soon as those consequences are removed, or even before, he will commit that very same sin again and with delight. Pharaoh was sorry for sin; yes, bitterly sorry for disobeying God every time one of those dreadful plagues came down upon him and his household and nation; and yet the moment the plague was removed Pharaoh was the same as before, and his heart was as hard against God as it had ever been. Again, a man may be sorry for sin, that is, for some particular sin, without being at all sorry for some other sins which bring him no difficulty, and at present no bitter consequences. Herod is a case in point here. It is written that the preaching of John the Baptist made quite an impression upon Herod. When he heard John, Herod "did many things, and heard him gladly." The inference is that, as a result of John's preaching, Herod laid aside certain of his external sins, that he reformed in certain particulars; but we know that, like Pharaoh, he never experienced repentance, for not long after, in a drunken debauch, he permitted the murder of the man whom he feared, and whose preaching he received apparently with such gladness of heart. Whatever repentance may be, it is not simply sorrow for sin.

JAMES M. GRAY.

A young girl who had run away from home was living a life of sin, and her mother wanted a friend to find her daughter. This friend took a number of photographs of the mother, and wrote down beneath the sweet face these words: "Come back." Then he took those pictures down into the haunts of sin and the mission stations, and left them there. Not long after this daughter was going into a place of sin and there she saw the face of her mother. The tears ran down her face so that at first she could not see the words beneath; but she brushed away the tears and looked, and there they were: "Come back." She went out to her old home, and when she put her hand on the latch the door was open, and when she stepped in her mother, with her arms about her, said, "My dear child, the door has never been fastened since you went away." The door of God's great heart of love has never been closed against his sinning and erring children; it is wide open.

J. WILBUR CHAPMAN.

Sometimes a sinner will be brought to realize his position and the need of immediate acceptance of Christ by showing him the uncertainty of life. I remember once talking to a young man before others. Said I, "I want you to promise me that you will not become a Christian for one year." "Oh my! No, sir!" said he. I shortened it a little: "Will you make it six months?" That seemed to sober him. "No," he said; "I will make it a month." "No, no." "I will make it a week." The Lord blessed that to his awakening. He realized that he was not sure of his life for a single day.

A. F. SCHAUFFLER.

Resist the devil, and he will flee from you.—James iv. 7.

Resist him when he comes with subtle doubts, with difficult questions, with hard and bitter things against you; drive him back by the sword of the Spirit and the shield of faith; quench all his fiery darts, and listen to the voice of God.

H. W. WEBB-PEPLOE.

Billy Bray, the Cornish miner whose rugged piety has been a blessing to so many of God's children, gives much instruction in his quaint way as to how to treat the temptations of Satan. He says that one day, when he was a little downhearted, he stood upon the brink of a coal-pit, and some one seemed to say, "Now, Billy, just throw yourself down there and be rid of all your trouble." He knew in a minute who it was, and, drawing back, said, "Oh no, Satan; you can just throw yourself down there. That is your way home; but I am going to my home in a different direction." Another time his crop of potatoes turned out poorly; and as he was digging them in the fall, Satan was at his elbow and said, "There, Billy, isn't that poor pay for serving your Father the way you have all the year? Just see those small potatoes." He stopped hoeing and replied, "Ah, Satan, at it again—talking against my Father, bless his name! Why, when I served you I didn't get any potatoes at all. What are you talking against Father for?" And on he went hoeing and praising the Lord for small potatoes—a valuable lesson for us all.

D. W. WHITTLE.

O wretched man that I am! who shall deliver me from the body of this death? I thank God through Jesus Christ our Lord.—Rom. vii. 24, 25.

The bitterest experience with most believers is the presence and power of sin. They long to walk through this grimy world with pure hearts and stainless garments. But when they would do good, evil is present with them. They consent to God's law, that it is good; they endeavor to keep it; but they seem as unable to perform it as a man whose brain has been smitten with paralysis is unable to walk straight. What rivers of tears have been shed over the penitents' psalm by those who could repeat it every word from the heart! And what regiments of weary feet have trodden the Bridge of Sighs, if we may so call the seventh of Romans, which sets forth in vivid force the experience of a man who has not learned God's secret!

Surely our God must have provided for all this. It would not have been like him to fill us with hatred to sin and longings for holiness if there were no escape from the tyranny of the one, and no possibility of attaining the other. It would be a small matter to save us from sinning on the other side of the pearly gate; we want to be saved from sinning now and in this dark world. We want it for the sake of the world, that it may be attracted and convinced. We want it for our own peace, which cannot be perfected while we groan under a worse than Egyptian bondage. We want it for the glory of God, which would be then reflected from us with undimming brightness, as sunshine from burnished metal. Thank God, we may have deliverance through Jesus Christ.   F. B. MEYER.

A great many people have consciences which are morbidly scrupulous. They are constantly asking, "Ought I to wear jewels?" "Ought I to go to this, that, or the other place?" What would a young man think if, when he came to spend one hour a week in the company of his loved one, she was all the while upstairs before the dressing-glass, putting on now this and now the other thing, and seeing how she looked in them, until the last three minutes of his hour, when she would come down, hoping that, on the whole, she would suit? Now a scrupulous conscience is always keeping the soul wondering as to what will suit Christ. You should ask Christ to show you what he would have you do. An enlightened conscience is the contrast, the antipodes, to a scrupulous conscience, and if you want to have an enlightened conscience, bathe it in the truth of God's Word. Some people think that the law of God is soap to cleanse them with. It is not soap; it is a looking-glass in which they may see themselves and compare themselves with God's eternal standard of rectitude.

F. B. MEYER.

We cannot be justified by the law which we have broken. Christ would have committed spiritual adultery if he had brought us into union with himself before he had broken the connection between us and our first husband. But Christ died in our place, that he might destroy him that had the power of death; and when he had overthrown him he rose triumphant, and in the power of an endless life he wedded the soul that believes in him. Now, in union with the risen Lord, the Christian brings forth fruit unto God. MARCUS RAINSFORD.

When God made this world he made laws to regu-
late it. This universe could not exist if it were not
for law, and there cannot be a law without a penalty
for its violation. The controversy of Eden is not
settled yet. God said, "The soul that sinneth, it
shall die." Satan walked in and said, "You will not
die if you sin." Adam believed Satan's lie, and that
is where he fell, and you and I are to rise on the
spot where he tumbled. The law has been broken,
and the penalty must be met. I must either die or
find some one to die for me. Why does God demand
blood? It is the life of all flesh, and all flesh has
sinned and come short of the glory of God; and how
can the law of God be kept, and how can God justify me without ignoring his law? It is an absurdity
to have a law without a penalty. Suppose that no
penalty should be attached to the law against stealing; some man would have my pocket-book inside
of five minutes. It is not the law that people are
afraid of; it is the penalty. I believe there was
one legislature that made a law and forgot to
attach a penalty, and it was the laughing-stock of
the day. Do you suppose God has made a law without a penalty? What an absurd thing it would be!
Now, there is a penalty; it is death. I must either
die or get somebody to die for me, and if that old
Book does not teach that doctrine it does not teach
anything. It teaches it from the beginning to the
end. If God turned Adam out of Eden for that
one sin, do you think he is going to allow us into
heaven with ten thousand sins?

D. L. MOODY.

Wherefore he is able also to save them to the uttermost that come unto God by him, seeing he ever liveth to make intercession for them.—Heb. vii. 25.

Christ Jesus is able to save forever and forever, because he is the same unchangeable priest; he is able to save—to save unto completeness; not simply to begin it and keep at it awhile, but to completeness. Oh, the wrecks in human history of things that men began with noble intent and sustained with high endeavor; but they died, and their work fell through and passed away. Our Saviour "is able to *complete* the salvation of them that come to God through him, seeing he ever liveth."

JOHN A. BROADUS.

A dear old woman lay dying, and an infidel came in to scoff at her, and said, "They tell me you are not afraid to die and are very happy." "Yes, thank God." "Do you believe in a God?" "Yes, I do." "Do you believe God punishes sin?" "Yes, I do." Then the infidel said, "I should like to know how you are happy, for if there ever was a bad old woman you are one. If what you say could be believed, it would be a great deal too good to be true." She looked him in the face and said, "It is—it is a deal too good to be true; but, bless the Lord, it is true, for all that!"

H. W. WEBB-PEPLOE.

Our repentance is far from being the condition of God's forgiveness; the fact is, our tears need washing in the blood of Christ before they can be acceptable. God was in Christ putting away the obstacles to our communion with him.   A. J. GORDON.

I give unto them eternal life; and they shall never perish, neither shall any man pluck them out of my hand.—John x. 28.

What a place of protection! But, as if to make it stronger, Jesus goes on to say, "My Father . . . is greater than all; and no man is able to pluck them out of my Father's hand. I and my Father are one." Here is our position, in the hand of Christ, the hand that swung the worlds off into space, the hand that brushes the tear from a weeping woman's face. Then just above us is placed the hand of the Father, the hand that holds the winds and turns them whithersoever he will; the Father and the Son are one in holding us safe. What protection—held between the hands of the Father and of the Son!

J. WILBUR CHAPMAN.

There are three classes of people who never ought to have assurance: those who have never been converted, but have joined a church to get assurance, those who believe but do not confess Christ, and those who are unwilling to work for Christ. God never intended a lazy person to have assurance. Somebody has said, "If you want to be discouraged, look within; if you want to be distracted, look about; but if you want to be satisfied, look up." Some people live on doubts, because they have nothing else to do. Just be occupied with the Master and his work, and you will have assurance. No matter what the feeling, the relation with God is the same, and even death cannot change it.

D. L. MOODY.

Now the God of peace . . . make you perfect in every good work to do his will, working in you that which is well pleasing in his sight, through Jesus Christ; to whom be glory for ever and ever. Amen.—Heb. xiii. 20, 21.

In order to this we must receive a complete baptism of the life-giving blood and yield ourselves unreservedly to its influence. According to the old Scandinavian legend, "Siegfried slew Fafnir, and in the hot blood of his foe he bathed himself, and so took on, as it were, an outer covering of new life, rendering himself sword-proof save at a single point, where a leaf of the linden-tree fell between his shoulders and shielded the flesh from the life-imparting blood."

Christians, you claim to have been baptized with blood,—the blood, not of a foe, but of your covenant Friend,—and it is life-giving blood, but is it a *full* baptism? Is there no linden-leaf betwixt your shoulders? Is there no unsurrendered sin that makes you vulnerable still to the assaults of Satan? The tragedy of many a life pivots on the reservation of some one cherished purpose. How many unbaptized dollars, how many unbaptized talents, how many unbaptized ambitions, might be found in the visible church? What is *your* reservation? What is the besetting sin that prevents *you* from demonstrating daily your identity of nature with the Son of God? Give it up! It is the death-spot in your armor! Invulnerable you cannot be until you bring the *whole* life under the influence of that shielding blood. Do that, and the very God of peace will sanctify you wholly, and your whole spirit and soul and body will be preserved blameless unto the coming of our Lord Jesus Christ.   W. W. MOORE.

284

Happy is he that condemneth not himself in that thing which he alloweth.—Rom. xiv. 22.

Apply that rule to your daily life and you will soon settle the questions about a pleasure or business. Can I go into partnership with one who serves man and the devil? How can Christ have fellowship with Belial? Do not deceive yourself with the idea you are going to do good. If you make yourself one with the world on the plea of raising the world to God, you know that you will have to pay for it in the day of the Lord's settlement.

H. W. WEBB-PEPLOE.

There is a subtle leakage of power in a man who is inconsistent with his best self. He may not show it, he may seem as devoted and earnest as possible, but there is a loss of the dynamics of spiritual force, and the devil knows it and says, "I need not worry; his sins are sufficient antidote for his work."

F. B. MEYER.

A man cannot have the kingdom of God first, and then at times, by way of relaxation, throw it off and seek his own enjoyment in the things of this world. People have an idea that life will become too solemn, too great a strain, if they have the kingdom of God first continually. Every one feels at once how wrong it is to think thus. The presence of the love of God must every moment be our highest joy.

ANDREW MURRAY.

Many Christians get cold warming themselves by this world's fires.   A. J. GORDON.

Your consecration is not so much a consecration
which you make to Christ as a consecration which
Christ makes of you to himself. The one conspicuous instance of consecration in the New Testament
is where Jesus says to the Father in his prayer, "Father, I consecrate myself." He could do it. To
consecrate means to appoint, to ordain, to separate
or sanctify. If Christ had been a modern preacher
he would have said, "Now, my friends, consecrate
yourselves." He did not say that, but, "I consecrate myself; Father in heaven, consecrate my disciples. I separate myself; Father, separate them."
If there is any consecration that is effective, Christ
must consecrate us to his service. There seems to
be a provision for a periodical consecration which
ought not to be in any calendar or any meeting.
Never appoint a time a month ahead for a consecration meeting. Well, but you say you may fall
away. Very well; but don't provide for it beforehand. If you expect to fall away before the first
Sunday of every month you will probably do it. If
sometime in the middle of the month you find that
you are faltering, come back and devote yourself
again to God; but do it feeling that you can live
a Christian life by the force of the Christ-life which
he gives to you. It is a dreadful thing that so many
people are trying to consecrate themselves and save
themselves and strengthen themselves and work
their way out through life. You must let God consecrate you and strengthen and support you. Not
all the good books in the world, not the Bible, not
the church, not the sacraments, without Christ in
them and working through them, can do you much
good.   ALEXANDER MCKENZIE.

Month of October

The nineteenth century is apt to quietly sneer us out of our faith in the miraculous. We feel the blush inclined to steal upon our cheeks, and "with bated breath and bated whispering humbleness" we would allow judgment to go by default, because we do not like to say that we do believe in the miraculous stories in the Bible. You remember how it was with Peden, the great Scotch prophet, in the killing times in Scotland when King James was the Herod. Poor Peden, for the faith and fear of Jesus Christ, was being persecuted, with a little band of his followers to whom he had been preaching in dens and caves of the earth in the south of Scotland. They were alarmed in time and determined to make a struggle for existence; they made a rush for safety. Their pursuers, being horsemen, gained on them, and when Peden and his little band had gone down into the hollow of a hill, for want of breath and for want of hope, he called a halt, and then he uttered a memorable prayer. "O God," he said, "it is the day and the hour of the power of thine enemies. They may not be idle, but hast thou no other work for them than to send them after us? Send them to pursue those to whom thou wilt give strength to flee; but as for us, our strength is gone. Twine them round the hill, O Lord, and cast the lap of thy cloak round Sandy and these puir things, and we shall tell to thy praise and glory what thou didst for us at sic a time." As surely as he prayed one of those dangerous, sudden, blinding mists for which our Cheviot hills are famous came down upon them. Their enemies with curses thundered past them through the mist and never saw them.

JOHN MCNEILL.

Rejectors of the gospel will often be heard saying, "Well, the Mohammedan has his belief, and the Hindu his belief, and the Parsee his belief, and the Christian his belief. They all have faith, and each one who is sincere in his faith will be accepted of God." If *faith* simply saved this might be so. But with the statement, "God hath given to us eternal life, and this life is *in his Son.* He that hath *the Son* hath life; and he that hath not the Son hath not life," before us, its fallacy is readily seen. If a man puts faith in a real, living person who has power to save him, and who engages to save him, he is certainly in a different position from the man who puts faith in that which has not life and which is not truth.

There were those in the time of Noah who undoubtedly had firm belief, as the rain commenced falling, that the hills would be just as safe a refuge for them as the ark. Their firm belief made no difference in their fate. Noah had a firm belief in God's word that the *ark* would save him. His belief led him to go into the ark, and the *ark*, not his belief, saved him. Christ is the ark in which we find salvation. D. W. WHITTLE.

When men ask us what we believe, our answer should be, "It is not *what* I believe, but it is in *whom* I believe." "I know *whom* I have believed." I should have a personal knowledge of the person in whom I believe. Christians have nothing to do with "its" in their belief. Our creed and our blessing are vitally connected with Christ; more than that, they are Christ himself.

H. W. WEBB-PEPLOE.

So long as there is a radical difference between truth and falsehood, and so long as truth sustains relations to life, it will make a difference whether men believe true or false doctrine. Doctrines are the roots of life. Great lives do not grow out of false beliefs. Doctrine is immensely important, but not all-important. The root does not exist for itself; it is a means to the tree and the fruit as an end. A Christian truth in the heart brings forth Christian acts in the life as naturally as the root pushes its stalk up into the air and the sun. Cut the stalk, fell the tree, and the root dies at length. A faith without works is soon dead. If our doctrines do not flower and fruit in Christian living, they die. Many a man's creed is a field full of stumps. There was life there once, but because the natural expression of that life was prevented, it perished. We have not overestimated the importance of *believing* the truth, but we have underestimated the importance of *living* the truth.

JOSIAH STRONG.

There can be nothing acceptable to God which does not begin with faith, but he who is contented with becoming a believer is like a man who expends all his strength in laying a good foundation and then ceases to build.

WILLIAM HENRY GREEN.

What the eye is to the body, faith is to the soul. You don't dig your eyes out to see if you have the right kind, but you are doing that to your faith.

D. L. MOODY.

289

Have faith in God.—Mark xi. 22.

What do they think God is who speak of the "good old times" or long for past hours when they better knew and enjoyed the blessing and fellowship of Christ? What kind of a God do they think we have? Does he not always keep the best things for the last? Is his love stronger than his strength, that we had the best things yesterday and the day before, and are not having yet better things to-day, nor to have better things to-morrow? A true theology insists that this month is the best month of our lives. Every day is the best day, and the next day will be better.

ROBERT E. SPEER.

Trust the providence of God, but do not tempt him by expecting too much. There are times when we have no right to dismiss a subject by saying, "God is God, and he will take care of his own." The question really, then, is this: We have a duty to perform, and God expects us to be of some use in the world. We must pray; but pray for that which will be for his glory. Do not ask God for things which it is not best for him to give. Be not dissatisfied when God says no to your request. There is a difference between the things which we are to receive and those which we are not to receive, and to discover this difference we need to pray especially for the indwelling Spirit of the living God.

RUSSELL H. CONWELL.

Faith is the golden key that unlocks the doors of heaven.   D. L. MOODY.

Let him ask in faith, nothing wavering: for he that wavereth is like a wave of the sea driven with the wind and tossed.— James i. 6.

The church is weak to-day because it has not come to appreciate the distinction between asking and taking, between praying and claiming. They may be parts of the same act, but alas! in too many cases life passes by in perpetually pleading with God to give certain gifts which all the while are waiting for the suppliant soul upon the outstretched palm of God, and all that the soul needs is to take. Say to yourself, "My Father has blessed me with all spiritual blessings in Christ," and then ask yourself whether you are not living a life that seems to be in the most distinct contradiction to the assertion of that text. Now it is either true that God has blessed you or has not blessed you with all spiritual blessings in Christ. You are bound to believe that God has put into Jesus Christ as your trustee his own unsearchable wealth, that he has vested in the hand of Jesus for every member of his mystical body, the church, his own divine fullness. Then how is it that your life is so threadbare? Do you live in your home day by day as a spiritual millionaire? Do you not rather live as a pauper? What is the result of your influence upon your family and upon others who know you best? Do you give them to feel that there is something within your reach that they have not yet touched, though they have all the riches of the Indies? If we were once to live as though we had something that they have not, we would not have to press men to come to us; they would come without pressing.

F. B. MEYER.

Human life is character-building; for remember that character means exactly what we are, while reputation is only what other people think we are. Every man builds his own character. Fix one fact in your mind, however, and that is, the better and stronger Christian you are, the more dearly you must pay for it. All the best things are costly. Jesus Christ laid down his life to redeem you from sin and death. "Free grace" for you meant Calvary for Christ. A strong godly character is not to be had gratis. THEODORE L. CUYLER.

The foundation of the spiritual temple that God is erecting, in which the Holy Ghost will dwell, is faith. Perseverance is the engineer that adds tier upon tier and stair upon stair. Brotherly love is the cement that binds all the stones together. Memory comes and hangs the walls with tender pictures of the past. Joy comes and fills every apartment with flowers plucked from the Paradise of God. Love comes and fills the halls with music, and at last hope comes and throws over the edifice a beautiful dome, through which aspiration looks up and longs for heaven. But even then, when man enters that edifice so divine, it only is to clothe him for better, nobler service here upon earth, and to prepare him for life eternal. M. D. HOGE.

We must not spend all our lives in cleaning our windows, but in sunning ourselves in God's blessed light. That light will soon show us what still needs to be cleansed, and will enable us to cleanse it with unerring accuracy. F. B. MEYER.

The best things in life have to be given freely, not from a sense of duty. You never can measure out friendship; you never can tell how much a man ought to do for his country; you never can tell what he should do for God. There is always that overflow, that abundance, which is chiefly valuable for us, and is valuable to God as it comes as the freewill offering of our hearts. You say of a certain person that he is just, implying you don't quite like him. You say of another person that he is generous, meaning that you do like him. It is because of that which he does beyond what he is obliged to do. If there is any life where this applies with the utmost force it is to the religious life. Your piety must make the cup overflow. If you do exactly your duty and nothing else, your life is no comfort to you and little help to any one else. You want something of joyousness and freedom in it and then it tells.

ALEXANDER MCKENZIE.

There is a Christian life which, in comparison with that experienced by the majority of Christians, is as summer to winter, or as the mature fruitfulness of a golden autumn to the struggling promise of a cold and late spring. This life should be the normal life of every Christian. It is God's thought not for a few, but for all his children. The youngest and weakest may lay claim to it equally with the strongest and oldest. We should step into it at the moment of conversion, without wandering with blistered feet for forty years in the desert.

F. B. MEYER.

It was only when Luther could say, "Martin Luther does not live here; Jesus Christ lives here," that God could use Luther. And it was only as Paul could say, "I am crucified with Christ: nevertheless I live; yet not I, but Christ liveth in me," that Paul could be used of God. We cannot truly say, "Whom I serve," until we have said, "Whose I am."

B. FAY MILLS.

A French officer whose ship had been taken by Nelson was brought on board Nelson's vessel, and he walked up to the great admiral and gave him his hand. "No," said Nelson; "your sword first, please." That is the gospel. Many people would take Christ's hand and say he is a noble character. Give up your rebellious will first; admit your guilt; then Christ will take your hand and never let go.

JOHN MCNEILL.

"The creature is dead, but he don't know it," said an Irishman, as he looked at the moving legs of a turtle whose head he had cut off a few hours before. "The flesh is dead in me," says the modern opponent of Paul; but the lively motions of the flesh that are often seen by the onlooker make him doubt if the flesh knows it. The remedy in all things for a believer is, to *know Christ*.

D. W. WHITTLE.

God hates the self-life dressed in sanctified clothes as much as when it is dressed in rags.

F. B. MEYER.

The sentence of death is on everything that is of
nature. But how many of us cherish it and try to
escape the sentence or to forget it! We do not
believe fully that the sentence of death is on us.
We must die daily. Jesus lived every day in the
prospect of the cross, and we, in the power of his
victorious life being made conformable to his death,
must rejoice every day in going down with him into
death. Take an oak some hundred years old. How
was that oak born? In a grave. A grave was made
for the acorn that the acorn might die. It died and
disappeared; it cast roots downward and shoots upward, and now that tree has been standing one hundred years in its grave. But all the time it has
stood in the very grave where it died it has been
growing higher and stronger and more beautiful.
All the fruit it ever bore and all the foliage that
adorned it year by year it owed to that grave in
which its roots are cast and kept. Even so we owe
everything to the death and grave of Jesus. Oh,
let us live every day rooted in the death of Jesus!

ANDREW MURRAY.

If a man is not willing to go to heaven by the
way of Calvary he cannot go at all. Many men
want a religion in which there is no cross, but they
cannot enter heaven that way. If we are to be disciples of Jesus Christ we must deny ourselves, and
take up our cross, and follow him. Do not think
that you will have no battles if you follow the Naza-
rene; many battles are before you. Men do not
object to a battle if they are confident that they
will have victory, and, thank God, every one of us
may have the victory if we will. D. L. MOODY.

How excellent is thy loving-kindness, O God! therefore the children of men put their trust under the shadow of thy wings.— Ps. xxxvi. 7.

Loving-kindness is love in action. "God is love." Then Jesus Christ is loving-kindness, God manifesting his love to us. Notice, "wings" is plural. The wing of God's power is to me no protection. I am afraid of power. Power let loose may destroy me. In the thunderbolt there is power that kills. God's omnipotence, viewed alone or linked with his justice, gives me no comfort; but linked with his love I find shelter beneath it. My danger is great in proportion to the power that may be against me. My safety is great in proportion to the power that may be for me. God's power linked with his love is for me; and I put trust under the shadow of the wings of his love and power.   A. C. DIXON.

People used to speak of God as a tyrant, and as if to be in his hands was to be next to all that was miserable and terrible. The hands that bled for me on the cross mean only to bless me. O hands of the Crucified, shall I dread to intrust my life to you? Nay; the misery of life will not be to be *in* the hand, but to be *outside* the hand of God. Never be afraid of God, unless you are sinning against him; always believe that behind what seems difficult and mysterious there is a heart as true and tender as the heart of the sweetest, gentlest woman that ever pressed her child to her bosom. Nay; all the love in all women's hearts together, compared to the love of his heart, is as a glow-worm's torch compared to the sun at noontide.   F. B. MEYER.

296

Behold, I have graven thee upon the palms of my hands; thy walls are continually before me.—Isa. xlix. 16.

Faithful Jews who were about to take a distant journey employed an artist to grave or paint a picture of Jerusalem upon the palms of their hands; so that when they were far away from the beloved city of the sanctuary they had but to open their hand and behold its memorial before them. In like manner, our Lord has gone into a "land of far distances." But he too has carried inside the veil the memorial of his beloved church. Those pierced hands remind him of his cross and passion and of the victory he has achieved over sin. And they are busy hands; every day and hour they are recording as with the graving of a diamond in the register of God the names of some new souls born into the kingdom of heaven.

GEORGE C. NEEDHAM.

Think what God is trying all the while to do for us, and see if it is not beyond our greatest thought. Christ is more than teacher. He is our divine Lord and Saviour, able to save to the uttermost. Oh, if the world were willing to take what he is so ready to bestow! If we desired more we should receive more. It is because our prayers are too narrow, because we only want to fill the cup up within an inch of the top, that we are poor; when we are willing that the cup shall run over there comes a springing out from heaven, a pouring down from above of that which fills the cup from the great wealth and mercy of our God.

ALEXANDER MCKENZIE.

·If ye abide in me, and my words abide in you, ye shall ask what ye will, and it shall be done unto you.—John xv. 7.

God is the source of the spiritual electric energy, and when we insulate ourselves from the world by prayer and communion with Christ it is precisely as it is with filling a body with electric energy : the spiritual power of God fills us. I have found in my own life that there is a very close proportion between the time I spend in communion with God and the amount of power that I have in dealing with men.

R. A. TORREY.

Every prayer should be actuated by a love for God and a desire to be used in his service. Every prayer should be judged by this standard: Will it be of use to the Lord God? Is it for his glory? "God, give me health to-day." Why? "Oh, because I shall feel better." Ah! that is not prayer; that is only presumption. "Lord, give me an ability that I have not now." What for? "Because I shall hold a higher place in the world's estimation." That is presumption. "Lord, help me to get such an education as shall give me influence with men, that I may be able to earn more money." It is tempting God. "Lord, keep my family alive." "Lord, preserve the life of my sick child, because I shall need that child's love by and by in order to be happy myself." It is tempting God. But the prayer that says, "Lord, give me health that I may glorify thee; give me wisdom that I may use it for thee; preserve the life of my child that I may bring her up for *thee*," is the prayer of faith.

RUSSELL H. CONWELL.

The hour cometh, and now is, when the true worshipers shall worship the Father in spirit and in truth: for the Father seeketh such to worship him.—John iv. 23.

No idea of prayer reaches a higher point than worship, which is the form which fills the Apocalypse. The soul is lost in thought of God. What new appreciation of adorable qualities! In Psalm xxix., that psalm of nature where the creation is seen as a temple, all nature is God's grand cathedral; the waters are the great organ with its deep diapason, and the thunders peal forth like the colossal pipes of the pedals; cyclones and whirlwinds are the choir with majestic voices; the lightnings are the electric lamps; giant oaks and cedars are the bowing worshipers; and the psalmist says, "In his temple doth everything shout, Glory!"

ARTHUR T. PIERSON.

In prayer there is worship, when a man just bows down to adore the great God. We do not take enough time to worship. I hope to spend eternity in worshiping God.

There is not only the worship of a king, but fellowship as a child with God. Christians think prayer is only asking and thanksgiving. If Christ is to make me what I am to be I must tarry in fellowship with God. I may put a poker in the fire twenty times in the course of the day, and leave it there two or three minutes each time, and it never will be thoroughly heated. If you are to get the fire of God's holiness and love and power burning in your heart you must take more time in his fellowship.

ANDREW MURRAY.

299

Lo, I am with you alway, even unto the end of the world.—
Matt. xxviii. 20.

Man when he promises for the future needs to
say, "I will do;" but God can say nothing stronger
than "I do" or "I am." Thus the promise of
promises of Jesus to his disciples as their ever-
present, all-sustaining Lord is, "Lo, I am with you
alway;" not "Lo, I *will be*," but "Lo, I *am*." So
God's covenant promise to Israel to be their loving,
guarding, and guiding God for all time to come is
in the words, "I am Jehovah thy God, which brought
thee out of the land of Egypt, out of the house of
bondage." HENRY CLAY TRUMBULL.

The Lord said to Moses, "Say unto them, 'I AM
hath sent me.'" Some one has said that God gave
him a blank check and all he had to do was to fill
it out from that time on. When he wanted to bring
water out of the rock all he had to do was to fill out
the check; it was the same when he wanted bread;
he had a rich banker. God had taken him into
partnership with himself. D. L. MOODY.

Herein it was that Israel sinned: they never could
take in the Godhead, I AM. They never could
realize that they were dealing with One to whom
past, present, and future are absolutely one. They
deigned to accept what God had accomplished, but
dared to doubt what God had promised.

The moment a man doubts the unknown future
he has boldly said to God, "Thou liest," and it is
the one sin there is no salvation for. Every sin can
be forgiven except blasphemy against the Holy
Ghost. H. W. WEBB-PEPLOE.

And this is life eternal, that they might know thee the only true God, and Jesus Christ, whom thou hast sent.—John xvii. 3.

Ignorance is the chief sin of our time. You say unbelief is. I think not. You say the great need is faith. But when we have intelligence we shall have faith. We need knowledge of God. I do think that people need most in this world to-day belief in God. It is a very rare man that truly and deeply believes in God. If you believe in God you see him in everything, in the birds and flowers and brightness and beauty as well as when the storms gather and sorrow sweeps over you. If a man believes there is a God his belief controls him all through his being. Jesus said, "Let your light so shine before men that they will glorify God." In order to make other men think of God we must believe in him and must have such a strong obedience coming out of our belief that men will take knowledge of us that we believe in God and know him.

ALEXANDER MCKENZIE.

We don't want the faith that comes by seeing, but the seeing that comes by faith.

JOHN MCNEILL.

When Christ said to his disciples, "Have faith in God," he did not mean, "Accept this moment all the doctrines which I have been propounding to you," though he well knew that that would follow from a surrender to him. What he meant was that they, personally, should surrender their lives in the absolute confidence of an unwavering trust to God.

ROBERT E. SPEER.

God has given us powers, and he means that we shall study to know what they are. Half the life-blunders come from not knowing one's self. If we overrate our abilities we attempt more than we can accomplish; if we underrate our abilities we might accomplish more than we attempt. In both cases life loses just so much from its sum of power. Not a few come to know themselves only through failures and disappointments. Strangers to their own defects,—perhaps also to their own powers,—they see how they might have succeeded only when success is finally forfeited. Their eyes open too late. A Southern orator tells of a little negro who very much wished to have a kitten from a new-born litter, and whose mistress promised that as soon as they were old enough he should take one. Too impatient to wait, he slyly carried one off to his hut. Its eyes were not yet open, and in disgust he drowned it. But subsequently, finding the kitten lying in the pail dead, but with open eyes, he exclaimed, "Humph! when you's alive you's blind; now you's dead you see!" Pity, indeed, if our eyes open only when it is too late to make life of use!

ARTHUR T. PIERSON.

Is your life what you want it to be? Is it satisfactory? I hear people sometimes say in prayer-meeting, "I want a few crumbs from the Master's table." Well, you may have them if you want to; crumbs are good for cats and dogs; but I am going for the *whole loaf*. The Lord doesn't want his people to live on crumbs; he is longing to give them a whole loaf.

D. L. MOODY.

When men are puzzled about the doctrine of the
Trinity they would do well to consider their own
nature, and discover in the spirit, soul, and body the
trinity in unity of the one personality of the individual. Man is like the Jewish temple: the most
holy place represented the spirit; the holy place,
where the priests did their work, the soul; and the
outer courts the body. In the unregenerate man
the holy of holies of the spirit, which was meant to
hold converse with God, is left dark and untenanted;
or with some the holy of holies, which was meant
for God, may be inhabited by the spirit of evil. I
am inclined to think that in most cases it is simply
untenanted, so that the natural man is a man the
holy of holies of whose spirit is empty; therefore
his nature is dominated entirely by the soul of his
natural life. We can easily understand, then, why
the body is not kept right, because nothing can
dominate the body but spirit. In regeneration the
Spirit of God becomes the Shechinah of the most
holy place, so that what before had been dark now
becomes illuminated. Even in a regenerate man
there is often failure because the man, whose
personality resides always in the soul, the holy
place, has the choice of living according to the
spirit in the holy-of-holies place, or according to
the flesh in the outer court, and chooses the latter
in preference to the former and so becomes a carnal
Christian. F. B. MEYER.

What this world wants is this doctrine thundered
out, *regeneration by the power of the Holy Ghost.* No
man is really born of God until he is brought into
harmony with God's plan, and then God can work in
him and through him. D. L. MOODY.

303

If you would go to heathen lands to work for Christ first satisfy yourself fully as to the inspiration of the Scriptures. Don't go to war with a quiverful of arrows the shafts of which are partly hickory and partly mullen stocks. If a missionary believes the Scriptures are inspired only in patches the heathen will trip up his heels as easily as if he were standing on ice. When you point to them the stupid cosmogony of their sacred books, and from thence argue their unreliability as religious guides, they will retort, "But you say there are scientific errors in your Bible, and that the Word of your God is contained in your Scriptures along with some rubbish. Now you know how to sympathize with us. The divine truths of our religion are contained in our "shasters." Unfortunately, our writers did not know everything, as you say yours did not, and some rubbish has crept into ours too." If you are lame and halting then better stay at home. We want strong and able-bodied men who know what they believe and why they believe it and are ready to assert it with vigor. WILLIAM ASHMORE.

What are soldiers good for if they don't know how to use their weapons? What is a young man starting out in the Christian work good for if he does not know how to use his Bible? A man isn't worth much in battle if he has any doubt about his weapon, and I have never found a man who has his doubts about the Bible who has amounted to much in Christian work. I have seen work after work wrecked because men lost confidence in the truth of this old Book. D. L. MOODY.

I know of nothing which would be more ridiculous, if it were not so lamentable and fraught with evil, than to see a man wise in his own conceit go on the cool assumption that the church, the Bible, Christendom, and the great God himself have no rights except such as first vindicate themselves to his lordly reason. Suppose the village poetaster should so treat "Paradise Lost," or the village architect should express grave doubts as to the excellence of the dome of St. Peter's. "Paradise Lost" and the dome of St. Peter's would not feel it much, but it would fix the grade of the architect and the poet.

CYRUS D. FOSS.

I believe that all the philosophy and literary criticism and the study of history, when rightly undertaken, will constitute an overwhelming argument in vindication of our belief in the Bible. I look for the coming of a good time when men who now disparage and despise and set at naught this Book will treat it as the inspired Word of God.

FRANCIS L. PATTON.

I would that every student of the Bible would take the motto which Bengel took for his guidance in study: "Apply thyself wholly to the Scriptures, and apply the Scriptures wholly to thyself." Learned critics are applying themselves wholly to the Scriptures with microscopic intensity of search and research, but they neglect the other half. We hear of some people who are famous at taking a sword and cutting up the Scripture, but we would like to see the Scripture, which is itself a sword, go through these men and cut some of them up.

A. J. GORDON.

305

> But the natural man receiveth not the things of the Spirit of God: for they are foolishness unto him: neither can he know them, because they are spiritually discerned.—1 Cor. ii. 14.

No one can so well explain the meaning of words as he who wrote them. Tennyson could best explain some of his deeper references in "In Memoriam." If, then, you wish to read the Bible as you should, make much of the Holy Ghost, who inspired it through holy men. As you open the book lift up your heart and say, "Open thou mine eyes, that I may behold wondrous things out of thy law. Speak, Lord; for thy servant heareth." F. B. MEYER.

The natural man discerneth not the things of the Spirit. This Bible is burglar-proof against unsanctified learning that seeks to penetrate into its mysteries. The violent have attempted to take it by force, but the Holy Spirit alone has the key to this treasure-house, and he only knows the combination of prayer and faith by which it can be unlocked and all the treasures of wisdom and righteousness therein stored be found out and appropriated. God forbid that I should despise any kind of learning. On the contrary, I put my strong emphasis on the importance of it. Modifying Augustine's phrase, let us remember that the sufficiency of learning is to discover that learning is insufficient. Your responsibility is that you make the Spirit of God your private tutor, and then you cannot be led very far astray. It is one thing not to know, it is another thing through the pride of unsanctified learning to be led to forget, that the Word of God is not to be comprehended by secular learning but by the guidance of the Holy Spirit.

A. J. GORDON.

Prophecy came not in old time by the will of man: but holy men of God spake as they were moved by the Holy Ghost.— 2 Pet. i. 21.

The consummate prophecy of Scripture is the Messianic. These prophecies were sufficiently remote in time to have made it impossible for the prophets to have influenced the results. Between the two Testaments was a space of four hundred years. There was absolutely no inspired prediction between Malachi and Matthew. As to minuteness of detail, Canon Liddon found three hundred and thirty-three distinct predictions concerning the Messiah. In order to estimate the chance of all these particulars meeting in one person, you must raise $\frac{1}{2}$ to the three hundred and thirty-second power, which is $\frac{1}{85,000,000,000}$, i.e., there is but one chance in 85,000,000,000! The promise that the seed of the woman shall bruise the head of the serpent is the germ of all Messianic prophecy. If there was to be but a single fruit to appear on a tree of over three hundred branches, and you must determine the particular twig on which that fruit should appear, every new ramification of the branches would make it more difficult to determine the exact twig. Of Adam's sons one must be the progenitor of the Messiah, and Seth is chosen. Noah has three sons; Japheth is chosen. Abraham has two sons; Isaac is chosen. Isaac has two sons; Jacob is chosen. Jacob has twelve sons, and one of the twelve must be Christ's ancestor—Judah. So the lineage ramifies indefinitely until we reach the very household in which Jesus Christ was born.

ARTHUR T. PIERSON.

In looking at the stars through a great telescope,
it is necessary first to put out every light until you
are left in total darkness. Every light sets the air
in motion, and disturbs the focus, and blurs the
vision of the stars. How often our vision of God is
blurred and dimmed by the flames of self-consciousness and sordidness that float around us! How
many times we have to put out the light of self-
seeking, earthly ambition and false pride of position
in order to look upward, and in the clear still air
know whither God's lights are leading us and what
God will have us to do!

W. H. P. FAUNCE.

It is difficult to convince men of anything which
they do not wish to believe. They demand evidence,
and what would afford proof to an unbiased mind is
often quite insufficient to convince men against
their will, while that which harmonizes with pre-
conceived opinion is often accepted with little or no
evidence. The narrower men are, the more difficult
is it to convince them of anything which runs
counter to their prejudices.

JOSIAH STRONG.

It is supposed by some, altogether falsely, that
faith is opposed to reason and that Christ does not
claim intellect. His very name is the Word and the
wisdom of God, and he demands the cultivation of
all our faculties, and he bids us prepare ourselves
in order that we may do his work.

A. C. A. HALL.

My friends, the outcome is bright. Men will keep on until they shall have circumnavigated the globe of thought,—these earnest men, these philosophical adventurers, these scientific discoverers,—and when they come back, as they surely will, to the old land from which they have set out, they will say with an earnestness they never knew before, "We believe in God the Father Almighty, Maker of heaven and earth." And when they get so far they will go on and say, "And in Jesus Christ, his only Son." The day of reconciliation between science and religion is not afar off. High authorities in philosophy tell us that agnosticism is on the wane. We look for the coming of the day which shall end the long estrangement, when science shall confess, "We know in part, but then we *know*," and religion will reply, "We know, but then we know only *in part*." FRANCIS L. PATTON.

We sometimes look upon this world and say, "It is no use; the race is corrupt and there is no promise." Stop! the promise is not in the men, but in the Word of God and the Spirit of God. Be faithful, consecrated, hopeful. Some day the world will be filled with the righteousness and peace of God. GEORGE C. LORIMER.

Thank God, the stone cut out of the mountain is growing and is going to come into collision with the image, which will become like the chaff of a threshing-floor. My friends, I am no pessimist, and I thank God for the outlook. I believe the time is coming when the voice of men will only give out the echo of God's voice, when Jesus Christ shall come to sway his scepter over the whole earth. D. L. MOODY.

309

For the kingdom of God is not meat and drink; but righteousness, and peace, and joy in the Holy Ghost.—Rom. xiv. 17.

The kingdom of God is righteousness; that represents the work of the Father. The foundations of
his throne are justice and judgment and peace;
that is the work of the Son; he is our peace, our
Shiloh, our rest. The kingdom of God is peace; not
only the peace of pardon for the past, but of perfect
assurance as to the future. Not only the work of
atonement is finished, but the work of sanctification
also is finished in Christ. The new man has been
completed, and I need only live out my life in him;
and then, if a kingdom is established in righteousness, there can be perfect rest. Then if there be
peace without and within there can be also joy, the
work of the Holy Spirit.

ANDREW MURRAY.

According to God's idea, the first element of religion is righteousness, and there are two kinds of
righteousness spoken of in the Bible: the imputed
righteousness and the imparted righteousness. The
imputed righteousness is that which was lived out
by the Lord Jesus Christ in a life of perfect devotion
to God and in a death that was substitutionary, and
that righteousness is imputed to every one who puts
his trust in the Lord Jesus Christ. The imparted
righteousness is that which is imparted to the soul
after it has believed in Jesus Christ, whereby it
grows in fitness for the life here and for the inheritance of the saints in glory.

W. W. MOORE.

Thou wilt keep him in perfect peace, whose mind is stayed on thee: because he trusteth in thee.—Isa. xxvi. 3.

There is the secret of peace; that was the source of Daniel's peace in the den of lions.

I can imagine Daniel walking through the streets of Babylon on his way to be cast to the lions, according to the king's decree. He was the greatest character that ever walked the streets of Babylon. He moved like a giant, like a conqueror; they cast him to the lions. There was no music in the palace that night. The king was in great distress; he could not sleep; and early the next morning you could see an unusual sight—the king abroad in his chariot; and you could hear the chariot go rattling over the pavements of the streets. What does it mean? I see that royal chariot sweeping up to the lions' den, and the king goes to the mouth of the den and cries to Daniel, "Is thy God, whom thou servest continually, able to deliver thee from the mouths of the lions?" And a voice comes up out of that den: "My God has sent his angels and shut the mouths of the lions." The calmest man in all Babylon that night, in my opinion, was Daniel. He prayed with his face toward Jerusalem, and after prayer took a lion for a pillow and lay down to sleep with a clear conscience. The king took him with him back to the palace, and then sent out a decree that the one hundred and twenty should be cast into the lions' den, and they were all devoured before ever they came to the bottom of the den. "There is no peace, saith my God, to the wicked," but the man who trusts in the Lord need never be troubled.   D. L. MOODY.

Christ came not alone to preach the gospel, but to *be* the gospel. When the cross was taken down scarcely any one knew that Jesus had ever been in the world, and his own disciples did not know clearly and fully why he had come. One thing was done to make the redemption of the world by Jesus Christ known to the world, and that was done in one instance by the Sea of Galilee. Jesus wanted something done, but he never hired any one and he never will. He said to Peter, "Simon, do you love me enough to do anything just because you love me?" Simon answered, "Lord, I do." Then Jesus said, "Simon, I have died for the world, and the world does not know it. Do you see those sheep? They are my sheep; I have been feeding them; and now I am going out of the world. Simon, will you take care of these sheep?" "Yes, Lord." "I shall depend upon you, Simon; those sheep will starve to death if you do not feed them." "But, Lord, what is John going to do?" "No matter about John. Simon, will you feed my sheep?" Simon said, "Lord, I will." Then Jesus went to heaven with no more anxiety; and if, when he reached heaven, some archangel had said, "Son of God, thou didst die for the world; does the world know it?" "Scarcely any one." "What arrangement have you made?" "Simon said he would go and tell the world that I have died." "And you trusted Simon?" "Yes." "But, Lord, you might as well never have left heaven if Simon fails you." "I know it. I depend upon him." Jesus knew that love never faileth, and so he went calmly to his eternal home. Then the Holy Spirit came, and men witnessed and preached.

ALEXANDER McKENZIE.

It seems to me as if there has been but one instance of faith. Jesus Christ went to heaven, not calling legions of angels, but trusting a handful of fishermen to tell men of his death on the cross for them. No men were truer than they; before those men had left the world there was scarcely a tribe upon the earth that had not heard of the redeeming love of the world's Saviour. It needed but to carry it on a little longer, and long, long ago the whole world would have heard the story, and foreign missions would never have been known.

But there came a time when the men disappointed this trust. The shepherds began to feed the sheep a little less, and presently the work of shepherds was to make the sheep feed them. An old writer has said that in the early days of the church they had wooden chalices and golden bishops, but now the church has golden chalices and wooden bishops. One of the popes said, "The time has gone by when the church had to say, 'Silver and gold have I none.'" "Yes," was the answer; "and the time has gone by also when the church can say, 'In the name of Jesus of Nazareth, rise up and walk.'"

Hear the appeal of Jesus Christ to you and to me: "Do you love me?" "What is the salary?" "I do not give any salary." A man may well count the cost, for you know what is coming next: "Do you love me more than money, more than ease, more than life?" And when one replies, "Lord, thou knowest that I love thee," there is always one answer: "I died for that man, and he does not know it; go and tell him." There are thousands of men and women who are without God and without a Saviour; go tell them.   ALEXANDER MCKENZIE.

313

Draw nigh to God, and he will draw nigh to you.—James iv. 8.

There is not a moment, not a talent, not a possibility of our being that should not be consecrated entirely to God and that should not be surrendered in tender, grateful, humble submission to his authority. We should feel that we could not afford to go out into the world and engage in its pleasures, its pursuits, and its ambitions, not because we have not the money, but because we cannot afford the peril, the temptation, the risk to the soul's peace and progress. Our ambition, our pleasure, should be to get nearer to God.

H. W. WEBB-PEPLOE.

God is the critic of the thoughts and intents of the heart, and I hardly can conceive of a better way of achieving saintliness than every night to sit still and let God say to you whatever he has to say. By the touch of his Spirit he seeks to mold men, but you must give the Spirit of God time. More blessing has been obtained among the hills and woods about Keswick than in the tent, though it has been the scene of the meeting of God and the soul in thousands of cases.

F. B. MEYER.

Conversion and consecration stand in marked contrast. In conversion the believer receives the testimony of God and sets his seal to it that it is true. In consecration God receives the gift we place upon the altar and sets his seal upon the believer that he is true.

J. WILBUR CHAPMAN.

And we know that all things work together for good to them that love God, to them who are the called according to his purpose.—Rom. viii. 28.

How wonderfully blessed to have everything that happens to me a pure blessing! A man may curse at me, an accident may injure me terribly, I may be brought to poverty; but if I once learn that there is the blessing of God in everything, what a life of blessing and love and joy unspeakable I shall have!

God sent the storm when Jonah went aboard the ship; God appointed a great fish to swallow him, and afterward to cast him out; God caused the hot wind to blow when the sun was sending down its scorching rays upon Jonah; God made the gourd to grow, God sent the worm to kill the gourd, and God sent the east wind to distress Jonah. If I am a child of God every circumstance of my life, every comfort and every trial, comes from God in Christ. So if I give up my whole life to Jesus and say, "Lord, I want grace to believe that thou art overseer," nothing really harmful can touch a hair of my head.

The secret of the Christ-life is this: such a consciousness of God's presence that, whether Judas came to betray him or Caiaphas condemned him unjustly or Pilate gave him up to be crucified, the presence of the Father was upon him and within him and around him, and man could not touch his spirit. That is what God wants to be to us. God first says to Moses, "I will bring you out," and then, "I will bring you in." Ah, God be praised! he has brought many of us out of the unconverted state; but has he brought us into the life of abiding communion? I fear not. November 10, 1980

ANDREW MURRAY.

315

Ye are bought with a price; be not ye the servants of men.—
1 Cor. vii. 23.

Jesus Christ has bought us with his blood, but
alas! he has not had his money's worth. He paid
for all, and he has had but a fragment of our energy,
time, and earnings. Of old the mighty men of Israel
were willing to swim the rivers at their flood to come
to David, their uncrowned but God-appointed king.
And when they met him they cried, "Thine are we,
David, and on thy side, thou son of Jesse." They
were his because God had given them to him, but
they could not rest content till they were his also
by their glad choice. Why, then, should we not
say the same to Jesus Christ?

F. B. MEYER.

It is the hardest thing in the grammar of life to
learn to put "mine" and "thine" in just the right
place. That is life's lesson. Paul had learned it when
he said, "Ye are not your own," and when he stood on
that deck in the storm and said, "God, whose I am
and whom I serve." The Christian man is the man
who has found to whom he belongs. The world
wants men who know where they belong and to
whom they belong.

W. W. MOORE.

One may use that which has been dedicated and
belongs to God, but in doing so he robs God. Ye
are not your own. Ye have been bought with a
price, and the price is the precious blood of Christ;
and ye were sealed with a seal, which is the Spirit
of God.

J. WILBUR CHAPMAN.

316

For ye are dead, and your life is hid with Christ in God.
When Christ, who is our life, shall appear, then shall ye also
appear with him in glory.—Col. iii. 3.

There are three truths upon which I try to live
every day: "I have died;" "My life is hid with Christ
in God;" and "When Christ, who is my life, shall
be manifested, I also shall be manifested with him
in glory." Do you believe that? If you have not
set to your seal that God is true in these great
statements, oh, for the Spirit of God to seal them
upon your heart!

MARCUS RAINSFORD.

Our life is a trust, not a gift; let us use it accordingly. ROBERT E. SPEER.

Some men talk of holiness as if it meant that it
was wrong to laugh, be bright, engage in manly
sports, play the piano, read any book but the Bible,
or follow certain pursuits for which we have natural
aptitudes. I believe that God in his Word will not
contradict the nature which he has given, and that
which is wrong in us is not our natural aptitudes,
but the self-life around which those aptitudes re-
volve. The life which God desires his children to
live is not a life of denial of anything which God
has imparted, but the transference of these from
the pivot of self to the pivot of not self, which is
Jesus Christ, incarnate love. The man who enters
this life is still a bright companion, a manly athlete,
still enters into all that home and friendship and
life may mean; but everything is hallowed, elevated,
ennobled, because revolving evermore round the will
of Jesus Christ. F. B. MEYER.

317

In the secret of his presence how my soul delights to
hide!
Oh, how precious are the lessons which I learn at
Jesus' side!
Earthly cares can never vex me, neither trials lay
me low;
For when Satan comes to tempt me, to the secret
place I go.

When my soul is faint and thirsty, 'neath the shadow
of his wing
There is cool and pleasant shelter and a fresh and
crystal spring;
And my Saviour rests beside me, as we hold communion sweet:
If I tried I could not utter what he says when thus
we meet.

Only this I know: I tell him all my doubts, my griefs,
and fears.
Oh, how patiently he listens! and my drooping soul
he cheers.
Do you think he ne'er reproves me?   What a false
friend he would be
If he never, never told me of the sins which he must
see!

Would you like to know the sweetness of the secret
of the Lord?
Go and hide beneath his shadow; this shall then be
your reward.
And whene'er you leave the silence of that happy
meeting-place,
You must mind and bear the image of the Master
in your face.

ELLEN LAKSHMI GOREH.

Month of November

NOVEMBER

But ye are not in the flesh, but in the Spirit, if so be that the Spirit of God dwell in you. Now if any man have not the Spirit of Christ, he is none of his.—Rom. viii. 9.

In the matter of consecration God said to an Israelite, "Now, if you wish to fully consecrate your life to me, to separate yourself unto the Lord, you are at liberty to do so for any period that you desire." The vow of a Nazarite might be taken for a year, or for five or seven years, for a half or a whole lifetime. God seemed to say, "You may just go in for as much consecration and blessing as you have the heart to." But under the new covenant God would have us all to recognize all through our Christian life that we are not our own, that we are bought with a price, and that he has a rightful claim to all we have and to all we are.

In like manner, under the old covenant the Holy Spirit was given for special service on special occasions, but it was needful for the receiver to pray, "Take not thy Holy Spirit from me." The Spirit was given to Saul, but was taken away, and we might find other illustrations of the same truth. But to the believer under the new covenant the Spirit is given as a seal upon a document, never to be removed—as an earnest not to be recalled until the redemption of the purchased possession. We may grieve the Spirit and lose the benefit of his guidance, but the Spirit does not leave the believer. What we want is to have the open ear always ready to hear and to obey the precious One who has taken his abode within us.

J. HUDSON TAYLOR.

Consecration is not the act of our feelings, but of our will. Do not try to feel anything. Do not try to make yourself good or earnest enough for Christ. God is working in you to will, whether you feel it or not. He is giving you power to will and do his good pleasure. Believe this and act upon it at once, and say, "Lord Jesus, I am willing to be thine;" or if you cannot say as much as that, say, "Lord Jesus, I am willing to be made willing to be thine forevermore."

Consecration is only possible when we come to the point of giving ourselves to God we are almost certain to become aware of the presence of one thing, if not of more, out of harmony with his will. Every room and cupboard in the house, with the exception of this, thrown open to the new occupant; every limb in the body, but one, submitted to the practised hand of the good Physician. But that small reserve spoils the whole. To give ninety-nine parts and to withhold the hundredth undoes the whole transaction. Jesus will have all or none. Who would live in a fever-stricken house so long as one room was not exposed to disinfectants, air, and sun? Who would undertake a case so long as the patient refused to submit one part of his body to examination? Who would become responsible for a bankrupt so long as one ledger was kept back? The reason that so many fail to attain the blessed life is that there is some one point in which they hold back from God and concerning which they prefer to have their own way and will rather than his. This one little thing mars the whole, robs them of peace, and compels them to wander in the desert.

F. B. MEYER.

There are three grades of Christian life. There is, first of all, the dissatisfied life; the life that knows there is something which it does not possess; the life that is perpetually discontented, and rightly so, with itself. There is, second, the life that is half and half, that now and then rises up to the Mount of Transfiguration, and then paces for long seasons over weary wastes of whitened ashes. There is a third life of satisfaction and contentment, of peace and power and rest; the life that has made Jesus Christ its one object; the life that every man lives who is able to say, in the fine phrase of Ignatius, "O Christ, thou art 'my inseparable life.'" The soul that has made Christ its one object has entered into rest and has entered into power; it has entered into a life of activity which no foe can withstand, and of contentment which no storm can ruffle; for over all the seas where it voyages speaks that voice which quieted the turbulent waves of the Tiberian Sea: "Peace, be still." Nothing can overcome or disturb the soul that is hid with Christ in God and has made Christ the one object of its life. ROBERT E. SPEER.

The difference in men is the way in which the truth gets hold of them and passes through them. The electric current passes through the wire easily and the wire is unaffected by it; but the carbon-point in an electric light holds the current and is deeply possessed by it; hence there flashes out the brilliancy of an arc-light. So the man that not only lets truth pass through him, but is charged, possessed, and held by that truth, becomes a point where truth is manifested and vivified. WILTON MERLE SMITH.

Yet a little while, and the world seeth me no more; but ye see me.—John xiv. 19.

When the sun goes down our hemisphere does not see it any more, but the moon sees it all night long, and the moon takes the sun's light and throws it down upon us. When the Sun of Righteousness set behind the hill of Olivet the world saw him no more; but the church, because it is seated in heavenly places in Christ, all the night long sees the Sun, and throws the light upon the world through the Holy Ghost. The world receives what light it has from the church, and the church receives it from Jesus Christ. A. J. GORDON.

Only Christ can influence the world; but all that the world sees of Christ is what it sees of him in the life of his followers. . . . So that a Christian's usefulness depends solely upon his relationship to Christ and the accuracy with which he reflects the divine likeness. HENRY DRUMMOND.

Those little things which fill up our lives when relaxation comes are spiritual tests. Do we choose spiritual pleasures, or are we living on unspiritual things? ROBERT E. SPEER.

What is needed in the church is simplicity of worship, a pure gospel, fervent prayer, unity of work, godly men, beauty of holiness, and prayer for return of the Holy Spirit. ARTHUR T. PIERSON.

We talk about drawing ministers; what we want is a few more drawing church-members!
D. L. MOODY.

I must work the works of him that sent me, while it is day:
the night cometh, when no man can work.—John ix. 4.

This world is a poor enough place for selfishness,
but it is a glorious place for denying self. The opportunities for doing good in this world are far beyond those in heaven. A very little light goes a
great way; so shines a good deed in a naughty world.
A rushlight in a humble home may guide a wanderer.
In the true spirit of consecration there is light. It
is a great thing to give light, even if it is in the
humblest home and goes no farther. But it does go
farther. The daybreak is a joyful prospect, but not
for those whose lights have smoked and died to ashes.
"If only I had let it blaze in the night, how many
wanderers it might have guided!" you lament.
"Work, for the night is coming;" but better yet is,
"Work, for the night is past." Make good use of
the night while it lasts. The light of love is greatly
needed. There should be no limit to great-hearted-
ness.   J. MONRO GIBSON.

Christians are constantly praying that they may
hear, "Well done," when the Lord comes to reward
his servants, while, as a matter of fact, they are doing nothing. They talk about entering into rest, but
what are they going to rest from? A beautiful verse
in Thessalonians referring to the rest of the saints
is, "Those that are laid to sleep through Jesus."
Dives was tormented with insomnia. If he had been
late to dinner because he was looking after Lazarus's
family, and had clothed a thousand children among
the poor, he might have had sleep; but because he
was self-centered he could get none.
                         A. J. GORDON.

The Bible is the most practical book in the world. It flies straight as an arrow to its mark and wastes no time on side issues. Its one design is to bring men into right relations to God, and so to save them from their sins and guide them into heaven. Therefore it is not a revelation of all religious truth; it reveals only what we need to know for our salvation. Consequently, also, it contains many statements which present only partial truths. As a rule, they present facts, not reasons; duties, and not the philosophy of religion. Hence there are many omissions of what would interest us greatly as to the history of the past, as to science, as to the biography of great men.

ADDISON P. FOSTER.

When Kepler was seeking to discover the true law of planetary motion, he made seventeen successive experiments before the hypothesis was applied which disclosed the true path of a planet's orbit. In the endeavor to unlock the mysteries of planetary motion he had tried seventeen different keys, and they would not work; but at last he said, "I will suppose the path of a planet around the sun to be not a circle, but an ellipse, with the sun at one of the foci." When he put that key in the lock the bolts were thrown back, the doors that had been shut for millenniums flew open; he flung up his hands in rapture and said, "O Almighty God, I am thinking thy thoughts after thee." That is the way to study the Bible. Take the biblical facts and seek to find God's key. When you have found that, it will perfectly unlock God's mysteries, and you will not need to go hunting around for a human locksmith.

ARTHUR T. PIERSON.

The unity of the Bible is fourfold. First, the same purpose runs through the Bible. The first two chapters describe the creation of the first earth, the last two chapters the creation of the new earth; the first two the birth of man, the last two the birth of the race; the first two the earthly Eden, the last two the heavenly Eden. And all the Bible between is the bringing of man from earth to heaven.

Second, there is the unity of the character of God. He is always holy, pure, sin-hating, the eternal Father, Saviour, and Comforter.

Third, the moral law of the Bible is always the same. The ten commandments are just as binding to-day as three thousand years ago, and as much enforced by the conscience of men. They smite every sin and crime of the nineteenth century as they did the sins of the past. The applications have been different, but they have the same hold on human nature. The ceremonial laws were not done away with, but fulfilled in Christ, and the spiritual truths thus taught are eternal truths. The laws are the scaffolding that falls away, and the truth is the temple that remains forever.

Fourth, there is a unity of the scheme of redemption running throughout the whole Bible, at first in types and symbols, in ceremonies and forms, for the training of the infancy of the race in the truths of salvation, and at last in the life of the Son of God and his atonement on the cross, to which all types and sacrifices pointed, and in which all were fulfilled. We will not understand fully the Old Testament and its sacrifices till we see them in the light shining from the cross, which they prefigured and foretold.

F. N. PELOUBET.

325

If any man will do his will, he shall know of the doctrine.—
John vii. 17.

Obedience, as Robertson puts it, is the spiritual
organ of knowledge, and if any man refuses to obey
what he knows, he shall know no more; whereas if
any man obeys what he knows, he shall be led
swiftly in the path of truth.

A. F. SCHAUFFLER.

The Bible rings with one long demand for obedience. The key-word of the Book of Deuteronomy is,
"Observe and do." The burden of our Lord's fare-
well discourse is, "If ye love me, keep my commandments." We must not question or reply or excuse
ourselves. We must not pick and choose our way.
We must not think that obedience in one direction
will compensate for disobedience in some other particular. God gives one command at a time; if we
obey this he will flood our soul with blessing, and
lead us forward into new paths and pastures. But
if we refuse we shall remain stagnant and water-
logged, make no progress in Christian experience,
and lack both power and joy.

F. B. MEYER.

There is only one way to get to know God, and it
is along the path of obedience, along the path of
bowing our stiff knees, and opening our lockjawed
mouths, and praying out of our hearts, and giving
our entire obedience to his will.

JOHN MCNEILL.

And that ye study to be quiet, and to do your own business, and to work with your own hands, as we commanded you.— 1 Thess. iv. 11.

Here St. Paul exhorts us to service conjoined with silence, doing the best we can and saying nothing about it. Some clocks strike the hours, and some tell the time of day only with their hands. So some Christians advertise their business, and others do it and say nothing about it. Two texts ought to be read together: "Do not sound a trumpet before you," and "Let your light so shine." God wants you to be ambitious to have good works that somebody can see; light travels faster than sound, and so, with Christians, you see the flash before you hear the report if they are the right sort. The ambition is, not that men may praise you, but that they may glorify your Father which is in heaven. You thus have an opportunity to be ambitious, and yet to be sublimely humble.

A. J. GORDON.

The first thing a man must do if he desires to be used in the Lord's work is to make an unconditional surrender of himself to God. He must *consecrate* and then *concentrate*. A man who does not put his whole life into one channel does not count for much, and the man who only goes into work with half a heart does not amount to much. We are living in an intense age, and if a man is to succeed he must set himself apart for the work and throw all his energy into it.

D. L. MOODY.

The Bible has very little to say about the end of
its heroes and heroines, but very much about their
beginning. The death-bed, the parting scene, the
final rapture—these things find small space in the
Scriptures; but the divine summons to service is related almost everywhere with minute and definite
detail. What was the end of the life of the Apostle
Paul? The last sentence in regard to him reads, "Paul
dwelt two whole years in his own hired house, . . .
preaching the kingdom of God, . . . no man for-
bidding him." But the conversion of that apostle
with his summons to his apostolate is related three
times with wonderful and startling vividness. The
last sentence with regard to Peter is simply, "And
Peter departed and went into another place." But
can we ever forget how the young Messiah, walking
by the Sea of Galilee, summoned the young apostles,
Peter and Andrew, to follow after him? Peter was
never weary of telling of that. So of Moses it is
said, "No man knoweth his sepulcher," but every
man knows his call. Did Amos pass away in peace?
What were the closing scenes in the life of Ezekiel?
What was the end of Jeremiah? The Bible does not
tell us; but every one of those prophets has related
with the utmost detail how at some time in his life
a divine hand was laid upon him, and a divine voice
was heard speaking to his soul. In short, the Bible
places tremendous emphasis on the fact that God
does summon men and women to specific forms of
Christian service, and that we may recognize his call.

W. H. P. FAUNCE.

There are three passages in which Christ speaks of the work we ought to do and where he teaches the principle of the overflowing cup. They are very remarkable. First, "As the Father hath sent me, even so send I you." Are you willing to be sent into the world as Jesus Christ was sent? We shrink back. I believe that it is true, and yet it is hard for me to believe that I am sent down into the town where I live as Jesus Christ was sent into the world. The next passage carries us a little further; it teaches that if you go into the world loving and trusting Christ you shall do the works that he did, "and greater works than these shall ye do." Have you worked any miracle to-day? We talk about Christ's miracles. He said, "You shall do greater ones." Think of that! Jesus opened the eyes of a blind man, and he looked up and saw the face of his Lord. Have you ever opened your friend's eyes so that he looked up into the face of Jesus? That is a greater thing. The other passage is the strangest of all. Christ said to the Father, "The glory that thou gavest me I have given them, . . . that the world may know that thou hast loved them as thou hast loved me." I believe with all my heart in the love of God. But here we see his royal bounty. Let us be willing to be loved as Christ is loved, and to love in return with all the heart and more.

ALEXANDER MCKENZIE.

We are workers together with God; do not let us forget God.

FRANCIS MURPHY.

Power belongeth unto God.—Ps. lxii. 11.

It is only as we have power from on high that we have spiritual power at all. Some people have a good deal to say about the latent power that exists in the church of God. There is no such thing as power, either latent or expressed, in the church of God. Power is just as distinct from the church as steam is distinct from the engine that it moves, or as life is distinct from the earth that seems to bring it forth.

B. FAY MILLS.

There is no such thing as a church of God in which the Spirit of God does not preside. There are a great many so-called churches of Christ which I believe Christ utterly disowns because the Spirit of God does not regulate those church organizations. They are mere churches of men—sometimes religious clubs, sometimes benevolent societies, sometimes social organizations, baptized with a religious name; but that alone is a church of God in which the Spirit of God rules and presides, and where his invisible headship is acknowledged and reverently submitted to in the fear of God.

ARTHUR T. PIERSON.

The Holy Spirit must have the right atmosphere to work in. You must have air to convey sound, and you must have the Spirit in order to carry home the truth to men's hearts.

D. L. MOODY.

All Christians, like all Scripture, should be God-breathed. A. J. GORDON.

330

If any man will come after me, let him deny himself, and take up his cross, and follow me.—Matt. xvi. 24.

I must deny myself and take Jesus himself as my life; I must choose. There are two lives, the self-life and the Christ-life; I must choose either of the two. "Follow me," says our Lord; "make me as your rule of conduct, give me your whole heart, follow me, and I will care for all."

ANDREW MURRAY.

The clay has no option but to be what the potter would make it; but, somehow, you and I possess the marvelous power of saying "Yes" and "No" to God. If you say "Yes," then you have the blessedness of the beatitudes; if you say "No," "Woe to him that striveth with his Maker!" God wants to make you, but you have the power to resist, and you have used it.

A great Christian worker, when dying, was asked the secret of his saintliness. He modestly disclaimed any title to saintliness, but he said, "The secret of my life is that I have said 'Yes' to Christ." I think I hear that clay saying "Yes" to the potter every time he touches it. With all your heart say "Yes" to Jesus Christ, and let him have a chance to make you over again.   F. B. MEYER.

We talk about being surrendered to the will of God. When you get into your carriage you surrender yourself to the horse, but you hold the reins and make him go where you want to. It seems that we surrender to God's will, but try to hold the reins and do God's will by doing our way.

A. J. GORDON.

331

There is more said in the Bible about praise than about prayer. I believe it is just as important that we sing with the Spirit as that we pray with the Spirit or speak in the Spirit, and if we could have all our worship in the Spirit, the Holy Ghost would work not only while we were preaching and praying, but while we were singing. Many a church has lost its power on account of the choir that has not been in harmony with God. A godless choir will keep the Holy Ghost from working in any church, or a choir that sings in an unknown tongue.

We don't thank and praise God half enough. That is one reason why so many of our churches are so dull and gloomy. When churches get into a backslidden state, they hire singers to stand away up in some organ-loft and praise God for them. How can we expect God to give us further blessings if we don't thank him for what he has given us? One of the best ways to wake a church up and start a revival is to hold a praise-meeting.

D. L. MOODY.

Cheerful tempers manufacture solace and joy out of very unpromising material. They are the magic alchemists which extract sweet essences out of bitter herbs, like the dear old colored saint in the smoky hut who was "glad of anything to make a smoke with," and, though she had but two teeth, thanked God that they were "opposite each other."

ARTHUR T. PIERSON.

God can do no more for you than he has done. All that God has is within your reach, but you must learn to take it. F. B. MEYER.

332

The work of the hands and of the head are subordinate to that of the heart. If you have been redeemed by Christ, renewed by the Holy Ghost, and your citizenship is in heaven, what is your principal business? It is to tell others about Jesus Christ, and bring them to the knowledge of his love and of his grace. Whatever else you do must be subordinated to that, and it is a shame and scandal in our nineteenth-century Christianity that so many business men get and live and labor and save, as if they understood that getting riches was the end of their existence, instead of getting riches in order to glorify God. I care not what your occupation is,—you may be a carpenter at the bench, a blacksmith at the forge, a merchant behind the counter, —your first business is to give the gospel to those that have not heard it. Does it look as though we regarded it as our principal business?

There are eight billions in the hands of Christians in America; that is, invested for the most part in bonds, mortgages, diamonds, silks, horses, carriages, houses, furniture, pictures, and a thousand other things—vastly more than in that which ought to be the principal business of the Christian, giving the gospel to the world. Some men say, "I believe that the world is getting better and better every day," although they have millions laid up, and yet you cannot get twenty cents out of them for the Lord's work. A. J. GORDON.

There is no other way to win a soul than by seeing in him one whom Christ loves, and whom Christ, your Saviour, would have you win to him.

L. W. MUNHALL.

333

Enthusiasm is the normal condition of a true Christian. Sometimes in the month of February, when the thermometer is away down at zero, an ignorant man says, "The sun doesn't give as much heat as usual; it must be burning out and cooling down." But on the very day when the thermometer is at zero, if you could send a pyramid of ice fifty miles in diameter flying toward the sun at the rate of two hundred and seventy millions of miles in a minute, it would melt as fast as it flew. We are at a different angle to the sun in February to what we are in July. If you are a cold Christian you are in a wrong attitude toward Jesus Christ; away from duty, away from prayer, away in worldliness, away in unbelief, indulging in some besetting sin. When you get into the right position with reference to Jesus Christ, the blessing will descend upon you most abundantly.

THEODORE L. CUYLER.

A great many people are afraid of enthusiasm. If a man is enthusiastic they raise the cry, "Zeal without knowledge!" I should rather have zeal without knowledge than knowledge without zeal. I know men as wise as owls without any fire in their souls. Enthusiasm means "in God"; and I can't understand how any man can realize his standing before God and not be on fire three hundred and sixty-five days in the year. Any man who goes into business and doesn't throw his heart into it doesn't succeed. Now why not go into the Lord's work as earnestly as into athletics?

D. L. MOODY.

334

The psalmist tells us that "the fool hath said in
his heart, No God, no God." It was a fool who said
it, and even a fool had to say it in his heart, for
even a fool's head knew better than that. Atheism,
of whatever kind, is a freezing void, an arctic breath,
a lifeless life, an atmosphere in which no wing can
soar, no heart can beat, and no soul rejoice. Atheism can transform a rare day in June into a raw
day in January. R. S. MacArthur.

A good theological definition of the nature and
effects of the labors and mission of an atheist or
infidel is, "The devil's whetstone to sharpen dull
preachers on." I. D. Driver.

Honest doubt is simply the absence of conviction,
and its remedy is evidence; dishonest doubt comes
from moral alienation, and its only remedy is repentance and submission to truth. You can no
more cure dishonest doubt by evidence than you
can cure cataract on the eye by an operation on the
ears. We should respect honest doubt which comes
from insufficient evidence; for we are not sponges
to be put a-soak in a tub of doctrine, and take up
whatever happens to be in the tub. But an honest
doubter will leave no stone unturned in order that
he may find out the truth. Arthur T. Pierson.

The most mischievous infidelity is not that which
men read out of books, but that which they read out
of professedly Christian lives. When church-members show that Christ is able to cast out the devil of
self, they will furnish the evidence which the skeptic
demands. Josiah Strong.

335

A small circle of usefulness is not to be despised.
A light that doesn't shine beautifully around the
family table at home is not fit to take a long way
off to do a great service somewhere else.

J. HUDSON TAYLOR.

Some men are afraid of being too religious.
What we need to-day is men who believe down deep
in their soul what they profess. The world is tired
and sick of sham. Let your whole heart be given
up to God's service. Aim high. God wants us all
to be his ambassadors. It is a position higher than
that of any monarch on earth to be a herald of the
cross; but you must be filled with the Holy Ghost.
A great many people are afraid to be filled with the
Spirit of God—afraid of being called fanatics. You
are not good for anything until the world considers
you a fanatic. Fox said that every Quaker ought
to shake the country ten miles around. What does
the Scripture say? "One shall chase a thousand,
and two shall put ten thousand to flight." It takes
about a thousand to chase one now. It takes about
a thousand Christians to make one decent one now.
Why? Because they are afraid of being too religious. What does this world want to-day? Men—
men that are out and out for God, and not half-
hearted in their allegiance and service.

D. L. MOODY.

What a cowardly religion it is to be afraid to
oppose the foe until Christ has vanquished him, and
then rush over his corpse and kick it and get all we
can from what Jesus has done, but never think of
him who gained the victory at the cost of his life.

H. W. WEBB-PEPLOE.

Sanctification is making real in our lives our condition in Christ. If we are sanctified in Christ, it is our business to be sanctified in ourselves. Make the real state correspond to the ideal. The gospel is the opposite from morality. Morality says, "I ought to be holy, therefore I will be holy." The gospel says, "Ye are holy in Christ, therefore be holy in yourself."   A. J. GORDON.

God's Word tells us that the Holy Ghost is already given as the universal income of the church. We shall know the full extent of our inheritance when we see Jesus as he is; meanwhile, the Holy Ghost is described as "the earnest of our inheritance." A man may possess a splendid income and yet may never have seen his magnificent property. What we enjoy of our income is the measure of holiness which we really possess and exhibit in this life. Holiness is, so to speak, the expenditure of income received through God's gift of the Holy Spirit. Hereafter the inheritance will be ours in its fullness; then we shall know as we are known.

H. W. WEBB-PEPLOE.

A man who is filled with the Holy Spirit will have an undoubted assurance of his sonship; moreover, he will be cleansed from the power and love of indwelling sin; he will be tempted, but will find that his inner nature is like a tinder-box which has become damp. The devil will still try to strike his matches upon him, but the man will not respond; he will be so saturated with the Holy Spirit that there will be no response as in other days.

F. B. MEYER.

337

It is more blessed to give than to receive.—Acts xx. 35.

This is true whatever be the character of our acquisitions. There are riches of learning; but what are the highest advantages of intellectual culture? Is one to study and travel, read and write, simply for the sake of being a student, a writer, a walking library of knowledge or an encyclopedia of information? Our instincts tell us that we are not to live simply to acquire; society does not want mere effigies, whether stuffed with bran or brains; but the world wants men, living, working, serving others, who acquire in order to impart, who have at heart the good of the race. ARTHUR T. PIERSON.

Inquire diligently what blood mortgage there is on your property in the interest of foreign missions—how much you owe to the heathen because of what you owe to Christ for redeeming you with his precious blood. It will go hard with you when your Lord comes to reckon with you if he finds your wealth invested in superfluous luxuries, or hoarded up in needless accumulations, instead of being sacredly devoted to giving the gospel to the lost.

A. J. GORDON.

The mistake of the Christian world is that they expect to have the beatitudes without fulfilling the conditions attached to them. How often do we pray that we may have the kingdom of heaven without thinking that we must first be poor in spirit. How often do we pray for mercy, without first seeking to be merciful. How often do we expect to be filled because we hunger and thirst, when we have never made sure that what we are hungering and thirsting for is real righteousness.

HENRY DRUMMOND.

But the fruit of the Spirit is love, joy, peace, long-suffering, gentleness, goodness, faith, meekness, temperance: against such there is no law.—Gal. v. 22, 23.

Let us not talk of the *fruits* of the Spirit; it is the *fruit* of the Spirit—nine grapes in one bunch. It is all of one Spirit who desires to work one and the same blessed fruit in us all. Here are nine beautiful grapes, and they all relate to character, rather than conduct. Perhaps you are longing for splendid conduct, wanting to go and do some great works. God wants you to begin with character. The Holy Ghost works character; then he can fill you for service; and assuredly God desires all to be thus blessedly filled. It is no man's special prerogative or gift, above his fellows, to be filled with the Spirit. But remember that, while the world "resists the Holy Ghost," even a child of God may "grieve" and "quench" him.

H. W. WEBB-PEPLOE.

The Holy Ghost comes to make Christ an actual, indwelling, always abiding Saviour. Christ saves me with a full salvation. Whatever delay there may be in the full enjoyment, if we trust Christ he will make his word true. Then rest simply upon the word of promise. Resting means abandoning yourself to the object upon which you rest. Abandon yourself to the living Christ; let your faith rest in the promise and the love of Jesus—that is your only safety, but that is a sure foundation.

ANDREW MURRAY.

It is remarkable how often maps have played a great part in the extension of the kingdom of God. The little haystack prayer-meeting in Williamstown was not simply a place for worship, but a place for the study of the map of the world. Carey's cobbler shop was not only a place for making shoes, not only a place of prayer; it was a place for the study of the world's map. If your map has less than the world on it, then you cannot truly decide on your field of Christian endeavor. I believe that no one field is better than all other fields, and no one form of Christian service is more acceptable to God than all other forms. Suppose we should take Charles H. Spurgeon, Phillips Brooks, David Livingstone, and Joseph Neesima, could any of you take those four lives and say which has been most blessed of God? We should be content with the song of little Pippa as she passed through the city singing:

"All service ranks the same with God:
. . . There is no last or first."

Every opening life should have before it the knowledge of the entire kingdom of God. We should keep before our eyes what God is doing in all parts of the world, and remember that the field is the world, and not simply a little part of it. The field is not the church; the church is simply the reapers thrust out into the field. God help *us* to keep before *ourselves* the map of his entire extended kingdom, and give *us* a heart that is willing to go anywhere. Until we are willing to go anywhere we are fit to go nowhere.

W. H. P. FAUNCE.

There is great need at home. Let no man in his zeal for the mission field minimize for one moment the need for Christian activity in this land. With a hundred thousand drunkards going down every year to the drunkards' hell; with a million voters unable to read the votes they cast; with four million children out of the public schools; with thirteen million children out of the Sabbath-school; with seventy-five per cent. of our young men never entering a Christian church—God knows there is need enough for Christian work in the United States! But enough for what? Enough to make us *ashamed* that there should be so much after two centuries of Christian activity. Yes, but *not* enough to justify us in nullifying the last command of Christ. Whose fault is it that there is so much work to be done in the United States? Is it the Hindu's or the Chinaman's or the African's fault? By what right do we shut them out of the kingdom of God because of a state of affairs for which they have no responsibility at all? The gospel was not given to them on condition that there was no need in America for the gospel. It was given to "every creature." Of course there is need for Christian work in the United States, but at whose door is the responsibility to be laid? God's? "All power is given unto me, and I hand it on to you." The heathen's door? They have not known there was any such country as this. No man can hide himself behind the sophistry that God's peculiar love for our nation, or the peculiar need for Christian work in this land, justifies us in neglecting the untold millions who wait that life whose dawning maketh all things new. ROBERT E. SPEER.

341

There is a world-wide difference between the falling of a sinner and the stumbling of a saint. The sinner habitually walks in the way of evil; the saint has deliberately chosen the way of good. When the sinner falls, he falls *in* the evil way that he is pursuing; that is to say, his uniform course is sinful, but his fall involves an *outbreaking* sin. Lust has been in his heart, but it breaks out in open impurity; latent hate has been there, but it betrays him into the sin of violence; secret avarice now becomes open overreaching or dishonesty. The sin is in accordance with the habitual life which he has been leading. On the other hand, when the child of God, who has chosen the good way and walked in it thus far, stumbles into sin, this is *not* in accordance with his ordinary walk; and when he is recovered by the grace of God, he pursues the same path, in the same direction, as before his error. The difference between these two is finely expressed in the Bible. James says, "Brethren, if any of you do err from the truth, and one bring him back." A brother is supposed to be walking in the way of the truth, and to make a temporary deviation from that way; and some one is to call his attention to the evil-doing, and bring him back into the right way. Again, the Apostle Paul says in his letter to the Galatians, "Brethren, if a man be overtaken in a fault, ye which are spiritual, restore such a one." Some old habit comes up, as it were, from behind, and, when he is incautious and unheeding, trips him up, so that he falls. Now you, says Paul, which are spiritual, go and help him up on his feet, and set him on his way again, with the help of your sympathy and prayer.   ARTHUR T. PIERSON.

How many men and women of ability there are in the church of whom we expect great things but who always disappoint us! What is the matter? Sin! Oh, if you would have a mighty work of God in your own soul, ask God to search your heart, and if God shows you some sin, give it up. No matter if it is like tearing out your heartstrings, out with it! It hinders a mighty work of God in your soul.   R. A. TORREY.

You are not responsible if disreputable persons ring at your door; but for the persons whom you systematically take into your home life you are permanently responsible. Just so for the thought that you dwell on, that you turn as a sweet morsel under the tongue, that colors and shapes the whole fabric of your life—for that thought you are responsible.   MERRILL E. GATES.

Have you gained the victory over the foes within you? There is jealousy. Would you overcome that? If you are jealous of any one, do him some good turn. There is a fable of an eagle which was jealous of another that could outfly him. He saw a sportsman one day, and said to him, "I wish you would bring down that eagle." The sportsman replied that he would if he only had some feathers to put into his arrow. So the eagle pulled one out of his wing. The arrow was shot, but didn't quite reach the rival eagle; it was flying too high. The envious eagle kept pulling out more feathers until he lost so many that he couldn't fly, and then the sportsman turned around and killed him. My friend, if you are jealous, the only man you can hurt is yourself.   D. L. MOODY.

For all that is in the world, the lust of the flesh, and the lust of the eyes, and the pride of life, is not of the Father, but is of the world.—1 John ii. 16.

Satan, the world, and the flesh are the three mighty foes of the child of God.

Man, led captive by Satan at his will, either denies his existence or clothes him with hoofs and horns, a creature to be dreaded and shrunk from; instead of remembering the warning that he appears as an angel of light, presenting to each a tempting bait, and luring on in pleasant paths the soul to hell. Never will you be in so great danger from Satan as when careless and unconcerned as to his existence, and even questioning his personality.

D. W. WHITTLE.

The defiled imagination is the devil's sharp-shooter secretly firing death-missiles into the souls of man from the domain of hell. By it he fetters the will, deadens the sense of right and duty, sears the conscience, hardens the heart, and destroys the soul. Using it as a banquet-table, he spreads before appetite, passion, and lust every allurement for evil which can be wrought out of the wine-cup, gambling game, lottery device, race-track scourge, unhallowed love, evil reading, and kindred vices. The defiled imagination fills the atmosphere of the soul with reeking odors; it deposits a deadly poison in the fountain of moral purity, corrupting the stream of life. As sewer-gas poisons and infects the atmosphere of the home, bringing disease and death in its wake, so the debauched imagination, the sewer-gas of hell, infects the domain of the mind.

ANTHONY COMSTOCK.

But now being made free from sin, and become servants to God, ye have your fruit unto holiness, and the end everlasting life.—Rom. vi. 22.

I have had people come to me again and again and say, "I would not, of course, go to a polished-floor ball, but I suppose there is no harm in a carpet-dance. I would not for anything go to see some of the impure plays of which I read or hear, but a good first-class moral theater I suppose is all right for Christian people, is it not?" I cannot stop to weigh worldly pleasures in the scales as a chemist or a physician would measure out poisons; to examine into the exact amount of grains that make up the difference between morality and immorality. My Lord has called me to preach a life full of privilege, when *all* is consecrated to God; a life of honor and of delight, in giving up everything to the Master. Such quibbling distinctions are only of the devil. We must not degrade our Christianity thus. We must ask ourselves just this one thing: "If I am consecrated to God from this day forward, for time and for eternity, and my profession is real, how can I prove it best by every action of my life, by every thought and every word that proceeds from me?" That is all that we need to inquire. It is not how near we may sail to the world in its pleasures and custom, and give the fag-ends to God from a sense of duty and necessity, but how we can delight our souls in him and his service. There are many Christians who seem to live upon earth, and now and then pay duty-calls in heaven; but the true privilege of the Christian is to live in heaven, and pay certain duty-calls on earth when God imposes the necessity.   H. W. WEBB-PEPLOE.

And hath put all things under his feet, and gave him to be the head over all things to the church, which is his body, the fullness of him that filleth all in all.—Eph. i. 22, 23.

Why did God say that Christ was the head to the church, which was his body? In the first place, the head is the seat of government so far as the body is concerned. It is an indication of a diseased spiritual condition when the church is not through and through governed by Christ. What a mighty work the church might accomplish through the power of God if it should awaken to the glorious truth that the Lord Christ is head over all!

Christ, as the head of the church, is the seat of wisdom. What a glorious thought that all the wisdom locked up in the eternal being of Jehovah is ours!

Suppose it were possible for the various members of the body to act independently of the headship. Suppose my right foot were to walk, my left foot to dance, my right hand to write a sermon, and my left hand to play the banjo; I should at least make a very suspicious-looking figure. Many a church in the sight of God's angels is just as ridiculous as that. In how many churches you find that instead of every organization being guided by Christ's wisdom and working in harmony, every member is pulling his own way.

Again, the head is the seat of the consciousness of joy and pain! What a comfort to feel that, however small the position we hold, Christ feels our joy and pain! In the physical body sometimes the brain gets out of order, needs sleep, so that it does not warn us of danger. But Christ never sleeps.

A. S. GUMBART.

Behold, how good and how pleasant it is for brethren to dwell together in unity! —Ps. cxxxiii. 1.

A great commentator on the Psalms says that it is not unity with one another that is meant, but unity with the great Head which makes unity with one another.   A. J. GORDON.

Three things are essential to the communion of the saints; first, their union to the Lord Jesus Christ by his Holy Spirit on his part and faith on their part; second, the simultaneous workings of love and hope and joy and peace and life and fullness of assurance of salvation in the souls of all believers; and third, the consciousness of the simultaneousness of these workings.

NATHANIEL WEST.

"Many as the waves, but one as the sea," is the motto of the true church of Christ. But equally true is it of the works of God and the Word of God.
F. N. PELOUBET.

Even among Christians, how often there are divisions and bitternesses among those who work together! The fruit of the Spirit, which is love, is often absent in Christ's own people. Jesus Christ can give us the victory over sin and can keep from actual transgression. I do not say that the root of sin will be eradicated and that you will not have any natural tendency to sin; but when the Holy Spirit comes not only in his power for service as a gift, but when he comes in divine grace to fill the heart, there is victory over sin; power not to fulfil the lusts of the flesh; ability to live peaceably among our brethren.   ANDREW MURRAY.

347

My cup runneth over.—Ps. xxiii. 5.

Now there is no use in a cup running over; if a
cup is full, that is enough; if it is nearly full, it is
more convenient; and yet it is the part of friendship
and it is the part of God to have the cup running
over. The Queen of Sheba came to see Solomon,
and when she went away the king, having given
her everything which she asked for, added something more; not because she had desired it, but because he had desired it; not out of her heart's seeking, but out of his heart's wishing to bestow. The
part he wanted to give is called the "royal bounty";
that is, the part that overflowed, and it was very
much the best part.

Christ always gives more than men ask for. At
Capernaum they brought a man sick with the palsy.
Jesus saw perfectly well what they wanted, but he
passed over that and said, "Son, be of good cheer;
thy sins are forgiven thee." That was enough. The
man would be able to walk in a few days; death
would heal him. But they were a little discontented, so Jesus healed him—threw that in.

Then he came to that miracle by the Sea of Galilee.
The disciples had toiled all night and taken nothing.
In the morning Jesus told them where to cast the
net, and they drew it in full of fishes—a hundred
and fifty-three fishes. But then there was a fire of
coals on the shore and fish laid thereon. That last
fish is the running over of the cup. That was the
best fish of all. That is what Christ is doing all the
while. He gives us a hundred and fifty-three to
sustain life and then he adds another—that is his
royal bounty.

ALEXANDER MCKENZIE.

Month of December

Let us lay aside every weight, and the sin which doth so easily beset us, and let us run with patience the race that is set before us.—Heb. xii. 1.

We all have what the negro called our "upsetting sin," but we don't always know what it is. I will tell you what is the besetting sin of every one of us. When man fell from God originally he fell into himself. There is your besetting sin—*self*. Self is the house devil, after all, that every one of us has to fight; smooth-tongued, suave, hoodwinking us all. "Oh, how much good I am doing!" Are you? Self whispered that. When they told a noted preacher at the foot of the stairs that he had preached a good sermon he said, "The devil told me that before I left the pulpit." I tell you, self in some form, my brother, will be an enemy all the time to be fought. We must get rid of self, or we can never be filled with the Spirit. Charles G. Finney said that when he went into the cities to begin his evangelistic work he would sometimes preach a day or two without one atom of power. What did he do? He just let himself down before God and prayed God to empty him of Charles G. Finney, as it were, to take the bump of self-reliance, self-trust, and self-seeking out of him. "Seekest thou great things for thyself?"—even in Christian work,—"seek them not." Let them be for Christ. When self is out there may be an inpouring of the Spirit. Pray that you may be so filled with Christ that there shall not be room for the house devil of self.

THEODORE L. CUYLER.

Brethren, if a man be overtaken in a fault, ye which are spiritual, restore such a one in the spirit of meekness.—Gal. vi. 1.

There we see two marks of the spiritual man: he will be a meek man and he will have power and love to help and restore those that are fallen.

ANDREW MURRAY.

Brethren, we are members one of another. Why, then, do we hurt and annoy one another? There ought to be no discord in the home or in the church, because we are called to be one body, and if I wound a brother Christian I am blighting my own life; I am spoiling the body which is one.

H. W. WEBB-PEPLOE.

To be a Christian a man must be born of the Spirit, born into the family of God. The Lord Jesus is the elder brother in this family, and we are all ordained to be conformed to the image of the elder brother. If you do not see the likeness to Christ in your fellow-Christians the trouble may be in the dullness of your eyes. You must get more of the Spirit of God as a medium through which the Spirit may shine upon the eyes of your understanding.

L. W. MUNHALL.

Some people will never know anything about Jesus Christ except what they see in the lives of his disciples. We must remind people of Christ by living the Christ-life ourselves. We must walk so close behind Christ that people will not see us, but Christ.

J. M. THOBURN.

350

My sheep hear my voice, and I know them, and they follow me.
—John x. 27.

True sheep know the voice of their shepherd. It
is a sick sheep that will follow a stranger. The
goats will follow anybody's voice, but Jesus is the
only one whom it is safe to follow in all things. If
you follow Abraham you are apt to get to lying; if
you follow Moses you are apt to lose your temper;
if you follow Elijah you'll get discouraged and sit
down under the juniper-tree; but follow Jesus Christ
and you will find that you are led in the path of
righteousness and peace.

D. L. MOODY.

When Garibaldi was raising his army he said, "I
have no money, no food, no clothing, no stores, no
resources; let every man that is willing to suffer
poverty, shame, hunger, disease, and death, and who
loves Italy, follow me." It is the measure of our
suffering that will enable us to be like the Master.
It has been said that when he died he left his purse
to Judas, his clothes to the soldiers, his mother to
John, his pardon to the dying thief, and his peace to
his disciples. Some one has said, "I look for the
world and I find it in the church, and I look for the
church and I find it in the world." You may try all
you please for the baptism of the Holy Ghost, and
unless you are willing to present your bodies a living
sacrifice to God, you cannot be filled with the Spirit.

D. W. WHITTLE.

Hope is a heavenly bird of passage, with faith and
love as its wings.

L. W. MUNHALL.

351

Kept by the power of God through faith unto salvation ready
to be revealed in the last time.—1 Pet. i. 5.

A great many are afraid that they won't hold out.
It is a good thing to remember that we haven't got
to hold on to Christ; Christ holds on to us.

D. L. MOODY.

Two little boys are walking along the road with
their father. One grasps hold of his father's fingers,
and finds that it is about all he can manage. The
other puts his hand right into his father's large,
strong hand, and the father holds it. Suddenly they
come to a ditch in the road. Both slip; the one who
is holding his father's hand loses his hold and goes
down; the other is held up firmly by the father's
strong grasp. You do the trusting and let God do
the keeping, and you will go safe through life and
enter into glory. H. W. WEBB-PEPLOE.

Christ in heaven is our hope in glory, and Christ
in the heart is our hope of glory. An anchor is
useless unless fastened at both ends, and Christ has
fastened one end in glory, while the Holy Ghost
comes down and fastens the other end of the anchor
in our hearts. In olden times the anchor used to be
brought in first and the ship came in afterward. So
Christ has gone in as the forerunner within the veil,
and we shall come in afterward. A. J. GORDON.

God may not give us an easy journey to the
Promised Land, but he will give us a safe one.
ANDREW A. BONAR.

That he might present it to himself a glorious church, not having spot, or wrinkle, or any such thing; but that it should be holy and without blemish.—Eph. v. 27.

In the body of his flesh through death, to present you holy and unblamable and unreprovable in his sight.—Col. i. 22.

Here are eight different terms to express the final state of the church: "glorious," "spotless," "without wrinkle," "without any such thing," "holy," "without blemish," "unblamable," "unreprovable;" and Jude has one more adjective—"faultless." Think of it. Even *you* are to be presented faultless before the presence of his glory. The presence of God's glory is so awful that when Daniel himself, the well-nigh perfect man in Babylon, was confronted with the vision of the glory, he says, "My comeliness was turned into corruption, and there remained in me no more strength." The very things that he had prided himself upon,—his virtue, his morality, the excellence of his character, and the blamelessness of his life,—when the glory of the Son of God beat upon him, lost their beauty, and his very *comeliness* was turned into *corruption*. And the holy man of God, John, who leaned on the breast of Jesus at supper, tells us that when he beheld the vision of the glory of the Lord he "fell at his feet as dead." And yet—astounding fact!—you and I are to be presented faultless before the presence of that same glory. It will remove the last taint or scar of sin, so that even God cannot find a remnant of sin, not a trace of guilt, not even a scar left by the wounds of sin on your soul, in your final, ultimate, glorious perfection.

ARTHUR T. PIERSON.

The wind bloweth where it listeth, and thou hearest the sound thereof, but canst not tell whence it cometh, and whither it goeth: so is every one that is born of the Spirit.—John iii. 8.

In condescension to the infirmity of our nature, God clothes his spiritual truth in material forms, making the kingdom of nature, which is seen, illustrate for us the kingdom of Christ, which is not seen. The greatest teacher of spiritual truth that ever lived cast nearly all his instruction in the form of parables. In like manner, when the Scriptures would give us some insight into the character and phases of the third person of the Trinity, they do it by a series of emblems drawn from the natural world. One emblem of the Spirit is that of fire, the illuminating agency in the world, as the Spirit is the only agency that can drive away the darkness of sin and let in the sunlight of God. Another emblem of the Spirit is water, the universal cleansing agent, as the Spirit is the only power that can cleanse us from the pollution of sin. Another emblem is oil, the old-time medicine, as the Spirit is the only being in the universe to bind up the broken heart; also oil is the consecrating element, and we cannot become kings and priests unto God until we have the Holy Spirit. But the most remarkable emblem of the Holy Spirit is the wind. There are three great points about the Holy Spirit stated in this verse which our Lord obtruded upon the mind of Nicodemus. The wind and the Spirit are both invisible to man, they are both indispensable to him, and they are both independent of him.

W. W. MOORE.

354

Where the Spirit of the Lord is, there is liberty.—2 Cor. iii. 17.

Some people think that this means liberty for them to do just about as they please. I never shall forget how I was startled when a Christian once asked me, "Do you always have a program made out for the Holy Ghost in your church?" In most of our churches everything is planned very exactly: a voluntary here, a response here, a sermon here, and so on—all fixed from beginning to end. It is the lack of liberty that causes so much deadness in the pulpit and deadness in the pew. Oh, for the liberty of the Spirit! A. J. GORDON.

When a man tries to speak for Christ without the help of the Spirit he will not have liberty; he is apt to be fettered, like Lazarus when he came out of the grave with a napkin bound over his mouth. If a man neglects prayer and his Bible he is not going to have liberty. I have seen ministers in the pulpit as dry as Gideon's fleece. Sometimes it is the fault of the minister and sometimes it is the fault of the people. Do you suppose there would have been anybody converted on the day of Pentecost if the one hundred and twenty had been criticizing Peter? Suppose James had said to John, "I do not think Peter is preaching as well as usual. It is the most influential congregation I have ever seen in Jerusalem. There is half of the sanhedrim, and more than forty of the leading rabbis, and half of the leading Sadducees; and yet Peter is giving a very ordinary sort of a talk." But Peter had not talked very long before there came gales from heaven and swept over that audience. Those one hundred and twenty were holding Peter up in prayer. D. L. MOODY.

355

Where two or three are gathered together in my name, there am I in the midst of them.—Matt. xviii. 20.

If Christ had said, "Where five or six hundred are gathered in my name, there am I in the midst," how anxious we should have been to attend great meetings, that we might get near the Lord! But he says, "Where two or three are gathered together." If he had said, "Where bishops or popes or great men are assembled, there will I be," we should travel the world over to attend such assemblies. But we go to the prayer-meeting, and we find only half a dozen, and we think it is best to adjourn. We say, "There will be no one there but that old lame brother, and that blind sister, and that deaf one," and so we stay away. When we believe what Christ has said we will not open a prayer-meeting by asking him to come and be in our midst, but we will come expecting to find him, and will simply say, "Speak, Lord; for thy servant heareth." H. L. HASTINGS.

Much of our strength in prayer and effort is exhausted in striving to induce God to agree with us and come to our assistance. Some one asked Abraham Lincoln to appoint a day of fasting and prayer, that God might be on their side. "Don't bother about that," said the man of common sense. "God is now on the right side; you simply get with him." The only way to command God is to obey him, just as the only way to command electricity and steam is to obey the laws that govern them. A. C. DIXON.

Be careful for nothing; but in everything by prayer and sup-
plication with thanksgiving let your requests be made known unto
God.—Phil. iv. 6.

In prayer the most important thing is to catch the
ear of him to whom I speak. Do not offer one petition until you are fully conscious of having secured
the attention of God. You need to have your heart
filled by the Spirit with the holy consciousness that
the everlasting, almighty God is indeed come very
near you. ANDREW MURRAY.

It is not necessary to make long prayers, but it is
essential to be much alone with God, waiting on his
will, hearkening for his voice, lingering in the garden
of Scripture for the coming of the Lord God in the
dawn or cool of the day. No number of meetings,
no fellowship with Christian friends, no amount of
Christian activity, can compensate for the neglect
of the still hour. F. B. MEYER.

It is possible to recite even as sublime a prayer as
the Lord's Prayer, and do it with as little thought or
emotion or appreciation as though one were reeling
off prayers by the yard. To repeat the alphabet or
multiplication table is not more thoughtless than
many formal prayers that have become mere reci-
tations. ARTHUR T. PIERSON.

He that saveth his time from prayer shall lose it.
He that loseth his time for communion with God
shall find it in blessing. ROBERT P. WILDER.

God loves us too much to give us all we ask for.
We sometimes pray for razors, and then complain
and say that God doesn't answer prayer.
D. L. MOODY.

357

The Bible is not specially concerned with the points wherein men differ. No; the Bible is busy with a matter of life and death. Suppose that men were drowning, and you were shouting directions by which they should escape. You would call them to seize the rope you threw them without stopping to explain to them that a rope which holds the end of a sail is called a sheet; you would tell them to swim to the ship without being particular to describe the vessel as a hermaphrodite brig, though that might be its technical name. So the Bible does not trifle with us by a display of learning or by delays to explain every trivial thing. It sweeps right ahead in an herculean effort to save life, and does not stop to palter over the length of geologic days, or the omission of a name here and there in a genealogical table. It tells no untruth, though on a multitude of subjects it does not commit itself, but presses straight on to pluck a brand from the burning.

ADDISON P. FOSTER.

What man made man may destroy; what God has made God will preserve. The grass of infidel oratory withereth, the flower of Christian interpretation often fadeth, but the Word of God shall stand forever.

R. S. MACARTHUR.

A foolish child can pull a flower in pieces, but it takes a God to form and paint a flower. Until a man can construct a book that equals the Bible he would better let the Bible stand in its solitary grandeur and power.

DAVID GREGG.

358

A Scotchwoman who received kind letters from her son found bank-bills inside them, but, having never seen such money, thought they were only pretty pictures and put them aside. Many people think the promises found in the Bible are very pretty pictures, and perhaps some of you have put them away in an old tea-pot. Is it not time to understand that they are drafts on the bank of heaven that will be honored night and day? God make us ashamed that we have such a poverty-stricken spiritual life, when all the resources of the Holy Ghost are ready to supply our need. God does not want us to be beggars, but sons.   A. J. GORDON.

God never deals out to men just so much as they need and no more. David said, "He maketh me to lie down in green pastures." But it would not be possible for him to lie down in a millionth part of the pastures. "He leadeth me beside the still waters." There were a hundred thousand water-brooks, and he could only wait by one to refresh himself. There are flowers in the woods where no man can enjoy their beauty. We could get along without beautiful birds and their warbling notes. Ah! they are the overflow of the cup. God gives us a great many blessings that we do not ask for. So some people say that there is no need in praying because God gives us what we need without our asking. Yes; but God lets us come to him and tell him our wants, and he gives more than we name. Then let us ask for what we need, and come back and thank him for that and for the royal bounty.
                            ALEXANDER MCKENZIE.

The most important of all things is the conception which a man has of God. Given a man's idea of God, and the degree of sincerity with which God is worshiped, and there can be no difficulty in discovering the moral quality of the worshiper. Find a man whose idea of God is low, and you find a heathen. Find a man whose conception of God is lofty, pure, tender, loving, and you find a life ennobled and enriched with proportionate thought and charity. A God infinite in power, and in wisdom, and in goodness, and in love, a God to whom sin is abominable, such a God ought to produce a man of purity, of dignity, of largeness of heart, and of nobleness of character.   DAVID GREGG.

God is true and righteous and holy; he is perfect in his equity and in his standards. Instead of turning away from the judgment of God as a blemish on his character, we ought to rejoice in it as another aspect of his benevolence. We must have in God the blooming valley full of beautiful flowers and with the purling streams of grace, and also the dark, frowning crags of divine judgment, the very intensity of whose shadow implies an intensity of glory, for you never can get shadow without light. Prostrate yourself before an engine, and the very qualities which make it a blessing make it an engine of destruction. God moves on a track of absolute and perfect equity and holiness, and the same qualities that insure that you would be borne forward into the eternal ages if connected with God make it sure that you would be ground to powder if you place yourself before his wheels of judgment.
                    ARTHUR T. PIERSON.

There is a sevenfold seal of God upon the Bible, which may be noticed in the following particulars: 1. Predictive prophecy, the seal of divine omniscience; 2. History and biography, the seal of divine providence; 3. Miracles, the seal of divine omnipotence; 4. Morality, the seal of divine righteousness; 5. Unity, the seal of divine omnipresence; 6. Accuracy, the seal of divine truthfulness; 7. Practical power, the seal of divine benevolence.

ARTHUR T. PIERSON.

It is not mere speculation of fancy to consider the tabernacle and temple as typical.

First, they were typical of heaven, God's true abiding-place, and, indeed, of the whole vast universe, which is a symmetrical temple perfect in every part, and in which are continually being sung praises to the almightiness, to the power, to the wisdom, and to the love of God.

Then the temple stands as a type of the incarnation of the Son of God and of the blessed Christ, the true meeting-place between God and man. Hence he could say, "Destroy this temple, and in three days I will raise it up again."

Then we know, from the Epistles to the Corinthians, that the tabernacle and temple are types of every Christian, for, "Know ye not that ye are the temple of God?" DAVID BARON.

If the early morning hours spent by Christians over the newspaper were given to the Bible, keeping the paper till later, what a change would be wrought in the tone of our Christian life!

ROBERT E. SPEER.

361

The believer's union with Christ is represented in the Scriptures in the form of similitudes because the human mind thus understands it better. To give the idea of security it is compared to the union of the stones of a building with the foundation-stone. But stones are inanimate, and to supply the idea of vitality it is further compared to that of the vine and its branches. But a plant has no consciousness and power of motion, and therefore the union between Christ and the believer is compared to that between the head and members of a body: Christ the head, the seat of intelligence and feeling, the source of vitality and volition, and all the members being united to it by a common set of nerves, and by the community of life and motion. But no affection is suggested in that figure, so this union is further compared to that between the husband and wife, united by a legal tie, and both thus becoming one. But between husband and wife there may be also a lack of perfect harmony; and so Jesus compares the union between himself and the believer to that between himself and the Father, the sweetest accord of perfect harmony. And in the eighth chapter of Romans Paul puts the capstone on this glorious structure when he pronounces the union between Christ and the believer to be everlasting, challenging all the sundering forces of the universe to separate us from the love of God, which is in Christ Jesus, our Lord. All these ideas are gathered up and expressed at once in a great general statement in Paul's first letter to the Corinthians, when he says, "But he that is joined unto the Lord is one spirit." This general statement means that the believer is identical with Jesus in the Holy Spirit.   W. W. MOORE.

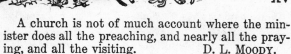
A church is not of much account where the minister does all the preaching, and nearly all the praying, and all the visiting.   D. L. MOODY.

A factory is sometimes linked by a belt to a power-house. Christ is the center and source of all power for his church. The Holy Ghost is the belt to the church, carrying up our needs and prayers, and bringing down Christ's answers and fullness. As I believe that wind-power is the best for sail-boats, and steam-power is the best for engines, so I believe that the Holy Ghost is the best power for churches. For a church to bring in an opera-singer or amusements and secular appliances to make the church go is as absurd as for an ocean steamer to uncouple its shaft from the engine and couple it on to the donkey-engine.   A. J. GORDON.

"Unto every one that entereth the house of the Lord, his daily portion." You have been looking ahead and have been fretting because you know not how the supply will come, how you can ever go through this or that trial or sacrifice. Beloved, God never said look ahead, God said look up; God never said look around, he only said look into the holy of holies; God never said look down, he only said look into the face of the living God; "Look unto me, and be ye saved, all the ends of the earth." As we look beyond to-day and say, "How can I expect that in the wear and tear of daily life this holy peace is to be sustained?" the answer is, "Unto every one that entereth into the house of the Lord, his *daily portion*."   H. W. WEBB-PEPLOE.

In the beginning was the Word, and the Word was with God, and the Word was God.—John i. 1.

A word is the manifestation of a thought. If I wish to communicate a thought to you that thought takes shape in words. You cannot see my thought, but what is there comes through the channels of speech, and so travels through your ear to your mind, and becomes part of your thought. Now Christ became the Word to take the thought out of the mind and heart of God, and translate that thought so that we could understand it, so that what was before invisible and inaudible and beyond the reach of our senses, comes into our minds and hearts as something that was in God's mind and heart, but now is in ours. Beautiful indeed is this as an expression of what Christ is to us. You want to know God; well then, study Christ, and you will know all about him. "He that hath seen me hath seen the Father," said Jesus.

ARTHUR T. PIERSON.

In the gospel story we find five great points of special importance—the birth, the life on earth, the death, the resurrection, and the ascension. An old writer has called them "the process of Jesus Christ" —the process by which he became our glorified King and our life. In all this life-process we must be made like unto him. In his birth he received his life from God. In his life upon earth he lived in dependence on God. In death he gave up his life to God. In his resurrection he was raised up by God. In his ascension he lives a life in glory with God.

ANDREW MURRAY.

Wherefore God also hath highly exalted him, and given him a name which is above every name; that at the name of Jesus every knee should bow, of things in heaven, and things in earth, and things under the earth.—Phil. ii. 9, 10.

The other names of Jesus express his relationships, offices, and work, but this name is most potent and precious. There is majesty in the name God; there is independent being in the name Jehovah; there is authority in the name Lord; there is unction in the name Christ; there is friendship in the name Immanuel; there is help in the name Advocate; but in the name Jesus alone is there salvation.

GEORGE C. NEEDHAM.

Between creation and the incarnation of Christ there is one small but important object, an altar of sacrifice. Between the first coming and the second coming is another small object, the table of the Lord. The altar of sacrifice refers back to the creation and fall of man, and forward to the incarnation and cross of Christ. Every victim that bled upon the altar reminded men of their sin, of Adam's fall, and of the disaster that overtook the race, and pointed forward to the Lamb of God that was to take away the sin of the world. Likewise the table of the Lord has a double reference—backward to the cross, forward to the coming of the Lord; and every time we sit down at the Lord's table the body and blood of our Lord, as represented in the bread and the cup, point back to his cross and forward to his second appearing. " As often as ye eat this bread, and drink this cup, ye do show the Lord's death till he come."

ARTHUR T. PIERSON.

Whoso offereth praise glorifieth me.—Ps. l. 23.

Christ here teaches that the highest object of money is not even to minister to the poor, but to glorify God and express the gratitude of a loving heart. ARTHUR T. PIERSON.

I am so impressed with the importance that God attaches to sweet voluntariness that I am often tempted to resolve never to beg a cent for God again, but rather spend my energy in getting Christians spiritualized, assured that they will certainly become liberalized. A. J. GORDON.

Gold has no value in heaven. They use it there to pave the streets with—better gold than we have down here—transparent gold. God can make gold as easily as he can make dirt; but he knows that man has his heart set on it, and what he wants is what your heart is set on. If you love him you will give him everything.

God told the children of Israel that if they hadn't anything else they might even bring goats' hair and it would be accepted. Thank God for the goats' hairs! Lots of people haven't any gold or silver or brass or fine linen, but they have a few goats' hairs. God wants every one to do something, as much as each one is able. D. L. MOODY.

The church is weighed down to earth by bags of gold, and cannot lift itself heavenward. You will have to give an account of that which God has intrusted to you to be kept for himself and not for yourself. DAVID BARON.

366

Be not wise in your own conceits.—Rom. xii. 16.

What God wants is men great enough to be small enough to be used.   H. W. WEBB-PEPLOE.

I used to think that God's gifts were on shelves one above the other, and that the taller we grew in Christian character the easier we should reach them. I find now that God's gifts are on shelves one beneath the other, and that it is not a question of growing taller, but of stooping lower, and that we have to go down, always down, to get his best gifts.

                     F. B. MEYER.

We have come so much to regard humility a cardinal virtue of Christianity that we may have forgotten that the Christian should be ambitious. I think he should be the most ambitious person on the earth. To whom is the promise of eternal life spoken but to those who, in patient endurance, in well-doing, seek for glory, honor, and immortality, than which there cannot be a much higher ambition? Humility is sometimes only pride turned wrong side out, just as you turn a garment, and dye it, and refit it. A person says, "If I can get into heaven at last I am willing to occupy a back seat." But Scripture very certainly indicates that you are to seek not only barely to get into heaven, but you are to seek "an abundant entrance" which "shall be given you into the kingdom of God." The back seats are all spoken for, and God wants us to get as near the throne as possible.   A. J. GORDON.

St. Paul says to the Philippians, "In everything and in all things have I learned the secret [Have you? What secret?] both to be filled and to be hungry, both to abound and to be in want"—the secret of perfect contentment. There sat the aged apostle, bound by a chain to a brutal Roman soldier. Nero might at any moment order his head to be cut off, or that he be thrown into the Tiber, or given to the lions. He has nothing but the comforts of a miserable Roman prisoner. He has not even a friend at times, and yet, with the galling chain upon his wrist, and facing a martyr's death, the man takes the pen and writes, "In all things have I learned the secret [blessed initiation into the mysteries of the kingdom!] both to be filled and to be hungry, both to abound and to be in want." He drops a little thing, only one, and gains more than all things; that is the secret. H. W. WEBB-PEPLOE.

The peace of Christ is not something that he puts into your heart, and that you must keep that it may keep you. If the peace of God is to rule in my heart it is because the God of peace himself is there.
ANDREW MURRAY.

How little have we accepted and made use of the legacy of peace and joy which Christ left to us! Instead of faces telling the world what a full salvation we have, how often a long face has suggested that men had better take their fill of happiness first before they leave it behind by becoming Christians! May God give us so to live winning lives that others will be allured to desire the same blessings we enjoy.
J. HUDSON TAYLOR.

"Woe to him that striveth with his Maker!"
Pharaoh did it, and was overthrown in the Red Sea;
Saul did it, and was deposed; Jehoiakim did it, and
he perished; Judas did it, and he hanged himself; the
Pharisees did it, and their city was destroyed; Julian
the Apostate did it, and, falling back upon the field
of battle, said, "Thou hast conquered, O Galilean!"

You can tell a man who has thwarted God if you
know much about him. Many old fossils give the
same experience twenty years after their conversion
that they gave the month after. In a prayer-meeting many pray the same stereotyped prayer year
after year. Some ministers are just where they
were in their doctrine and the expression, and in
their very sermons, as when they commenced their
ministry—arrested, dwarfed. F. B. MEYER.

We must coöperate with God. If there is any sin
in my heart that I am not willing to give up, then I
need not pray. You may take a bottle, and cork it
up tight, and put it under Niagara, and there will
not a drop of that mighty volume of water get into
the bottle. If there is any sin in my heart that I am
not willing to give up I need not expect a blessing.
D. L. MOODY.

These are the things that hinder a mighty work
of God in the individual man: present sin; unconfessed and unrectified past sin; an unforgiving spirit;
fear of surrendering unreservedly to the will of God;
pride; unbelief. Which of them is the hindrance in
your case? Be in earnest; find out the hindrance,
and ask God to take it away. R. A. TORREY.

Cursed be the man that trusteth in man, and maketh flesh his arm.—Jer. xvii. 5.

Trust in yourself, and you are doomed to disappointment; trust in your friends, and they will die and leave you; trust in money, and you may have it taken from you; trust in reputation, and some slanderous tongue may blast it; but trust in God, and you are never to be confounded in time or eternity.

D. L. MOODY.

The Scriptures not only tell us that the Christian religion has come to inform us how we are to be saved, but that our faith in Jesus Christ conditions our salvation. It is not as it might have been—that the salvation came, and that we can get the benefit of it whether we know anything about it or not, whether we have any creed or not, whether we repudiate the whole thing or not, whether we believe in it or not. It is not like the tide, that rises whether you care about the moon's influence or not. Our destiny is connected not simply with the fact of Christ's atonement as recorded in the Bible, but is conditioned on our acceptance of it. There is no question of greater moment to you in your intellectual life than this obligation to believe something definite about Jesus Christ, as to what he was, what he did, and how the doing of what he did stands related to the divine economy of men's salvation.

FRANCIS L. PATTON.

Unless our faith is manifested in righteousness, we must beware lest we think it is genuine when it is not; there must be in it the seed of all holy life.

TEUNIS S. HAMLIN.

The seed is the Word of God.—Luke viii. 11.

The seed is the perfect fruit of the flower, to which all parts of the flower are subservient, and the flower must die to develop the seed in its completeness. The gospel of Christ is the seed to which everything in God's Word is subject. Not till Calvary did we have a complete gospel, which is therefore the final product of God's thought; and Christ himself is the rose of Sharon and the lily of the valley. It was necessary that Christ should die that you and I might have that seed which contains the very life of God. We cannot find the product of God's thought in any other character. Therefore, though we ought to know the whole of the Word of God, we ought to study it only in connection with this thought, that we are somehow to be led to the clearer and fuller understanding of the Word of God, which is the seed.

The seed is composed of two parts—the shell, or outer part, without life, and the inner part containing life. The gospel of Christ consists of two parts. There is the shell, the printed Bible; and there is the inner part, which contains the life and the spirit. What is the shell for? So far as the seed is concerned, for the protection of the life within and for the conveyance of that which makes the life within. If you destroy the shell you destroy the life. The shell of that seed which is the Word of God has been given us for the protection of the life within and for its conveyance.

God intended the seed for dissemination. Is this gospel to stay in your heart or town? No; wherever there is a human heart there is where God expects this seed to be planted.   A. S. GUMBART.

God seeks to mold us by circumstances, and you must believe that God has put you down just where you are because your present position is the very best place in the universe to make you what he wants you to become. He could have made you a king or a bishop, a millionaire or a statesman; but he passed all these by and has put you just where you are. You may be a stableman, a cook, or a housemaid; but God had the whole universe to choose from, and he wanted to do his best for you, and he put your soul just where it is because he knew that there you would be surrounded by the best conditions to make you what he wanted you to become.

F. B. MEYER.

Jesus Christ is a very, very peculiar Saviour to meet the very, very peculiar need of very, very peculiar sinners, in all our very, very peculiar circumstances, and to bring victory to our very, very peculiar souls, under all the very, very peculiar difficulties under which we, in our very, very peculiar circumstances, may be called to pass throughout our lives.

H. W. WEBB-PEPLOE.

When a young man is converted he is almost always inclined at first to say, "I know I could do far more good if I was a preacher, so I'll leave my business and become a preacher of the gospel." But very often mistakes are made just in this way. God may have given you some work to do for him in the position in which he has placed you which no one else could do if you were to leave it undone. We should be very careful how we wish to change from whatever position in life into which God has seen fit to put us.

ANDREW A. BONAR.

I wonder not that the scorning skeptic so often mocks at Christians because he says that they cowardly cringe at the foot of the cross, ready to take God's gift like a sneak, but show nothing as a fruit of that blessed gift. Remember that God demands, and where God demands he enables, and where God enables he expects us to fulfil.

H. W. WEBB-PEPLOE.

When Leonard Woods, president of Bowdoin College, was in France, he was invited to dine with the king. He presented himself at the palace, and was met by the king with his accustomed courtesy, who said, "We did not know that we were to have the pleasure of your company to-day. You did not answer our invitation." Leonard Woods said, "I thought the invitation of a king was to be obeyed, not answered." When the Spirit says "Come" it is equal to a command, and we would better put off all other engagements and come. No matter how gently and winsomely the invitation comes, let us never forget that there is a voice of royal, imperial, imperious urgency and authority behind it.

JOHN McNEILL.

We must not only accept God's will as revealed in his Word, but we must accept it in every providence. Whether it be a Judas that betrays or Pilate in his indifference who gives you up to the enemy, whatever trouble or temptation, vexation or worry comes, see God in it, and accept it as his will.

ANDREW MURRAY.

373

It is time that the church of God should awake to her responsibility. We have been acting as though we had an eternity in which to do the work, and the people whom we seek to reach an eternity on earth in which to be reached.

ARTHUR T. PIERSON.

Did you ever think, my brother, my sister, that if it were not for missionary work you would be serving idols to-day? Suppose that Paul and those who labored with him had been directed to go east in place of west. How shocked you are when, in some picture, you see a mother throwing her child into the Ganges! It might have been you, my sister. Have you no pity for the fellow-beings that are dying at the rate of one hundred thousand a day?

W. E. BLACKSTONE.

In China are tens of thousands of villages with small trace of Bible influence, but hardly a hamlet where the opium pipe does not reign. It does more harm in a week than all our missionaries are doing good in a year; it is the sum of villainies. It debauches more families than drink and it makes more slaves than the slave-trade.

J. HUDSON TAYLOR.

The world is open to Christian woman as it never has been before. She must write; for a literature must be created for the women of the East. She must teach; for the convert must be trained and the heathen won. She must evangelize; for her feet alone can carry the good tidings of peace to her sisters in their seclusion. J. M. THOBURN.

The more your religion costs you, the richer re-
turns it will bring you.

THEODORE L. CUYLER.

Men talk much of giving their spirits to God; they
talk somewhat of giving their souls; and they think
that they can satisfy God and man by saying that
they present their spirits, which no man can lay
hold of, and their souls, which are only observable
in their outward acts; but they refuse to give their
bodies, for the most part, because this would cost
them something palpable; this would involve what
even men call "self-sacrifice."

H. W. WEBB-PEPLOE.

Christ is our life. The air is our life, and is everywhere. Is the air nearer to us than Christ? Verily,
no! Christ is around us on every side. Nothing in
heaven or earth or hell can keep the light of Christ
from shining into the heart that is empty and open.
Then take him in his blessed meekness and gentleness. When he has taken possession of you there
will be blessed fellowship with him day by day.

ANDREW MURRAY.

Hercules could not kill the monster against which
he contended until he lifted him from earth, his
mother. We are engaged in a violent struggle with
evils that are of the earth, earthy, and we shall
never kill those things within us and of us till we
lift them away from that in which they were born
and cleanse them in the atmosphere of spiritual
union with Christ. W. W. MOORE.

375

Before any work for God there always comes the vision of God. To behold him, to be lifted up above our troubled hearts, above our worries and discords, and to be absolutely sure that we have spoken with God and he has spoken with us, this is the indispensable preliminary of doing anything whatsoever in God's service. If a servant of God is uncertain of his Master he will be uncertain of everything that follows in his service. If you and I have no doubt about having seen God, then our divine service will grow sweeter and clearer and easier every year we live. I have had men say to me, "Didn't Paul's Christian life begin with the question, 'What wilt thou have me to do?'" No, it did not; no life begins with that question. It began with the question, "Who art thou, Lord?" When Paul had settled that it was the risen Christ who appeared to him, then came the much easier question, "What wilt thou have me to do?" We cannot feed the multitude out of an empty basket; we cannot present the Lord until we have seen the Lord.

W. H. P. Faunce.

When God beckons you forward he is always responsible for the transport.   F. B. Meyer.

When God almighty linked himself with Moses' rod it was worth more than all the armies in the world. If God can use an old, dried-up, withered rod he can use you and me. It was not Moses nor Moses' rod that brought the plagues on the Egyptians, but it was the God behind the rod.

D. L. Moody.

Point to without trying to prop up the cross.
Theodore L. Cuyler.

Remember there are few, if any, cases where in judgment much is made of sins committed; for they are purged away by the blood of Christ. Men are judged because of what they have not done, more than because of what they have done. As a Christian said on his death-bed, when asked by a friend who saw him weeping if he was afraid to die, "Oh no; I am not afraid, but I am so ashamed to die, for I have done so little for my Lord." What have you done for him in return for what he has done for you?

H. W. WEBB-PEPLOE.

Napoleon sought to rule men; Washington aimed to serve them. You see the results of the two systems in what is left of them. At Waterloo to-day you find a great waste desert, in the center of which is simply a mound to commemorate a great battle. But around the field of Bunker Hill sprang up the great city of colleges and schools, and those influences that went out through all the world; that is the result of the service which Washington rendered in contrast to the domination of Napoleon. You find at Mount Vernon a very plain structure for the tomb of Washington, scarcely to be noticed, except one goes out of his way to see it. Napoleon's tomb is in the heart of Paris, and a marble casket holds his remains. Washington's remains are as broad as the continent. That is the result of service as opposed to self-seeking.

ALEXANDER MCKENZIE.

A man who would have God's guidance must be willing to make spiritual things his main business.

H. C. MABIE.

377

To every truly established Christian there ought
to be a fixed standard of faith and duty, a great
revelation from God of his privilege and obligation
in every respect from the beginning to the end of
eternity. We must put God to the front, and then
remember that the standard of holiness which we
are to attain must never be lowered to meet the
necessity of man's circumstances, but must remain
the same, the absolutely true and perfect standard
of God himself. If God were ever to lower his
standard to meet my requirements there could never
be satisfaction through eternity for us creatures,
because we hope to rise higher and higher, to be
nearer and nearer to God. If I found that God had
lowered his standard of holiness to meet my ideas
down here in my imperfection, how could I reverence
him as the absolute and all-perfect one?

H. W. WEBB-PEPLOE.

The conscience sustains to the will of God some
such relation as the eye sustains to any work that
we have to do. Your eye may be very accurate,
but who would trust you to build a wall if you have
no dependence but your eye? You must drop the
plumb-line alongside and lay the level upon your
work, and then the united action of eye, plumb-line,
and level helps you to make a perfectly upright wall.
In the matter of truth and duty your eye is the
fallible conscience, the plumb-line and level the
revealed will of God, and the action of the two together enable you to build a character and to do
works that are according to the will of God. Christ
had to come as the prophet to supply us with the
plumb-line and level. ARTHUR T. PIERSON.

378

That is to be the common, every-day experience of the believer, not his life only at set times. Did ever a father or mother think, "To-day I want my child to love me"? No; they expect the love every day. So God wants his child every moment to have a heart filled with love by the Spirit. In the eyes of God it is most unnatural to expect a man to love as he should if he is not filled with the Spirit.

ANDREW MURRAY.

It is only when we begin to love other people, and become rooted and grounded in love to them, that we learn to know what Christ's love is to us. You must love a woman that you may understand what Christ feels for his church; you must love a child to know how God feels to his children; you must love a friend to know how Christ feels to his friend. Every time you do an unselfish, gentle, tender thing it is another window into the love of God. You must go lengths to understand the length of his love, which is everlasting; you must go depths to the infamy and degradation of such as you would help if you would understand the depth of the love of Christ; you must go breadths outside the narrow limits of your charity to understand his broad expanse of love; and you must climb to heights, bearing up some languid, fainting soul, if you will understand something of the upspringing of Christ's love that bears us in his ascension climb. Love men if you want to know the love of Christ.

F. B. MEYER.

The love of God is shed abroad in our hearts by the Holy Ghost which is given unto us.

ROM. V. 5.

TEXTUAL INDEX

TEXTUAL INDEX

TEXTUAL INDEX

TOPICAL INDEX *

* Italicized words refer to kindred topics in the Index.

TOPICAL INDEX

385

TOPICAL INDEX

TOPICAL INDEX

TOPICAL INDEX